BLOGGING AMERICA

BLOGGING AMERICA

The New Public Sphere

Aaron Barlow

New Directions in Media
Robin Andersen, Series Editor

Westport, Connecticut
London

Library of Congress Cataloging-in-Publication Data

Barlow, Aaron, 1951–
   Blogging America : the new public sphere / Aaron Barlow.
     p. cm.—(New directions in media, ISSN 1939–2494)
   Includes bibliographical references and index.
   ISBN-13: 978–0–275–99872–1 (alk. paper)
   1. Blogs—Social aspects. 2. Blogs—Political aspects. 3. Blogs—
Religious aspects—Christianity. I. Title.
   HM851.B368 2008
   303.48′33—dc22   2007029029

British Library Cataloguing in Publication Data is available.

Library of Congress Catalog Card Number: 2007029029
ISBN-13: 978–0–275–99872–1
ISSN: 1939–2494

First published in 2008

Praeger Publishers, 88 Post Road West, Westport, CT 06881
An imprint of Greenwood Publishing Group, Inc.
www.praeger.com

Printed in the United States of America

The paper used in this book complies with the
Permanent Paper Standard issued by the National
Information Standards Organization (Z39.48–1984).

10 9 8 7 6 5 4 3 2 1

When I tell any Truth, it is not for the sake of Convincing those who do not know it, but for the sake of defending those that do.

—William Blake

It is because they are compelled to act without a reliable picture of the world, that governments, schools, newspapers and churches make such small headway against the more obvious failings of democracy, against violence, prejudice, apathy, preference for the curious trivial as against the dull important, and the hunger for sideshows and three legged calves.

—Walter Lippmann in 1922

CONTENTS

PREFACE   ix

1   AN INTRODUCTION TO THE BLOGS   1
2   THE BLOGS IN SOCIETY   35
3   THE BLOGS FROM WITHIN   59
4   THE BLOGS, POLITICAL ISSUES, AND THE PRESS   85
5   THE BLOG IN POPULAR CULTURE   113
6   ONLINE COMMUNITY, ONLINE UTILIZATION: THE CHRISTIAN BLOG   137

CONCLUSION   159
BLOGROLL   161
NOTES   165
BIBLIOGRAPHY   177
INDEX   181

PREFACE

Blogs and Other Online Entities Discussed in the Preface

Andrew Keen: On Media, Culture, and Technology, http://andrewkeen.
  typepad.com

Crowdsourcing, http://crowdsourcing.typepad.com

Nomades Advanced Technologies Interactive Workshop, http://www.natiw.
  ch/blog

Rosenblumtv, http://rosenblumtv.wordpress.com

Shadmia's World, http://shadmia.wordpress.com

The Unconventional Truth, http://theunconventionaltruth.blogspot.com

When he had finished looking over the manuscript of my last book, *The Rise of the Blogosphere*, Dan Harmon, my editor at Praeger, felt that he only had half the story. What I'd given him was a history, the backgrounds in American journalism leading up to the blogs—but with little on the blogs themselves. I think he felt a little cheated. Though he did like the book, he wanted more.

What Dan had been hoping for was something that also explored the blogs as they have become today—but that, we soon agreed, was too much to try to add to the one book. Another book was needed, a different one and with a new focus, a book on what the blogs are doing today, and why.

With that in mind, I began this project, which I first envisioned as simply a look at the blogs as they were in 2007. But, as usual, I was drawn to the past, for I cannot see the blogs or any aspect of any culture existing alone simply as part of a particular time. Therefore, though I have kept my look at the blogs fairly focused on what is going on as I write, my search for understanding often takes me back to earlier times.

It is impossible to cover all of the blogosphere. It is too big, too dynamic, and too responsive to change for anyone to say much about it beyond "this is what I found in this particular place at that particular time."

In fact, the blogosphere is way too big for even a brief survey in any one book. For that reason, I have limited my examinations in a number of ways, many of which will become apparent as one reads the book (the only blogging community I really provide any sort of portrait of, for example, is that of Christian bloggers).

One of the areas I have avoided is that of the big commercial blogs. Even many of the small blogs, these days, do make a little money out of advertising, but it isn't much. Some of the larger blogs, however, are commercial enterprises from start to finish. I do mention MySpace and Facebook in passing (while making distinctions between social-networking blogs and those dedicated to extant, offline communities, for example), but do not delve into them. The intersection between the blogs and commerce, fascinating though it is, still has not shaken itself out into a form that I am comfortable drawing conclusions on. That, I think, will not happen for a couple of years.

In addition, the commercial blogs operate on premises different from those of the individual. Though I do look at ChronCommons.com, part of the online presence of the *Houston Chronicle*, in relation to place-based citizen journalism, I do not really explore the blogs that have become such important parts of commercial news media entities in general. These deserve a book or two by themselves, preferably by someone with a background in both journalism and business.

The blogs have also become much more of an important part of the online presence of businesses in general. They can be used to generate interest in product roll-out, for complaints, and for all sorts of other discussions relating to products as they are, as they have been, and as they may be. Because blogs are not so tied to temporal immediacy and sequence, they are beginning to replace the phone connection between the business and its customers. No more waiting on hold! Simply place a query on the blog, and a response will come. This has advantages even over email, for its public nature proves useful to both the business (it doesn't have to repeat the same thing endlessly) and the user (who may just be able to find their answer through a search of the blog).

The focus in this book is on that most notorious aspect of the blogosphere, the personal blog. To me, these blogs are the most interesting, for they show an aspect of individual relations to technology that could not really be seen until the advent of the World Wide Web and the rise of the blogs. If the blogs are changing our culture, it is because of the individual bloggers, not because of the other uses that have been found for the blogs, no matter how fascinating these may prove to be. If nothing else, the blogs are changing our relationships with technology, making them more personal and active than ever before—in the political realm, certainly, but elsewhere as well.

Chapter 1 presents a background for understanding the blogs in terms of political discussion and language, using the work of Jurgen Habermas, B. F.

Skinner, and Walter Ong as a background to understanding just what is going on in terms of the blogs and the Web. It is here that I talk of *neteracy*, a new set of skills that do not replace literacy, but that will be increasingly necessary as more and more human activities acquire Web-connected aspects.

Neteracy is more than skills, carrying with it an entirely new set of attitudes towards ownership of the items carried by the new communications media. While copyright and patent regulations are revised to cover the Web, they still reflect older ideas of protection and rights, ideas that are already clashing with what is becoming standard usage on the Web. It will be a long time before this conflict is resolved, for each side has strong arguments in its favor.

The second chapter presents the blogs in the larger American society and as they are seen by those who are not directly involved in them, either as writer or as reader. Because of their high visibility in the media (and their impact on political discussion), the blogs fall victim to descriptions that often have little to do with their reality. Some of these descriptions arise from those who feel threatened by the blogs and the Web, though the truth of the matter is that the Web doesn't really increase the danger to anyone on its own.

In chapter 3, I discuss the blogs from a view within the blogosphere, trying to capture just how the bloggers see their relationships to the wider communities around them. Bloggers don't view themselves as entering a virtual world when they write, but simply as the utilizers of a new set of tools for dealing with situations in the "real" world. On the other hand, their imagined expansionism sometimes is little more than a new way to talk to the same type of people they would be talking to anyway, the expansion being only in number and not in type. This does not mean, however, that the blogs do not have impact—they have, and will continue to—simply that it will rarely be in converting an audience to the blogger's belief.

Also in this chapter is discussion of the fact that no blog exists alone—that is, each is part of a greater conversation that includes comments, links, and other blogs (among other things). The blogger creates no discrete work, but adds to conversations already in progress.

As a great deal of discussion concerning the blogs has focused on their impact on journalism and politics, chapter 4 presents a picture of just how those interact. Professional journalism certainly is not going to die as a result of the blogs, but it will not remain the same as it has been for the last several decades. The same is true of politics.

What is happening through the blogs, for both politics and journalism, is the carving out of a new place in the universe of organization and authority. Over the past century and more, both have become increasingly hierarchical, top-down. The blogs, much more egalitarian in focus, are forcing recognition that the old model of organization will no longer suffice, that there needs to be a way of encompassing individual ideas and initiatives while not giving up all control. This is a process that is probably still in its early days, and the tensions between the "grass roots" of the blogs and the established journalists and politicians have yet to be completely resolved—if they will be at all.

In chapter 5, I focus on communications technology in popular culture (with an eye on the blogs), comparing the views of fifty years ago with the situation today. At that time, communications technology (outside of the telephone) was primarily one-way, coming from a centralized point of creation and dissemination to members of a public that were seen as little more than passive receptacles. Today, of course, those same individual audience members have become part of the creative process, taking more and more power each year.

Finally, in chapter 6, I present a survey of one blogging community, that of Christian bloggers. In some respects no different from other blogging communities, this one shows great breadth and depth, along with a great desire to use the blogs for personal and community growth.

The importance of what is happening in the blogosphere was brought home to me just as I was finishing this book, when I ran across a post on the blog of Andrew Keen, a critic of the blogs who blogs himself. After participating in an online panel, Keen wrote:

> I learned that blogs are boring. I learned that we need to get beyond arguing about blogs versus *The New York Times*.... But all anyone wants to discuss, it seems, is the well trodden terrain of bloggers versus traditional news reporters.
>
> Enough of blogs and enough of bloggers! It's bad enough that there are 70 million of them out there, littering the Internet with fast breaking news about what their authors ate for breakfast. But blogs are just one piece in the digital media revolution. They are boring to write (yawn), boring to read (yawn) and boring to discuss (yawn).
>
> What I really want to discuss is the impact of Web 2.0 on truth, education, memory and power. I want to debate the increasingly Orwellian role of Google in our information economy. I want to talk about the way in which the Internet has unleashed a plague of pornography, gambling and intellectual dishonesty on our youth. I want to discuss the future of the book.[1]

Enough? Let us tease apart what Keen is saying to see if there is any substance there:

First, he assumes a rivalry between the blogs and *The New York Times* that no one cares about any longer. "Been there, done that," he seems to be saying regarding the tensions between bloggers and commercial news-media entities. But he does not seem to recognize that the debate has been a good one for our American public sphere, that the boundaries of journalism have been expanding, and that we are developing new means of research, information retrieval, and debate that are, as yet, not fully formed. What seems to him "well trodden terrain" is really just preamble to a new type of journalism not based at all on an either/or between the amateur and the professional but on a melding of the particular possibilities each brings to news gathering, analysis, and distribution.

It is easy to disparage something (especially something new) through undemanding stereotypes and the simplistic conceptions presented by a commercial news media that looks for the quick and easy phrase for encapsulating any new phenomenon. The pajama'd blogger writing of cereal bowls is as rare as the image is common—and would only be an example (and a poor one, at that) of one type of blogger out of many, the social networker. Most bloggers have a point to make, something to say to a group wider than friends, family, and colleagues.

Though many blogs are *bad*, poorly written and researched, and often thoughtless, they are never boring. If they create a yawn, the cause is probably inside the yawner. As our mothers told us when we were young and complained of being bored, "Use your imagination! Boredom is your responsibility; it comes from within you. Find something to do, and do it." A blog is boring to write only if you haven't explored yourself carefully enough to find something to say, then explored outside, to see what others have said. A blog is boring to read only if you think you've found all the answers already, and won't discover anything new. A blog is boring to discuss only if you aren't open to discovery and new ways of approaching a topic.

A blog is only as boring as any piece of writing.

I would argue that there's a subtext in calling the blogs boring, and that is belief that there's an elitism to knowledge. The only ones who really "know" are those with the certification from the establishment. The blogs, with so many millions coming at almost any topic from so many different levels of skill and knowledge, are always going to be difficult to plow through, but any worthwhile search is difficult, taking diligence and patience. They are only boring if you believe nothing will really be found there.

If Keen wants to discuss "truth, justice, and the American way" in terms of Web 2.0, adding in "education, memory, and power," he certainly can do so. He could quickly come across statements like this about Web 2.0: "In the early days the web was a static medium. Early web shops were like a shop front or foyer leading to vast operations out back. In contrast, web 2.0 is about fluidity and change; the web itself is the business."[2] The implications of this statement on education and memory are tremendous. Or he might find this: "The open source dictum, 'release early and release often' in fact has morphed into an even more radical position, 'the perpetual beta,' in which the product is developed in the open, with new features slipstreamed in on a monthly, weekly, or even daily basis."[3] The implications here, too, are extensive, on truth and power and on much more. Want to discuss Google and Orwell? Out of the thousands of posts discussing both, you will find many asking if Google really springs from Orwell's imaginings in *1984*: "Google's motto is 'Don't be Evil' but its ubiquitous presence on the Internet is near monopolistic and history has shown that monopolies, whether government-sponsored or private enterprise do not have a good track record."[4]

If Keen wants discussion on the Web that's not boring, he need only Google himself and his book *The Cult of the Amateur: How Today's Internet Is Killing Our Culture*. The day after its release on June 5, 2007, there were already several hundred blogs that had written on it. Much of it was negative and dismissive, with the reactions, at their best, being on the level of this, addressed, really, to Keen:

> As the wise Heraclitus once wrote, "much information does not teach wisdom."
>
> So do not be afraid of much information. Or much mess for that matter.
>
> It's a sign of a healthy culture.
>
> Free presses are messy. They are supposed to be. Democracy is messy. They are also supposed to be. It is fine, in fact it is healthy to have lots and lots and lots of voices, as opposed to a few state controlled or corporate controlled "voices of truth."
>
> As Justice Louis Brandeis wrote, the answer to bad free speech is more free speech.[5]

Not exactly boring, uneducated, or referencing breakfast.

Clearly, countering someone like Keen concerning the blogs is like shooting a gnat with a cannon—if the conversation continues online. But, as *Wired*'s Jeff Howe writes, Keen isn't really addressing the blogosphere: "Keen's arguments will sound mightily persuasive to a significant constituency who *do* believe the Internet is primarily a repository of porn, spam and corrosive amateurism. Failing to recognize that the choir to which Keen preaches might just be larger than our own congregation is an arrogant, and potentially irreversible blunder. While Web 2.0 insiders might love to hate Keen, many in the world at large will love to love him."[6]

One purpose of this book of mine, though most of it was written before Keen's book appeared, is to bring discussion of the blogosphere to those who might not be in the choir Howe refers to. Though there is much here that might be of interest to those of us perfectly comfortable online, I want to expand the universe of discourse to include everyone in America and everywhere else where the blogs have become an important force. One of my main points is that there is no real divide between "reality" and "virtuality," and so I don't want to address people as if they are so divided in their interests and possible knowledge.

Keen's premise, that the Internet is killing "our" culture, is paltry in its implied conception of knowledge and culture, containing within it the same logical fallacy behind the argument that increased literacy weakens culture, for it lowers the average level of knowledge and skill among the literate. Neither argument recognizes that expansion does not actually make the people counted stupider or less learned—it simply brings more people into the equation. The Internet does not limit culture. On the contrary, it expands it by increasing possibilities.

One of the bloggers quoted previously references Brandeis on the fact that the way to counter bad speech is not to limit speech, but to increase it. The same holds true for other aspects of our culture—as this book, I hope, demonstrates.

Chapter 1

AN INTRODUCTION
TO THE BLOGS

Blogs and Other Online Entities Discussed in Chapter 1

The Academic Blog Portal, http://www.academicblogs.org/wiki/index.php/
   Main_Page

Assignment Zero, http://zero.newassignment.net

The Club for Growth, http://www.clubforgrowth.org

Daily Kos, http://www.dailykos.com

Diaryland, http://diaryland.com

Drew's Marketing Minute, http://www.drewsmarketingminute.com

Grasping Reality with Both Hands: Brad DeLong's Semi-Daily Journal,
   http://delong.typepad.com

Informed Comment, http://www.juancole.com

The Little Professor: Things Victorian and Academic, http://littleprofessor.
   typepad.com

LiveJournal, http://www.livejournal.com

Pixel Press, http://www.pixelpress.org

Second Life, http://secondlife.com

Startling Bleats of Tomorrow, http://lileks.com/bleats/index.html

TPMCafe, http://www.tpmcafe.com

University Diaries, http://margaretsoltan.phenominet.com

The Weblog Awards, http://2006.weblogawards.org

Any understanding of the blogs becomes more fulsome when it includes a little background in language and culture, for blogs are not simply a function or result of the technology that distributes them. Nor are they merely a new trash pit, a place for all the detritus of human thought that amounted to nothing and had previously been hidden from sight. Internet development may have unleashed them, but blogs are also a new and original cultural phenomenon, reflecting more the changes and needs in society than simple realization of technological possibility.

For the purposes of this introductory chapter, I've chosen to provide a little of the cultural background that has led to the rise of the blogosphere through glimpses (along with other discussions) at the thoughts of three twentieth-century scholars, Jürgen Habermas, B. F. Skinner, and Walter Ong. Other thinkers could be used as easily, but these three connect neatly and together cover a great deal of the relevant ground. Through a look at them, it should be clear that the blogs are not only changing our cultural landscape, but that the direction may be much more positive than many have assumed. Each scholar has a unique perspective, yet, taken as a trio, they provide a context for effective understanding of the contemporary communications revolution in its cultural, though not its technological (that is another topic completely), aspects. Because the subtitle of this book, "The New Public Sphere," is taken from a phrase Habermas created, I will start with his work.

In *The Structural Transformation of the Public Sphere*, Habermas describes and defines the "public sphere" through an examination of cultural shifts and developments in eighteenth-century Europe when, he argues, the public sphere first developed. Though the public sphere, as he claims, has been tremendously constricted since, his definition stands today: "The bourgeois public sphere may be conceived above all as the sphere of private people coming together as a public; they soon claimed the public sphere regulated from above against the public authorities themselves, to engage them in a debate over the general rules governing relations in the basically privatized but publicly relevant sphere of commodity exchange and social labor."[1] Habermas illustrates what he means through a chart:[2]

Private Realm		Sphere of Public Authority
Civil society (realm of commodity exchange and social labor)	Public sphere in the political realm	State (realm of the "police")
	Public sphere in the world of letters (clubs, press)	
Conjugal family's internal space (bourgeois intellectuals)	"Town" (market of culture products)	Court (courtly-noble society)

The public sphere exists within a tension between what might be called "private" or "familial" or "personal" authority (what I will call, later in this book, the horizontal) and public authority (which I look upon as the vertical)—once the private has gained a certain parity with the public. It covers matters of politics, the arts, and commerce—or about all that might fall under the rubric "culture,"—and it is where, today, the blogs reside. The weakness of the public sphere is that it is protected only by the will of the public and not by any institutional structures. The First Amendment to the U.S. Constitution, for example, doesn't guarantee a public sphere; it merely protects it from government interference.

As Habermas reiterates throughout his book, the public sphere, though it may have evolved out of the tensions between states and society, remains firmly within the "private realm." Governments could not and did not protect the public sphere as commercial forces grew to dominate western societies. Yet the private sphere could have evolved "into a sphere of private autonomy only to the degree to which it became emancipated from mercantilist regulation."[3] This is a central conundrum of the public sphere: it can't be a creature of government, but it needs government if it is to exist at all.

Left pretty much to its own devices, over the course of the nineteenth and twentieth centuries, the "public sphere in the private world of letters was replaced by the pseudo-public or sham-private world of cultural consumption."[4] In the United States, this was most noticeable in the growth of centralized communications media that eventually took control of the public sphere, leaving much of the public only as passive observers of actions on a commercial stage. "When the laws of the market governing the sphere of commodity exchange and of social labor also pervaded the sphere reserved for private people as a public, rational-critical debate had a tendency to be replaced by consumption, and the web of public communication unraveled into acts of individual reception, however uniform in mode."[5] Possibly, the advent of the blogs, a free, easily used, and accessible venue for public discussion, is changing that, technology acting as a buffer (temporarily, at least) against public-sphere domination by commercial forces and even allowing it to be opened up again. It is too early in the life of the blogosphere to assess that absolutely, but that does seem to be the current direction. However it may prove, Habermas's examination of the constriction of the public sphere in the past provides the basis for my argument, made elsewhere,[6] that the taking back of the public sphere through the blogs is, in some respects, nothing more than a return to the type of debate and journalism practiced in the United States before the tremendous growth of the commercial news media starting in the 1840s.

Beyond that, what exactly is this "public sphere"? In discussing eighteenth-century coffeehouses and other nodes of the growing public sphere, Habermas identifies three "institutional criteria" that can also apply to the modern public sphere:

First, they preserved a kind of social intercourse that, far from presupposing the equality of status, disregarded status altogether.[7]

Just so, status (professional or otherwise) doesn't matter on the blogs—not, at least, in terms of access. Reputation, of course, is as important on the blogs as it is elsewhere, but status coming *into* the blogs can only take one so far. Blogs operate through the words on the screen, and these become the movers of judgment, all supposedly equal, though there are plenty of means of heightening their exposure, most requiring either money or extensive work within the blogosphere but outside of the particular blog (commenting on other blogs, providing links, manipulating search-engine searches, etc.).

Well-known politicians may post on a group blog such as Daily Kos, but their posts will look like any other, and commenters will react to them in a manner not far removed from how they react to any other poster. The fact of expertise established outside of the blogs (possession of a Ph.D., for example) is always trumped by expertise *demonstrated* through the blogs. The "democratization" of discussion broadens debate far beyond what can be found in traditional news media, where the only venue for most people's expression is a letters-to-the-editor ghetto. Were a group blog like Daily Kos a newspaper, it would have a front page of featured opinion pieces, a body of nothing but letters-to-the-editor, and a reference section consisting of things like AP wire stories.

> *Secondly*, discussion within such a public presupposed the problematization of areas that until then had not been questioned. The domain of "common concerns" which was the object of public critical attention remained a preserve in which church and state authorities had the monopoly of interpretation.... To the degree, however, to which philosophical and literary works and works of art in general were produced for the market and distributed through it [they, and the ideas contained, became] ... in principle generally accessible.[8]

Discourse in the late twentieth century tended to fall more and more to chosen pairings of disparate views, generally represented by figures raised from and by the news media. Before the blogs, these were on the way to becoming the representatives of a new authority, one representing the state but provided through commercial venues. The blogs are an overt rejection of this trend, an unconscious attempt to bring discussion back under popular (and not centralized) control.

In addition, before the blogs, the topics for debate, more and more frequently, were brought *to* the public rather than arising *from* the people. In the blogosphere, stories arising through popular interest and exploration, called "crowdsourced" by *Wired* magazine's Jeff Howe and journalism scholar Jay Rosen[9] (whose "Assignment Zero" is an attempt to experiment with crowdsourcing and provide it the framework of professional support that he believes will help sustain it), develop cohesion and popular interest together, providing the sense of drama sometimes lacking in stories force-fed to the public by the commercial and professional news media.

> *Thirdly*, the same process that converted culture into a commodity (and in this fashion constituted it as a culture that could become an object of discussion to begin with) established the public as in principle inclusive.[10]

The very nature of commerce makes it nearly impossible, at this point, for political or economic forces to curtail the blogs. When culture has become commodity, and a commodity becomes the vehicle for unfettered public discussion of culture, it is difficult to restrict that discussion to a privileged few. Once that genie is let out of the bottle, it is extremely difficult to get him back in. Future restrictions on the Internet by government regulators may allow commercial forces greater advantage on the Web than they now enjoy, but the Web has taken "commodity" in new directions, decentralizing it, making it something more open to action, and not simply reception, on the part of the public. Mass media, in a sense, has now become "massed" media—and will remain that for the foreseeable future.

What the blogs have managed to do, in some respects, is *re*-establish the public sphere much in the way that the coffeehouses, salons, broadsheets, and pamphlets (and more) first established it three hundred years ago. As its critics emphasize, beyond technological manifestations, it could be argued that there is little in the blogosphere that is really new. Blogs may carry debate (debate that may have been stifled, but debate in the public sphere, nonetheless) to a new venue, but there is nothing revolutionary in what the blogs are *doing*.

Aggressively cultural in orientation (and covering the entire spectrum from the private to the public on Habermas's chart), the blogs, significantly, have little resemblance to the MMO (Massively Multiplayer Online) games that have also attained a certain degree of popularity online over the past few years, games that establish online worlds that are aggressively distinct from the "real" one. Though many of those most passionate about the online "world" of Second Life resist the idea that it may be an MMO (it lacks much of the structure, particularly the iron-clad hierarchy, of games) it does, like the games, create a fictional world, and activity centers on that world in a way that may prove unlike anything we have seen before, making it (possibly) quite revolutionary, and making it worth noting in a discussion of the blogs—if for no other reason than to make a distinction.

As Philip Rosedale, founder and chief executive of Linden Lab, the producer of Second Life, sees it:

> Second Life competes in many ways with the real world, offering better ways to collaborate, meet people and build things. In the past few months 4,000 IBMers have flooded into Second Life to brainstorm, hold meetings for workers dispersed around the globe and prototype new shopping experiences for customers. Starwood Hotels tried out its upcoming Aloft hotels by building one in Second Life and hosting virtual parties where "guests" wandered through the hotel and gave design feedback. Most inspiring, thousands of people from all over the world are making a secondary income, creating businesses and selling things in Second Life with no more required of them than their own ingenuity and a PC.[11]

The blogs, on the other hand, don't move into any completely new arena, certainly never competing with the real world. They don't want to focus on something *like* the real world, but on the real world itself, even though the very venue for discussion they establish is often seen as "virtual."

The communities associated with the blogs do not, for the most part, arise through the blogs, though they are facilitated by them. As tools for participation in the reinvigorated public sphere, the blogs do not fit well into any model that effectively removes itself from direct public-sphere participation—and the MMOs do just that, though Second Life does style itself in such a way that its activities can be said to provide an entrance *back* into the "real" world. If anything, however, it creates a new and separate (and essentially fictional and restricted) public sphere rather than providing an amplification of the public sphere of the quotidian world.

Current interest in the possibilities of Second Life is based on the possibility that an ersatz Web world can (and does) exist, and that it need not have clear correlation to quotidian reality in order to be of real value to the people who utilize it. Its proponents see Second Life as, among other things, a petri dish for examining aspects of "real" life in isolation, as experiment. The Second Life Web site describes it:

> Second Life is a 3-D virtual world entirely built and owned by its residents. Since opening to the public in 2003, it has grown explosively …
>
> • From the moment you enter the World you'll discover a vast digital continent, teeming with people, entertainment, experiences and opportunity. Once you've explored a bit, perhaps you'll find a perfect parcel of land to build your house or business.
> • You'll also be surrounded by the Creations of your fellow residents. Because residents retain the rights to their digital creations, they can buy, sell and trade with other residents.
> • The Marketplace currently supports millions of US dollars in monthly transactions.[12]

Though Second Life currency can be exchanged for U.S. dollars in certain circumstances, the "world" is almost entirely "removed" from offline reality. For example, threats in it would pertain (in theory) only to that world; people who might be vicious rivals "there" could be best friends "here."

Proponents of Second Life or of platforms of similar concept believe that the "avatar" and the "visual" online world will take over from the current word-based model (where sound and image are relative adjuncts) as the standard for the Web—which would move blogs into an entirely new "place" altogether, something even beyond the "vlogs" (or video blogs). The idea behind this may be that the virtual world is easier to negotiate when analogous to, but distinct from, the "real" world rather than when seen as an extension of non-Web ways for understanding. The problem is that nonvisual means of learning about the world were developed precisely because they mediate between the world and the way the human mind works and not because they mimic the "real" world. As Second Life apes the "world," though in a somewhat cartoonish fashion, and provides a mask for the individual, it may well prove to be more a barrier than a mediator, providing unneeded obstacles rather than helpful bridges.

A lack of "real"-world grounding can have other consequences, as the science-fiction writer Philip K. Dick pointed out in a speech in 1978: "Fake realities will create fake humans. Or, fake humans will generate fake realities and then sell them to other humans, turning them, eventually, into forgeries of themselves. So we wind up with fake humans inventing fake realities and then peddling them to other fake humans."[13] Start making a "meta" world, and you open the door to all sorts of problems, taking one down a rabbit hole with a technological Alice. Dick describes what it could be like:

> I once wrote a story ["The Electric Ant"] about a man who was injured and taken to a hospital. When they began surgery on him, they discovered that he was an android, not a human, but that he did not know it. They had to break the news to him. Almost at once, Mr. Garson Poole discovered that his reality consisted of punched tape passing from reel to reel in his chest. Fascinated, he began to fill in some of the punched holes and add new ones. Immediately, his world changed. A flock of ducks flew through the room when he punched one new hole in the tape. Finally he cut the tape entirely, whereupon the world disappeared. However, it also disappeared for the other characters in the story ... which makes no sense, if you think about it. Unless the other characters were figments of his punched-tape fantasy. Which I guess is what they were.[14]

Second Life promotes itself as "Your world. Your imagination,"[15] and its proponents sometimes imagine that all of us will one day have an "avatar," "your persona in the virtual world."[16] That virtual world becomes a place, a destination. Yet, as such a "place" it becomes immediately suspect. Mark Poster describes it:

> Virtual reality is a computer-generated "place" which is "viewed" by the participant through "goggles" but which responds to stimuli from the participant or participants. A participant may "walk" through a house that is being designed for him or her to get a feel for it before it is built. Or s/he may "walk" through a "museum" or "city" whose paintings or streets are computer-generated but the position of the individual is relative to their actual movement, not to a predetermined, computer program or "movie." In addition, more than one individual may experience the same virtual

reality at the same time, with both persons' "movements" affecting the same "space." What is more, these individuals need not be in the same physical location but may be communicating information to the computer from distant points through modems. Further "movements" in virtual reality are not quite the same as movements in "old reality": for example, one can fly or go through walls since the material constraints of earth need not apply. While still in their infancy, virtual reality programs attest to the increasing "duplication," if I may use this term, of reality by technology. But the duplication incurs an alternation: virtual realities are fanciful imaginings that, in their difference from real reality, evoke play and discovery, instituting a new level of imagination. Virtual reality takes the imaginary of the word and the imaginary of the film or video image one step farther by placing the individual "inside" alternative worlds. By directly tinkering with reality, a simulational practice is set in place which alters forever the conditions under which the identity of the self is formed.

Already transitional forms of virtual reality are in use on the Internet.... As a result, a quasi-virtual reality is created by the players. What is more each player adopts a fictional role that may be different from their actual gender and indeed this gender may change in the course of the game, drastically calling into question the gender system of the dominant culture as a fixed binary. At least during the fictional game, individuals explore imaginary subject positions while in communication with others.... One participant argues that continuous participation in the game leads to a sense of involvement that is somewhere between ordinary reality and fiction. The effect of new media such as the Internet and virtual reality, then, is to multiply the kinds of "realities" one encounters in society.[17]

As I have said, its enthusiasts often feel that the concepts and manifestations of Second Life will expand to cover the entirety of the online world, that all of us will have "avatars" that we use in our online existences. But it doesn't satisfy: we do not want to be Garson Pooles, even in our imagination; most of us want single identities—and want them in a world we can have confidence in. In Piers Anthony's science-fiction novel *Macroscope*, one character is able to create another, who he then "allows" to occupy "their" body. That character only agrees to this because he has committed so awful a crime that his own existence (access to the body) is forfeited—and his creation becomes the controller. Outside of what are clearly "game" situations, few of us want a second existence in any real way; for all our flaws, we want to remain essentially as we are, not as we might imagine in our fantasies. Yet Second Life makes it all but impossible for any but celebrities to develop an "avatar" that directly reflects their "real" existence on the assumption that we would rather be represented by an idealized being than by ourselves. One has to be someone else in Second Life, a barrier that, at least for now, I suspect, will keep out of the experiment a number of those who now use the Internet for community, for participation in (and expansion of) the "real" public sphere.

Though it is true that many people take advantage of the possibilities for online anonymity to create a persona that is quite different from their "everyday" selves, this is not the case for most of us, and certainly not for the majority of bloggers, most of whom only use pseudonyms as a means of protection and not as a way of creating a new identity. They see what they are doing as extensions of themselves, not as new selves. The very idea of a further remove from the real world makes many, especially those who want to use the Web directly for real-world public-sphere purposes, shy away, though others are drawn to it.

Most Web communities do not spring from the Web, but from affinities existing in individuals beyond the Web. The Internet acts simply as a facilitator, not as the "home" of community itself (as in Second Life). The renewed Habermasian public sphere does not reside on the Web, but has found in the Internet a tool for providing participation in the debates of our time for those who might have previously felt themselves marginalized into a passive spectator status. Furthermore, the public-sphere participants who have taken so to the blogs do not do it just to learn about the public sphere, but to participate in it directly. There is no "game" aspect to the blogs (though there are plenty of blogs about games), and no sense that blogging is itself an experiment. It is a tool and, in the eyes of most of its users, only a tool.

Though he is not as critical to my thinking on the cultural foundations of the blogosphere for this book as have been Habermas, Skinner, and Ong, one of the writers whose thoughts have been with me as I have considered the cultural changes of the current communications revolution has been Kenneth Burke. His *Permanence and Change* has proven once again insightful, though from an era long passed (and from a man with something of a reputation as a technophobe). The blogs, after all, are a symptom of change. Burke's thoughts on change, then, do apply to the development of the online aspects of communities built around the blogs, especially in relation to one of his main foci, changing perceptions and possibilities—and to language itself. Burke writes, for example, "When a superstructure of certainties begins to topple, individual minds are correspondingly affected, since the mind is a social product, and our very concepts of character depend upon the verbalizations of our group. In its origins, language is an implement of action, a device which takes its shape by the cooperative patterns of the group that uses it."[18] Sometimes, people are led to try to sweep everything away in the face of the new, but the fact remains that *both* permanence and change are real and constant. Along with the Internet and the new possibilities it represents ride social structures and groupings as old as humanity—and so "the verbalizations of our group" (exactly what the blogs are providing) become increasingly important in a context of increased bombardment by "information" of all sorts and to all senses—especially as they are among the only things that can ease the fear of change.

A game or experiment like Second Life tries to supplant language from the place of centrality where Burke (and, as we shall see, Skinner and Ong—though in differing ways) place it. To some extent, each of them follows the old conclusion of linguist Edward Sapir that "It is quite an illusion to imagine that one adjusts to reality essentially without the use of language and that language is merely an incidental means of solving specific problems of communication or reflection. The fact of the matter is that the 'real world' is to a large extent unconsciously built up on the language habits of the group."[19] And it is this, in my opinion (along with its separation from the public sphere), that will restrain the Second Life visual model from becoming *the* Internet standard: language will no more be superseded by image on the Web than it is in our heads, for language, more than image, is at the heart of who we are—in terms of group identity, certainly.

I suspect that it is more likely that the aspects of human community that will survive and grow through connection with the Internet are those that have both a verbal base and a "real world" (public sphere) connection. The image of bloggers is of pajama'd isolators who have little interest in real interaction with the physical world and less skill with words—even though recent events have shown them to be directly concerned with that world and active within it, using the Internet and their blogs as tools for amplifying their effects on the world and for allowing them to deftly manipulate debate within the public sphere. The wide use of the blogs as a means for furthering political ends is probably the most high-profile example of how the blogs become tools, but religious organizations, academics, and even people in business are finding ways of making the blogs work for their own "outside" activities, doing so through what are their generally sophisticated *verbal* (and not visual) skills.

One of the changes in attitude toward the written word represented by the blogs is a devaluation of the grapheme, the visual grammar, and all the other aspects of the word as produced on a page or screen. These rose to importance over past centuries along with print culture and its emphasis on the artifact of the page. Though they generally use words, the blogs reduce the importance of the printed word itself, replacing the "thing" (the printed spoor, so to speak, of the word) with a dynamic unavailable to previous physical manifestations of verbal works, a dynamic in keeping with B. F. Skinner's conception of "verbal behavior."

Text messaging, email, and the blogs have provided something to the *printed* word (actually, the *published* word, for it is dissemination that is important in this context) that it has never before had to the extent possible today, a sense of *immediacy.* Not even the typewriter gave the writer such a feeling of the possibility of immediate response. There was almost always a remove, a distance between writer and audience. This made writing (especially writing for publication) qualitatively different from talking; it created one of the great problems (and advantages) for the written word. It also brought up one of the situations Skinner had to cover in his behavioral (stimulus/response/reinforcement) model for verbal activity, the delayed (or even non-existent) reinforcement received by an author:

> The writer is particularly likely to suffer from a lack of clarity in the audience as a controlling variable, but he can often compensate for this by finding a reader or listener who immediately reinforces him. An effective audience not only selectively reinforces particular kinds of behavior, it raises the strength of behavior in general. Sometimes this seems to be the only recourse of the writer suffering from the "abulia" of extinction. A writer who finds it difficult to "put his thoughts on paper" may be able to emit the behavior in the presence of a favorable audience.[20]

Or, at least, in an imagined presence of one—the creation of which is quite a sophisticated feat in itself. Of course, this, the lack of immediate response and reinforcement, is something writers have wrestled with since the advent of pen and ink. As Herbert Gans, writing about moviemaking (though the point is the same), says, "the creator not only anticipates his audience, but tries to create or attract one for his products. In order to do this, the movie-maker concentrates on the product itself, and tries to make a 'good' movie. He may succeed if his work on the product (and his audience image) are sensitive to the predispositions of any party of the total movie audience."[21] When an audience is directly before one, it is easy to react to *their* reactions, expanding, changing or clarifying ... or even shutting up. One could even argue that "writer's block" may be nothing more than a temporary inability to envision an audience. "Talented" writers and other artists, disciplined and experienced (like Gans's successful moviemaker), have always been good at creating imaginary audiences, "people" who are constantly reading over their shoulders, so to speak. But this is a developed skill at the very least, and one that takes practice and familiarity with the experiences at the other end of the process, that of the reader.

Sometimes, the fact of an "imaginary audience" for a writer spills over into the "reality" of the blogs, especially when the writer discovers that he or she is not as skilled as imagined and the "real" audience does not react as he or she had thought it would. Faced with this, a few bloggers go so far as to try to make their imaginary audiences seem real, something that was not possible with such immediacy before. Lee Siegel, an editor and writer for *The New Republic*, found himself suspended from his job after it was discovered that he had created what had become known as a "sock puppet" to comment on his own blog posts.[22] Writing under the name "Sprezzatura," Siegel lavishly praised his own writing and attacked those who disagreed with him. Sock puppets can become such a problem on group blogs that some, like Daily Kos, discourage the use of them—sometimes to the point of banishment.[23]

Even without sock puppets, most bloggers manage to bring back at least a sense of both a real and an immediate audience to themselves as writers, allowing even those who have not yet reached the level necessary for becoming an effective solitary writer to compose—sometimes even with skill and great effect. Not all blogs allow comment, of course, and most receive few, if any. But any blogger can determine quite easily how many people have looked at a post, and how soon after posting, providing a certain type of reinforcement. The fear that nobody is paying attention is certainly there, but it is immediately verifiable—and new avenues for attracting an audience are nearly always available.

It may be the *possibility* (and not the reality) of immediate response that has led to the quick growth in popularity of the blogs, at least partially. Certainly, it is the very fact of response that makes Skinner's conception of "verbal behavior" so useful in coming to an understanding of the blogs. Skinner's *active* model supplants the idea of discrete *things*, books and magazines, and so forth, as the center of significant (or lasting) verbal activity, replacing these with the *dynamic* of the verbal interaction.

The basic Skinnerian model for verbal behavior is based on recognition that our use of language is not grounded in grammar but arises from effect, and from evaluation of whether or not the effect matches expectation. With that in mind, Skinner created a new vocabulary for talking about language, relying not on nouns and verbs but on *tacts* (from *contact*) and *mands* (from *demand*), among others, on words that reflect the dynamics of the language act, not the artifacts of language itself. These new words are an attempt to place language acts within a behavioral context rather than a structural one, moving the emphasis to the transaction and away from the actual word used. This is particularly significant today as Skinner's model helps make possible a deeper understanding of the utilizations of language through such things as text messaging, email, and the blogs, for the conversational continuum is much tighter through these new communications tools than is possible through more traditional print media, reducing (again) the importance of the artifact and increasing focus on the conversation. No, it is not true that the blogs, any more than older written forms of language, simply represent "spoken language in visible form,"[24] but the newer possibilities do bring to the fore aspects of spoken language that have been slowly eclipsed by the rise of print-centered culture since the time of Gutenberg.

Some people, particularly parents and teachers, have been expressing concern over what they see as the devaluation of the word that they see showing through the new technologies. And they are right: the word-as-thing *has* been devalued. A kind of shorthand has grown up around Internet Instant Messaging (IM) and telephone text messaging, increasing the speed and ease of communication, but nearly erasing (in this context) the place of honor that the text itself has held for centuries. The worry is that the reliance on abbreviations and acronyms will bleed over into other sorts of writing. The fear is that formal academic papers will one day including phrases like "cn u c y?" This is not really likely—in part because of the differences in editing, drafting possibilities, and in the controlling of speed of response between the new and the old. Also, the word, in each case, is used differently—and the people using it are generally aware of the difference (or can be made aware of it). They know when to treat the word as a thing and when to use it as a tool.

Though the editing one does in a verbal (or IM) environment is substantially unlike that done on the page, it is still editing and still a part of the verbal process that relies on the demands (and strictures) of the response community. Skinner writes:

> The traditions and practices of editing which prevail within a verbal community are in part responsible for the extent of the verbal behavior shown by its members. The reticent or laconic differs from the voluble or effusive, in part at least, because of differences in the consequences of verbal behavior. Within a given community a speaker will show various degrees of editing in the presence of various special audiences. This fact is used by the speaker himself in encouraging his own verbal behavior when he seeks out a favorable audience.[25]

And the degree and type of editing depend on the specifics of the relationship between the speaker and the community (which will determine the acceptability—or lack of it—of things like IM shorthand). In certain laid-back atmospheres of conversation and general agreement, speakers (and writers, especially now, when audience reaction can be almost immediate and when text itself, in IM and text messaging situations, may disappear quickly from sight, reducing its importance as record) tend to relax, speaking with less care and, sometimes, with greater enthusiasm. In fact, we often find that it is enthusiasm that is tamped down through many editing processes, often reduced or edited out, certainly, when that most extensive editing process of formal writing is involved. Skinner, again, says:

> The functions of the speaker in generating and editing the raw material of his verbal behavior suggest the traditional distinction between ecstatic and euplastic composition. Wholly unedited behavior is ecstatic. The heavily wrought and thoroughly considered end-product is euplastic. Sometimes these functions are usefully separated in time. A writer may find it most effective to produce large quantities of behavior under the relaxed conditions of editing … and then to work this material over under totally different circumstances.[26]

In print, for the most part (except, of course, in works of art), we expect to see enthusiasm contained, and we expect to see something as close to accepted grammatical standards as possible (except in instances where use of other standards is signaled). Time and skill, we assume, have been used in preparation of the manuscript, making it a finished product on presentation to us in print. As with speech, there is little time for editing in text messaging (where response can come instantly, even requiring a quick reply for continuation of the conversation) without running the risk of extinguishing the exchange. Blogs and emails contain a similar (though not so dramatic) immediacy.

As I have indicated, the distinction between text messaging and other writing is not always well understood by educators, some of whom do worry that students are losing the ability to write well as a result of constant text messaging (instead of seeing it as an opportunity for starting with what writing students are already doing and developing that into the standard model). This worry even found its way into a report evaluating English test results by the Irish State Examinations Commission:

> The emergence of the mobile phone and the rise of text messaging as a popular means of communication would appear to have impacted on standards of writing as evidenced in the responses of candidates taking the exam. Expertise in text messaging and email is affecting spelling and punctuation in particular. Text messaging, with its use of phonetic spelling and little or no punctuation, seems to pose a threat to traditional conventions in writing.[27]

Language changes, as this passage's use of "impacted" shows, and it certainly may be true that text messaging will lead to alterations in the "conventions in writing." But the conventions of text messaging may just as likely have impact akin to those of the conventions of shorthand. The job of the teacher, in relation to Instant Messages, may be more to keep students aware that different conventions apply in different situations than to stifle use of one convention in favor of another. There is only a "threat" when these two means of verbal behavior are conflated or otherwise confused.

There is a significant imperative to respond quickly to a comment on one's blog, to a response to a comment on another blog, or to an IM, for implied in a lack of response is either acceptance of what the other has said or recognition that one's own initial statement was somehow lacking. Yet it is also true, and, rather frequent in "off the cuff" conversation (either through voice or online), that no response is possible:

> Even when return stimulation is not lacking and when there is time to respond to it, the speaker may nevertheless fail to respond. He does not edit because, to put it roughly, he "does not know what he is saying." The stimulations generated by the speaker's own behavior, whether public or private, has simply not been effective. The spoken slip may not only not be seen when emitted, it may even be denied when pointed out later.[28]

Sometimes we simply blow it—and recognize that it is time to bow out. This is an accepted fact of life in blogging, especially in comments. Again, this shows the closer relationship between verbal behavior and the blogs than between verbal behavior and most other writing.

Though blog diaries themselves can be edited after publication, comments, like emails and text messages, generally cannot be, making these *even more* like speech, where the words, once said, can only be amended through an overlay of other words, not revoked or revised through an editing process that keeps them from being seen until "ready." As in speech, this requires careful attention to audience and situation for the writer in a fashion not needed where another draft is possible:

> If editing is to occur, the speaker must react as a listener to his own behavior. If he cannot do so, he cannot edit. When behavior is executed with speed, either because it is very strong or because speed has been differentially reinforced (compare the student answering a question rapidly in order to be the first to answer it), the response affects the listener as soon as the speaker himself. The speaker cannot prevent the response, though he may later revoke it. The slip which is not "caught" but immediately "seen" after emission is characteristic of rapid speech.[29]

This is characteristic of rapid writing, especially when the writing can be "sent" or "published" almost immediately after composition. In both cases, this is acceptable in a manner not allowed for much other written work, for rarely, in the past, was a written communication so immediately irrevocable. So clearly recognized is this in the blogosphere that comment on grammatical errors in the comments in not considered polite or warranted.

Though we equate the danger of hitting the "send" or "submit" button too early with the age of the Internet, my own family has the story of my great-grandmother regretting her written and mailed "yes" to my great-grandfather's proposal of marriage. She waited by the mailbox to retrieve it from the postman—who refused to give it back to her (he was a friend of my great-grandfather). With the written acceptance soon "public," she did not feel she could revoke it. For the most part, however (until, at least, that post box door closes), written language has always contained within it a defense against immediacy and precipitous verbal action—up to the advent of the Internet, that is. Today, one of the most common complaints about email is just that ease of "send."

The other side of this ease of transmittal is the possibility of quick response, confirmation of understanding of a sort that could not come along with past composition as it did with speech. This new possibility enables immediate reinforcement of the writing act, and that comes in ways more reminiscent of speech than of writing. Skinner notes: "Scientists who study conditions of vocal communication usually accept an accurate restatement as evidence that a vocal response has been understood. This is possibly something more than a purely echoic response either as auditory mimicry or as a reproduction of conventional speech sounds."[30] On group blogs such as Daily Kos, there are a number of ways of saying both "I understand" and "I approve" immediately. One is by clicking a "recommend" button that can help bump the particular diary up in the hierarchy of the blog. Another is by posting a comment echoing the diarist's point, particularly in such a way that will elicit a new response from the diarist. A third is to rank highly the comments of others that reflect the point the diarist is trying to make.

Though it breaks with many of the conventions of written English, Internet writing behavior has quickly developed its own set of conventions, many of which are as strictly enforced as is subject/verb agreement in the prescriptive grammarian's classroom. Certain acts of writing for blogs, IMs, and emails have come to be considered incorrect and warranting of negative response. The use of capital letters only, for example, is seen as akin to shouting, and is frowned upon. Of course, conventions like this are nothing new in verbal behavior of any sort: "Certain properties and responses are aversive to others and likely to bring punishment. Among these are too loud a voice, a rasping tone, undue sibilance, heavy alliteration, singsong, and such defective execution as bad spelling, stuttering, or incompleteness."[31] Not only are there clear ways of expressing disapproval with the means of expression on the blogs, but there are also other behaviors that can be used to express disapproval, in ways analogous to other types of punishing verbal behavior, and these often provide a way for doing so without having to take direct responsibility for the disapproval (it is extremely easy, after all, to hide one's identity in a comment section). They are analogous to similar aspects of speech:

> In a group the speaker may *murmur* his dissent or *hiss* his disapproval. These responses do not conspicuously employ the speech apparatus, and the sounds are not easily traced to their source. (The *whisper* is a different kind of modification of response because it involves multiple audiences.) The anonymous letter is the written counterpart of the murmur or hiss but susceptible to the normal variety of forms. In all these ways the speaker avoids punishment.[32]

The anonymous comment on a blog (an easy thing to post) can make its point even more clearly than an anonymous letter, for it can become a direct part of an immediate conversation. The murmur can be seen in the comment that is off topic, the hiss in the snide remark.

As often as not, successful bloggers get involved in the comment discussions on their diaries, clarifying, explaining, and arguing in a way that, in the past, has been generally associated with verbal conversation and not the written word. The blogs, certainly, often act like verbal group discussions:

One of the principal effects of verbal behavior, then, is the strengthening of corresponding behavior in the listener. The verbal stimulus does not impart information available only to the speaker because of his special point of vantage, nor does it create new behavior in the listener. Instead, it clarifies and strengthens behavior which has already been available to some degree. This is often for the benefit of the listener; but it may have indirect effects in shaping and maintaining the behavior of the speaker. We learn to speak to be understood.[33]

Maybe, were Skinner writing now, he might also say, "we learn to blog to be understood."

It should be clear by now that the blogs require a different model of understanding and analysis than we have been using for print over the past centuries. They probably also need something different from Skinner's "verbal behavior" model, but whatever is developed should be able to encompass the dynamics of speech as they are reflected in the blogs as well as the more familiar (in terms of our analyses of words) print.

The blogs, with their "residue" (the fact that they can be returned to easily, that they do not "slide down into oblivion" quite so quickly as a text message or IM—or the unrecorded spoken word) have a conversational sustainability that the more ephemeral new uses of text lack. This advantage of the blogs can also be a bit of a different problem for the less substantial of Web communications. Simon Dumenco, writing in *Advertising Age*, says, "I'm sorry, but endless messages that read 'Hey, dude! Thanks for adding me [as a friend]' are not content—or at least not monetizable content. Just because something has been typed on a screen (a computer screen, a cell phone screen, whatever) does not automatically make it media or content. The vast majority of messages typed on MySpace (and Facebook and other social-networking sites) will never, ever be read again after they scroll off users' main pages. MySpace is all about what 'friends' said five minutes ago or five days ago—not five months ago."[34] Dumenco has a point, which is at the heart of why conversation through these devices will not replace blogging, which (in turn) will not replace more traditional texts, for both have different, more public, and more substantial purposes altogether than the more "conversational" uses of the Internet.

Not all reactions to speech, to writing, or to the blogs are positive or helpful, sometimes resulting in something other than the desired behavior. Skinner presents four effects of punishment on verbal behavior: concealing identity, recession to covert expression, talking to oneself, and disguised speech.[35] The first two are related, and here I shall deal with them as one. The last two are not really relevant to the blogs (though an argument could be made that disguised speech is). However, Skinner's main point about the punishment of verbal behavior applies to the blogs absolutely:

Verbal behavior is usually punished—if only by its ineffectiveness—when it is under poor *audience control*. Both vulgar and highbrow expressions are punished in the contrary environments. Some responses—such as obscenities, blasphemies, and so on—are fairly generally punished, but evidently not by the verbal environments which set them up. In general, movement from one group to another fosters punishment.... Another punishable insensitivity to the audience is exemplified by the response which is too obvious, too commonplace or shopworn, or simply too often repeated by the present speaker.[36]

Because quick response is so critical to the blogs, clear understanding of audience is even more important for the average blogger (who is no media professional) than it is just about anywhere else in verbal activity. Unlike in face-to-face (or even telephone) conversation, there are no visual or aural clues to help one figure out the audience and its reaction, making the ability to imagine an audience accurately (as I wrote of at the beginning of my discussion of Skinner) extremely important.

Though there is much more to Skinner's *Verbal Behavior* than is relevant to my discussion here, his work, if used by future scholars, will provide a model that can assist in coming to an understanding of the blogs and of the word in a new communicative context. Brought back into conversation in ways never expected in the past, the word today makes different demands on the user and does so in new ways. Today's email exchanges are not directly analogous to the letters of the past—so changes in the language used for mail cannot be ascribed simply to factors (such as education, cultural importance, etc.) outside of the venue of conversation. The changes in letter-writing style are, in part at least, determined by the way the newer technology relates the correspondents— and by the ways the correspondents want to be seen through their texts. This is not so much technodeterminism, however, but is technology allowing a reversion to, or recapturing of, another type of conversation in a new context. The technology does not "make"; it simply "allows." Just as the telephone inspired new forms of verbal etiquette and style, but without altering the language (for the most part) beyond adding to it, so will likely be the case with the blogs, email, and text messaging.

Because he examines all verbal behavior on the basis of its fit into his stimulus/response/reinforcement continuum, Skinner's work allows us to see the blogs for what they are, a heightening of an old means for the use of words within a new technological context, and not as simply a qualitatively new type of conversation. Just as the blogs also hearken back to a type of newspaper discussion superseded by the rise of the commercial press from the 1840s on, they reflect a conversational style (and consideration of words) that has been with us *in speech* since language began. That it uses the *written* word instead of the *spoken* becomes a less important distinction—as does the visual representation of the word—than it has been since before the advent of print. The question remains, though, where are the changes we are experiencing now taking us? They may be a means of incorporating the old, but that is not the full extent of their impact, either on language or on culture.

Benjamin Whorf, creator (with his mentor, Edward Sapir) of what has come to be known as the Sapir-Whorf Hypothesis that languages structures and culturally mediated understanding of the world are intrinsically related, wrote the following in an essay for a volume dedicated to the memory of Sapir:

> How does such a network of language, culture, and behavior come about historically? Which was first: the language patterns or the cultural norms? In main they have grown up together, constantly influencing each other. But in this partnership the nature of the language is the factor that limits free plasticity and rigidifies channels of development in the more autocratic way. This is so because a language is a system, not just an assemblage of norms. Large systematic outlines can change to something really new only very slowly, while many other cultural innovations are made with comparative quickness. Language thus represents the mass mind; it is affected by inventions and innovations, but affected little and slowly, where to inventors and innovators it legislates with the decree immediate.[37]

Making use, in part, of just this idea (though he saw Sapir's own conception of *written* language as simplistic), Walter Ong traces the development of language and culture from pre-Gutenberg times to the eve of the current communications revolution, focusing on the interactions of technology, culture, and language. Through his centuries-long focus, he makes it clear that, though technology certainly can have immediate impact (as Whorf claims), its real influence may take hundreds of years to manifest itself in the culture.

Chapter 5 of Ong's *Orality and Literacy*, "Print, Space and Closure," though predating the blogs, constructs another background that can help one understand just how the blogs work and why. What follows is a quick walk through that chapter, updating Ong's comments on print culture in light of new technological developments and showing a little of how Ong's observations pertain to Internet culture.

The first section of the chapter, "Hearing-Dominance Yields to Sight-Dominance," opens with the claim that "print both reinforces and transforms the effects of writing on thought and expression."[38] By the same token, the new Internet possibilities also reinforce and transform, but do so to the effects of *print*. Ong sees a shift from a sound "space" to a visual one—and what we are experiencing now is a further shift, to a virtual space, malleable in ways the print space is not. In both cases, the change is greater than simply an alteration in presentation that has no impact on the interaction between the communicants, but is one with huge effect on "thought and expression" as well.

The changes wrought by print are well-known and understood, at this point—at least, they should be: we have had more than five hundred years to study these changes even while going through them. The changes wrought by the Internet are not yet so open to identification, for we are likely still within the early days of the very process of change. The blogs in particular, and the Internet in general, are certainly providing a new means of communication that amplifies the old in much the same way that print amplified script or that the typewriter amplified personal correspondence, though the new may not reside so much in the technology as in new flexibility *in terms of* communication.

Our very conception of the word itself changed, of course, with print. "Print suggests that words are things far more than writing ever did."[39] The rigidity of the printed word gave it a remove, a separateness that even handwritten words never commanded and that spoken words certainly lacked. In addition, the multiplicity of the page and the individuality of type both contributed to the new way of considering the word: "Alphabet letterpress printing, in which each letter was cast on a separate piece of metal, or type, marked a psychological breakthrough of the first order. It embedded the word itself deeply in the manufacturing process and made it into a kind of commodity."[40] Today, even the spoken word (of course) has been commodified. As Habermas shows us, almost all communication has been commodified (along with everything else), but the blogs are breaking that down once more, from a *mass* commodity to an individual one.

If hearing dominated the art of the word before the printing press, and sight did the same once the newer technology had taken root in the affected cultures, what is dominating the new Internet culture? This question intrigues many today, people wishing to see a linear continuum from orality to literacy to the new paradigm. For lack of a better word, I will refer to this new step as *neteracy*—the ability to negotiate the Internet with relative ease and skill. Gregory Ulmer has suggested another term, *electacy*,[41] for the replacement (or augmentation) of *literacy*, for most certainly electricity and election are basic factors in the new paradigm, no matter how it is otherwise viewed. The problem with his offering is that the new communications technologies have rooted themselves culturally in both hearing and sight, changing not the dominant sense so much as amplifying each and providing new interactions between them. Whatever term is settled upon needs (I believe) to encompass those senses rather than to merely point out the technological needs behind that central act of encompassing. The weakness of Ulmer's term is that it simply suggests a movement to a limited concept based on technology and choice, ignoring the new and broader paradigm of the Web. The progression is no longer linear, but it does not take a turn into another area either. Instead, it might be best described as taking Ong's progression into a third dimension, giving us the same as we had before, but heightened.

Through the example of one early (1534) English book, *The Boke Named the Gouernour* by Sir Thomas Elyot, Ong convincingly argues that the mindset of oral culture lasted well into the print era, with the importance of the visual aspect of the printed product (of the word as thing) only slowly coming to dominate. Early on, the type size used for a word, for example, did not reflect the importance of the particular word (as soon it would) but simply the aesthetics of the page itself. Later the word and the meaning it carries would become an integral part of that visual aesthetic. Just so, most of us still approach the Web page with sensibilities developed through the printed page and its apparent immutability. Ong writes: "Printing from 'hot metal' type (that is, from cast type—the older process) calls for locking up the type in an absolutely rigid position in the chase, locking the chase firmly onto a press, affixing and clamping down the makeready, and squeezing the forme of type with great pressure onto the paper printing surface in contact with the platen."[42] As one who grew up as a "hot type" printer, I can certainly attest that the process of creating a document for distribution on the Internet is much more plastic, allowing a flexibility in product that is only now, fifteen years after the commencement of the World Wide Web, being successfully or seriously experimented with in ways that are more than trivial.

Second Life, whatever the outcome of its attempt to introduce a "virtual/visual" model as the standard for the Web, is certainly trying to move away from the old concept of the page. Fred Ritchen's Pixel Press, often using simple Web-page devices such as the "rollover" (where mouse placement changes or adds to what is on the page), tries to present a new type of integration of image and text—and often succeeds. But, for the longest time, most Web pages looked like little more than online print pages.

The blogs, of course, are one of the items involved in this change away from static, print-like pages, for they have never centered on a rigid presentation. Generally laid out with newest entry on top, they can ensure that the page itself is different almost every time it is visited—especially if comments on the entries are common. Though the building blocks of the Web, HTML code and its extensions, are fairly rigid, there are ways of working around and through the limitations—with new ones appearing regularly. Even were this not true, the fact would remain: the "product" on the Web has none of the stasis of a product in print. It can be revised, manipulated—even completely re-thought—without the major retooling required in print, and this can be done instantly (a factor whose significance should not be underestimated). So fast and frequent are revisions to these pages, in fact, that most Web sites have given up attempts to provide a record of versions—and style sheets now generally accept "date viewed" over any other means of sorting or establishing version.

At the end of this section of his chapter, Ong points out, "Manuscript culture is producer-oriented, since every individual copy of a work represents great expenditure of an individual copyist's time. Medieval manuscripts are turgid with abbreviations, which favor the copyist although they inconvenience the reader. Print is consumer-oriented, since the individual copies of a work represent a much smaller investment of time."[43] The Web is oriented to both, bringing a dynamism to the relations between producer and consumer that has never before been seen. The low cost of Web page creation allows producers to indulge themselves and not just their readers. Ease of response, on the other hand, allows those same readers to quickly and effectively express approval or disdain.

In the next section, titled "Space and Meaning," Ong discusses usage of the visual space (the canvas, so to speak), first as manuscript, then as printed page. It is the fact of the visual features of the page, Ong argues, that has allowed for the development of lists, for example, and indexes as well as other alphabetized items, all representative of the new conception of the word. "Alphabetic indexes show strikingly the disengagement of words from discourse and their embedding in typographic space."[44] One of the results of this disengagement has been the growth, over the past centuries, of a new ontological view of the word in print. As it is no longer part of discourse (in this aspect), it has developed its own sense of what amounts nearly to self-verification: "If it's in a book (a newspaper, a magazine), it *must* be true."

The awe of the word in print that divorces it from the word in discourse has carried over onto the Web in a paradoxical fashion that is frustrating for teachers of research, to say the least. Students, many of whom use the plasticity of the Web in their informal interactions, still tend to see much on the Internet as final product when it does not involve them directly in the discourse. Thus, Web searches (super indexes) provide, in their minds, fixed and "real" data, not simply entry into an ongoing conversation. This is the heart of the problem for many teachers with Wikipedia, the online encyclopedia that anyone can update or alter: Wikipedia is process, not result. The student who uses it needs to see it as a dynamic and not as a source, entering into the discussion presented but reaching to other places for verified (and verifiable) "information" when that is desired. Yet many do not yet make the leap from the older print-based mindset to the new Web dynamic, even though they participate in that dynamic through their own blogs and by comments on the blogs of others. As Ong points out, over time, the book became a thing and not an utterance[45] as print culture developed. By analogy, the tendency to also see a Web page as a thing and not a process may be receding but still remains, though it will probably continue to fade as neteracy expands and the net-based culture grows in general influence.

Ong points out the various uses of the page itself, including the white space, with such use becoming part of the "meaning" of the page, something that could not really have been part of earlier oral culture. The process has grown stronger the longer print culture has dominated. Twentieth-century movements in literary theory, for the most part, have concentrated on the page (and the word upon it) as the center of concern, from the New Critics, whose "close reading" removed most everything except the text (and the page) itself from consideration, to Deconstruction, which Ong saw as "tied to typography rather than, as its advocates seem often to assume, merely to writing."[46]

The static nature of the page here again facilitates such attention, for the page is also infinitely reproducible. The Web page is, too, but without assurance that what one person gets will be identical to what another receives. The page changes because of the particulars of an individual's screen and browser (or device), for example, and not only because someone has deliberately altered the page.

Ong saw a precision in verbal description developing through the coupling of word and image in print culture as it grew, a coupling allowing exact, unbending detail of a sort not available before (even though, before moveable type, illustrations could be reproduced exactly, the words, copied by hand, would be prone to error). This, he argues, led to the increasingly careful observation associated with eighteenth- and nineteenth-century scientific cataloguers and even literary writers beginning with the Romantic era. The attention to detail so engendered has made the jump to the Web, though much of what is written and presented is initially sloppy, at best. The most successful bloggers are constantly revising or adding as new information is brought to their attention—or error becomes apparent—refining by taking advantage of the plasticity of the Web that allows change to be made so easily. The sheer mass of information migrating to the Web makes error commonplace—but the Web, unlike a book, contains within itself the means for correction. As time passes and neteracy becomes more commonplace, details of Web presentation—even on the blogs—will probably receive more attention both from creators and critics.

The impact of print on culture, according to Ong, is nearly endless, in everything from the development of extensive dictionaries and prescriptive grammar to the sense of personal privacy prevalent today in American culture. The impact of the Web is proving just as extensive, taking almost every area of print impact and amplifying it. The single dictionary, for example, becomes a plethora, soon to attain a depth not even *The Oxford English Dictionary* will be able to match, for the available instances of any usage will be legion, and will extend back to the dark beginnings of the language—something the breadth of the Web, unlike a discrete and limited book (even one of more than twenty volumes), can easily accommodate, ever-changing as new usages arise and older ones are clarified.

Our relationship to grammar is changing too, as a result of the Web. Dedicated blog readers are discovering that they cannot use the presence of accepted grammatical styles as a shorthand means for determining the value of a particular piece, for the word itself is migrating back from its position as idolized "thing" to a simpler place within the discourse, and it is discourse that is at the heart of the blogosphere. So, the fact that a comma appears outside a quotation mark or "a lot" is spelled as one word becomes irrelevant to any judgment of the writer, a belated recognition of the truth of Charles Sanders Peirce's aside that "when the general mob of writers attend so much more to words than to things, this error is common enough."[47] Oddly enough, this is a loosening that runs counter to the increased tightenings that are seen more and more on the Internet. This is especially apparent in the growing sense of ownership of a broader range of "products," including Web items, than we had seen—along with tighter copyright and patent controls.

Of greater significance than a loosening of the grip of grammar may be the carry-over fact arising from print culture that print "creates a new sense of the private ownership of words. Persons in a primarily oral culture can entertain some sense of proprietary rights to a poem, but such a sense is rare."[48] Plagiarism, a great sin of print culture, perplexes many of today's adherents to Web culture, where borrowing is easy and, in many eyes, the reverse of harmful. After all, when the word is no longer a thing, it is harder to justify ownership of it.

In fact, one of the greatest questions facing the Internet and the blogs *is* ownership—of words, images, and sounds. Many bloggers feel they should be able to import complete texts or videos or songs into their blogs or to sites like YouTube, which then allows the product to be imbedded in the individual blog, feeling they aren't stealing, but using—even amplifying—making the object more valuable through their usage than it once was. Ownership of the items makes little sense to them, especially since few bloggers see themselves operating within a commercial sphere and the items are reproducible at almost no cost to anyone. The owner may not get rich, but he or she is not harmed.

The next section of Ong's chapter, "Print and Closure: Intertextuality," deals with that sense of finality necessitated by the physical aspect of the printed word, a finality that was never part of oral culture and that, today, is foreign to the dynamism of the blogs, where the chance to make changes is always present (though so are the superseded versions, much to the chagrin of people who have tried to erase earlier "mistakes" from the Web). It also presents the changes in intertextuality engendered through print, where originality and creativity could almost be said to be fetishized, a result of the fact that the unmalleable older texts in print (unlike the oral texts that had no exact physical referent) remain present and immediate. The borrowing taken for granted in an oral culture becomes stealing in a print one—a perception that, so far, has carried over into net culture, with predictable cacophonic results. How societies will react to such "borrowings" in the future remains to be seen, but the nearly absolute protectionism of human creations will likely loosen.

In many respects, intertextuality is at the heart the blogs. According to media scholar Jonathan Gray, there are four models of intertextuality[49]:

1. As simply the result of influence;
2. As a cooperative venture between and among texts but without differentiated functions;

3. As a cooperative venture among texts but with differentiated functions;
4. As a fabric of sometimes interactive and cooperative but sometimes competitive "texts working on each other's ground, setting up shop in each other's offices and working through and sometimes against one another's work."[50]

The fourth of these is the most significant for the blogs, operating on the Internet where the boundaries of print (essentially, the book or magazine, etc., cover) have been superseded by a new screen-determined set of limitations. Because they link to each other with ease and regularity, allowing readers/ viewers to slip from one to another and back as easily as turning a page, it is not surprising that the blogs often seem to be all over each other. And, just as unsurprisingly, the place of the viewer/reader in this is also significant. "Within such a system, understanding an utterance involves placing it into a context of other utterances.... Effectively, every utterance reaches us lifeless with thousands of protruding wires. For that utterance to make sense, for it to come alive, we must hook it up to active wires already-possessed. And those already-possessed wires will in turn have formed as a result of previous meaning-making activities."[51] And possession of those wires is, of course, part of what makes one *neterate*.

In the last section of Ong's chapter, "Post-Typography: Electronics," he comes closest to grappling with the effects of this new technological change on culture. He writes: "The new orality has striking resemblances to the old in its participatory mystique, its fostering of a communal sense, its concentration on the present moment, and even its use of formulas.... Like primary orality, secondary orality has generated a strong group sense, for listening to spoken words forms hearers into a group, a true audience, just as reading written or printed texts turns individuals in on themselves."[52] What is striking about this in terms of the blogs and neteracy is that the new orality Ong posited from video culture is now being quickly subsumed into a Web culture that takes from primary orality, secondary orality, *and* print culture, building on all three to create something that, while familiar in many of its aspects, is also proving to be startlingly new and different in just the sort of ways print culture did, starting half a millennium ago.

If we posit a new move in the pattern of from orality to literacy, that is, one of from literacy to neteracy, we can begin to see the place of the blogs in the imaging of the world through the communications revolution of the twenty-first century. What this new cultural paradigm will be called—what it will *be*—is not yet determined, as I have said, and a neterate society is only one of many possible descriptions, another being the earlier-mentioned "electacy." Others abound. Whatever it will ultimately be called, the change will happen—though it will not, as many fear, replace literacy. Instead, it will encompass it in a new, more extensive whole.

In an audio essay entitled "The Transmission of Experience,"[53] executive producer of the radio show *The Infinite Mind* Bill Lichtenstein makes a case for the next step involving experience rather than information, seeing the Second Life model as offering the possibility of the actual transmission of experience, arguing that, through use of the virtual world of Second Life via an "avatar," one can now experience what others have experienced—to him, a radical new possibility (though many readers and even film goers may disagree). Second Life founder Rosedale agrees: "But unlike the Web, this is a living space filled with other real people behaving much as they do in the real world. In other words, it's a lot more than a videogame. It's a place where real companies and real entrepreneurs can try out new product designs, hold press conferences and get feedback from customers. You can go on to Second Life and test-drive a Toyota Scion."[54] Lichtenstein and Rosendale see the approximation of experience as somehow "real" and as an essential difference between Second Life and the Web as generally constructed, though they both beg the questions of how this "experience" is ultimately any more authentic than, say, a television show (or actually driving a car), or how this overcomes the question of the unknown, which is what makes a true experience distinct from a carnival ride.

Other possible models for the replacement (or enhancement, as I think it will be seen) of "literacy" will arise, and it will be fascinating to see how the culture and definition of it evolve. Any way it does go, though, the blogs (or something descended from them) will be part of the transformation.

But what, exactly, *are* these blogs? We have established a background and context for them, but it remains to establish their extent. At its simplest, a blog is a personal chronicle generally presented with the most recent entry first and usually allowing room for comment. It has become much more than that, however, encompassing almost anything on the Web that has either an interactive aspect or frequent addition. The best way, therefore, to define the blog may be to describe its extent.

Since 2003, The Weblog Awards, "the world's largest blog competition, with over 525,000 votes cast in the 2006 edition for finalists in 45 categories,"[55] has been collecting votes for the best blogs in a growing number of areas. Among these are photo, culture, gossip, video, and music blogs, as well as ones dedicated to media, technology, sports, military, law, business, lesbian-gay-bi-transsexual (LGBT), parenting, education, and science. As these are just the most popular categories for blogging (outside of the political, which is by far the most extensive topic for the blogs), it should be obvious that blogs now cover just about any subject anyone can imagine—or would want to write about.

Interested participants in various areas of blogging have even gone so far as to create *wikis*, freely alterable Web sites, listing relevant blogs so that others may partake of an extent of possibility that is now impossible for any one person to catalogue. Among these is the Academic Blog Portal, which takes up the description of the academic blogosphere "as a kind of Invisible

College—this site is supposed to help make the College a little more visible to itself and its readers. It is a work in progress and will remain that way."[56] Because of problems with malicious changes and spam (generally attempts to draw viewers to commercial sites through improved search-engine rankings), the Academic Blog Portal requires anyone wishing to add or alter to register with a valid email address, standard practice, now, for most group blogs and wikis.

The "invisible college" concept, from the incredible breadth that the blogs promise, stems from and was coined by Brad DeLong, an economics professor at the University of California at Berkeley, whose blog is called Grasping Reality With Both Hands. Writing in *The Chronicle of Higher Education*, he says that he has looked around his beautiful campus but:

> I want more. I would like a larger college, an invisible college, of more people to talk to, pointing me to more interesting things. People whose views and opinions I can react to, and who will react to my reasoned and well-thought-out opinions, and to my unreasoned and off-the-cuff ones as well.... Aggressive younger people interested in public policy and public finance would be excellent. Berkeley is deficient in not having enough right-wingers; a healthy college has a well-diversified intellectual portfolio. The political scientists are too far away to run into by accident....
>
> Over the past three years, with the arrival of Web logging, I have been able to add such people to those I bump into—in a virtual sense—every week. My invisible college is paradise squared, for an academic at least.[57]

Much of the academic blogosphere shares DeLong's attitude, seeing a chance for academia to claim at least that *virtual* territory well beyond classroom and laboratory walls.

A good representative of academic blogs is Miriam Burstein's The Little Professor: Things Victorian and Academic. Burstein lists both her current reading and personal favorites and presents links of all sorts, starting with libraries and related sites and continuing to a section devoted to Burstein's specialty, Victorian Studies—followed by a few other academic areas, general academic blogs, and "just for fun." Burstein uses her Web site to put her blog and her academic work on a personal basis (something most academic bloggers tend to do—rarely will you find an academic blog written in the third person). Her posts include book reviews, comments on life with her cats, and even advice to graduate students. She says about her blog:

> For me, the blog offers a chance to "talk" to both scholars outside of my field and to non-academics. I'm often surprised by who turns out to be reading it (historians, English professors, scientists, professional critics, editors, librarians, the occasional novelist or poet). I think I'm better known for the blog than I am for my scholarship—understandably, there's a bigger

audience for generalist writing than there is for studies of Victorian religious fiction!—which sometimes bothers me, sometimes amuses me. That being said, readers learn about my work from my blogging, and I've certainly had some professional opportunities come my way courtesy of the blog, so in that sense the blog has extended my professional identity.[58]

Not all images of academic blogging are as positive as Burstein's experience as a glimpse at The Little Professor might lead one to believe. In 2005, a professor using the name "Ivan Tribble" published a piece in *The Chronicle of Higher Education* where he argues that blogging, seen from the view of a search committee, might be bad for academic careers:

> A [job] candidate's blog is more accessible to the search committee than most forms of scholarly output. It can be hard to lay your hands on an obscure journal or book chapter, but the applicant's blog comes up on any computer. Several members of our search committee found the sheer volume of blog entries daunting enough to quit after reading a few. Others persisted into what turned out, in some cases, to be the dank, dark depths of the blogger's tormented soul; in other cases, the far limits of techno-geekdom; and in one case, a cat better off left in the bag.
>
> The pertinent question for bloggers is simply, Why? What is the purpose of broadcasting one's unfiltered thoughts to the whole wired world? It's not hard to imagine legitimate, constructive applications for such a forum. But it's also not hard to find examples of the worst kinds of uses.
>
> A blog easily becomes a therapeutic outlet, a place to vent petty gripes and frustrations stemming from congested traffic, rude sales clerks, or unpleasant national news. It becomes an open diary or confessional booth, where inward thoughts are publicly aired.
>
> Worst of all, for professional academics, it's a publishing medium with no vetting process, no review board, and no editor. The author is the sole judge of what constitutes publishable material, and the medium allows for instantaneous distribution. After wrapping up a juicy rant at 3 A.M., it only takes a few clicks to put it into global circulation.[59]

"Tribble" has a point. It takes a great deal of confidence to put oneself "out there" to the world without any sort of vetting process—some might call it "foolhardiness." As a result, the most successful academic bloggers tend to be those in secure, tenured positions, or ones who keep a careful anonymity.

On the other hand, it may be that the timidity that "Tribble" advises is just what the academic blogs are fighting. As a whole, academia can be accused of speaking only to the converted, of working within carefully defined circles of the like-minded, and of avoiding the controversies of public debate. The blogs may be a way for changing that, and it could be that academic bloggers are on the leading edge of creating not just an "invisible college" but a broadening of education as a whole, taking it beyond boundaries of departments and universities to all who might wish to join in on any particular topic or question. Certainly, a blog like Margaret Soltan's University Diaries does attempt to take on the assumptions of academia, if not just those of the public beyond. The academic blogs may also provide something of the services gatekeepers can provide, though coming from a nonrestrictive angle. Because of the expertise of the academic bloggers, their sites can be relied upon more readily in their areas of specialty—and their links can be considered something of a vetting for the sites listed.

Business blogging, coming from the other end of our cultural spectrum, got a later start than academic blogging, which came close on the heels of personal blogging. This is not surprising. Not only was the image of the blogger tainted in the mind of the broader population, but there seemed little to be gained for a business in the blogosphere. But individual entrepreneurs were quick to catch on that something unusual was happening, and the corporate world was not far behind. A 2005 *Business Week* cover story caught the tenor of the changing perception of the blogs in its first paragraphs:

> Most of you are sick to death of blogs. Don't even want to hear about these millions of online journals that link together into a vast network. And yes, there's plenty out there not to like. Self-obsession, politics of hate, and the same hunger for fame that has people lining up to trade punches on *The Jerry Springer Show*. Name just about anything that's sick in our society today, and it's on parade in the blogs. On lots of them, even the writing stinks.
>
> Go ahead and bellyache about blogs. But you cannot afford to close your eyes to them, because they're simply the most explosive outbreak in the information world since the Internet itself. And they're going to shake up just about every business—including yours. It doesn't matter whether you're shipping paper clips, pork bellies, or videos of Britney in a bikini, blogs are a phenomenon that you cannot ignore, postpone, or delegate. Given the changes barreling down upon us, blogs are not a business elective. They're a prerequisite.[60]

The writers, here, have taken the step that "Tribble" could not: the blogs are here to stay, so it makes for good business (just as it makes for good education) to find ways to make the best of them. No longer, even in 2005, did it make sense to complain about the blogs in business any more than in academia. Instead, as the article says, it was time to make *use* of them.

Like blogs of all sorts, business blogs are extremely difficult to categorize. They range from blogs about business to blogs trying to drum up business to blogs meant to help provide better customer service—and more, of course. One exemplary blog about business is Drew McLellan's Drew's Marketing

Minute, where advice about marketing also serves the purpose of promoting McLellan's own activities as a marketing specialist. One of the things McLellan has done is retain the features of nonbusiness blogs, retaining the sense of individual and of network that has been so important to the success of the blogosphere as a whole. He keeps the blog personal and humorous, adding in enough detail on his own life to ensure that his readers do not mistake his for some faceless corporate offering. In an email to me, he explained his rationale:

> My blog is a living demo of our brand and our work. Marketing and brand-ing aren't linear processes and so my blog reflects that. One day, I am using a blacksmith shop as an analogy for why branding matters and the next post I'm quite subjectively reviewing a book or a new social media tool. Some-where along the way, I'll respond to a blogosphere phenomenon, the meme, and post a picture of me that shows a different side of my personality.
>
> What I love is that it all feels a little random and yet, there is a grand plan. For example, I only respond to memes on the weekend and I always add a meaty, marketing-focused post on the same day. My promise to my readers and the community is every day that I post, I will give them some-thing to think about and something that will help them grow/improve their business. If they get a little extra some days, I'm okay with that.
>
> The other unique aspect of blogging is the camaraderie on what is typi-cally a dog eat dog competitive playing field. I love being able to bounce ideas, start collaborative e-book projects and pick the brains of other mar-keting and branding pros. Riffing off of each other makes us all smarter and in the end, means we serve our clients better.
>
> The ultimate goal for my blog is to raise the visibility of my agency/myself and to set the table for what prospective clients/speaking opportuni-ties should expect. The greatest compliment I get from a blog reader who I speak with on the phone or in person is when they say, "you're just like your blog." That means I am genuinely conveying our brand. Which of course means that we're living what we teach. That matters to me.[61]

McClellan exemplifies the attitude of almost all successful bloggers, seeing the blogosphere as both a tool and a playing field, a place where he can both pro-mote what he does and learn new things, bettering himself and all those with whom he comes in contact. In this sense, the blog is quintessentially Ameri-can, harkening back to the days of everyone pitching in, even if the particular resulting structure is not for them. The blogs may seem "libertarian," but they really are not. They are places for the individual in community, not for the individual alone.

The "faceless" corporations have come to recognize this, and are now using the blogs to develop a face, to show themselves as individuals operating respon-sibly within the larger community. Among other things, the blogosphere is becoming an important place for the solving of public relations problems and responding to customer complaints:

> Companies such as Lenovo Group, Southwest Airlines, and Dell have specialists dedicated to engaging or co-opting their critics. Dell has made blogger outreach into such a discipline that the company's team, including refreshingly straight-talking blogger-in-chief Lionel Menchaca, recently sat down for drinks, nachos, and fried zucchini at an Austin (Tex.) pub with blogger Jeff Jarvis. He's the man who ignited the original Dell Hell customer-service crusade with his rants about the company. (Jarvis picked up his own tab.) "In a flash he transformed the borgish image of Dell for me," says Jarvis. That wasn't all. At Davos in January, Michael S. Dell sought out Jarvis at a cocktail party and apologized to him.[62]

A recognition of the personal nature of blogging allows the blogosphere to become the perfect venue for a company that wants its customers to feel they are dealing with an individual and not a bureaucracy, something telephone help lines are no longer able to do.

Commercial utilizations of blogs are going even further. As Andrew Keen writes, "Blogs are increasingly becoming the battlefield on which public relations spin doctors are waging their propaganda war. In 2005, before launching a major investment, General Electric executives met with environmental bloggers to woo them over the greenness of a new energy-efficient technology. Meanwhile, multinationals like IBM, Maytag, and General Motors all have blogs that, under an objective guise, peddle their versions of corporate truth to the outside world."[63] Though most neterate users of the Web are quick to identify examples of corporate manipulation, it will be easy to use the Web to fool people until a much greater percentage of the population becomes neterate on at least a rudimentary level.

Just as other blogs cross boundaries, so do business blogs. One doing so is the pro-business Club for Growth political blog. It describes itself as "a national network of thousands of Americans, from all walks of life, who believe that prosperity and opportunity come through economic freedom. We work to promote public policies that promote economic growth primarily through legislative involvement, issue advocacy, research, training and educational activity. The primary tactic of the separate Club for Growth PAC is to provide financial support from Club members to viable pro-growth candidates to Congress, particularly in Republican primaries."[64] The blog is primarily written by Andrew Roth, keeping it more focused than the group political blogs that feature any number of diarists. Tightly controlled, the Club for Growth blog attempts to be a source of information for its members more than a place of discussion.

Another blog with a definite political slant that is tightly controlled in terms of content is Juan Cole's "Informed Comment," one of the highest profile blogs of its sort, a cross between the political and the academic. Cole, a professor of modern Middle East and South Asian history at the University of Michigan, combines his professional expertise with a decidedly political slant on Middle Eastern affairs. There's nothing humorous or personal in what Cole offers, simply analysis of current events based on his extensive knowledge of the most contentious area of the world.

The successes of other individual political blogs are generally based on expertise brought to the blogs but demonstrated *through* the blogs, as in Cole's case. Due simply to the overwhelming numbers of blogs, few bloggers have become popular on their own—unless they were early into the field or have first been part of one of the group political blogs, establishing a reputation there and extending readership into the individual blog. Josh Micah Marshall, one of the first journalists to make a name for himself through the blogs, added an adjunct to his Talking Points Memo blog in 2005 called TPM Café to be "a public meeting place to read about and discuss politics, culture and public life in the United States. The site hosts both blogs and public discussion areas."[65] TPM Café provides a "front page" of invited celebrity bloggers and a section open to anyone who cares to blog there. Like Markos Moulitsas, whose Daily Kos has become the most read of the political blogs, Marshall has allowed his blog to become a venue for much more than his own opinions, creating a springboard for other bloggers. In Marshall's case, however, he has kept his Talking Points Memo more under his own (and his staff's) control than Moulitsas has at Daily Kos, keeping the look and the feel of TPM Café distinct from his main blog.

Aside from the discussions they carry, blogs are beginning to serve a research function as aggregators or filters, picking out items on the Web that the particular bloggers find significant and linking to them for others. This has not yet reached its full potential, and may never do so, for it begs the question of trust of the aggregator—and there seems little hope of clearing the barrier that question raises. This function of the blogs, however, may not be as pervasive or important as it at first might seem: "Although filter blogs in which authors link to and comment on the contents of other web sites are assumed by researchers, journalists and members of the blogging community to be the prototypical blog type, the blogs in our sample are overwhelmingly of the personal journal type (70.4%), in which authors report on their lives and inner thoughts and feelings.... This result is all the more notable in that we excluded journal sites such as LiveJournal.com and Diaryland.com [two social-networking blog sites] from our data collection, so that their popularity would not overshadow the other blogs in the sample. Even so, filter blogs account for only 12.6% of the sample."[66] The problem with simple categorization such as this, though, is that most blogs defy pigeon-holing. The best of the blogs always function in part as aggregators or filters, in part as sources of new ideas, in part as places of commentary, and in part as social arenas.

Though the personal blog, the rantings and ruminations of the individual blogger on whatever happens to cross his or her mind, has become a smaller percentage of the blogs as the blogosphere has expanded (and continues to expand) into new areas, it is still growing and going strong. James Lileks's blog *Startling Bleats of Tomorrow*, which he calls "dashed-off tripe,"[67] won the 2006 Weblog Award for best Individual Blog. It has turned into a commercial enterprise and is, again, tightly controlled—there is no room for comment or discussion. Lileks, however, is a talented and funny writer, able to keep his work amusing when others fall into repetition or trivia.

The few blogs mentioned in this chapter, of course, provide no more than a small taste of the possibilities offered by the millions of blogs now online. The only way, really, to understand them and to know what is going on in the blogosphere is to visit them and follow the links they provide to other blogs. This isn't really a refusal to define or avoidance of a difficult task, but recognition that what the blogs are today in 2007 is not what they will be—*by definition*—in 2008.

As should be clear by now, one of the major attributes of neteracy is plasticity, the ability to deal with manipulation and change. People, if they have the ability to alter something, will do so, to make it suit their needs. Others need to learn to adapt to that change, to accept its inevitability, and to evaluate it—or to not comment about it.

The blogs, which arose through people and networks and not through any controlling or centralized vision, will never give up their elasticity—not and remain blogs, that is. Some of the things now called blogs will spin off into their own cohesive universes, as is already happening with the social-networking blogs (MySpace, for example, is already distinguishing between its main personal pages and the blogs they can carry—eventually, the blogs will probably migrate elsewhere). Others may disappear completely or find themselves assimilated into existing paradigms—as may happen with the blogs that many corporations have set up as interfaces with customers for complaints, questions, and any other concerns that once were handled by telephone or by mail. Once these have become commonplace, there won't be need of a distinctive term for them on the Web sites—nor will the businesses want one. They will simply be the expected interactive feature of the sites.

What is thought of as the blogs will likely continue to be those sites dedicated to particular topics or personalities, retaining aspects of those things (like business and social-networking blogs) that have taken their own paths, but remaining distinctly related to individual concerns with "real world" matters. The process of defining aspects of the blogosphere will never be over, as new things will necessarily come into being and other parts will either atrophy or grow in other directions. As are all aspects of the Web, after all, the blogs are process and not result.

Chapter 2

THE BLOGS IN SOCIETY

Blogs and Other Online Entities Discussed in Chapter 2

Assignment Zero, http://zero.newassignment.net
BlogHer, http://blogher.org
Creating Passionate Users, http://headrush.typepad.com
Creative Commons, http://creativecommons.org
Creek Running North, http://www.faultline.org
Daily Kos, http://www.dailykos.com
Digg, http://digg.com
ePluribus Media, http://www.epluribusmedia.org
O'Reilly Radar, http://radar.oreilly.com
Technorati, http://www.technorati.com

A s of April 2007, Technorati, a major blog monitoring service, claimed to be tracking more than 75 *million* blogs. And the number is growing. Even if only half of these are legitimate, the blogosphere is huge. Though many within it come from outside of the United States, the figure still makes it clear that there can be few Americans without a family member or a friend who is involved in some way with the blogs. "If we keep up at this pace, there will be over five hundred million blogs by 2010," writes Web contrarian Andrew Keen, "collectively corrupting and confusing popular opinion about everything from politics, to commerce, to arts and culture. Blogs have become so dizzyingly infinite that they're undermining our sense of what is true and what is false, what is real and what is imaginary."[1] Of course, the pace will not continue, and the blogs have yet to be shown to be damaging to the popular discourse—and an increasingly *neterate* population is quickly learning how to sift noise from information—but Keen's view remains popular among many.

Indeed, even with all of the ballyhoo and the incredible popularity of the blogs, there are still plenty of people who know nothing of them or who look askance at them, coming to their views from any of a number of perspectives, philosophical and otherwise, their opinions sometimes formed out of lack of online experience, but often (as in Keen's case) not. Some see the blogs as nothing more than newsletters *writ large*. Others believe they provide little more than does a release valve, acting as vents simply for letting off steam. Some believe they isolate people. A few of these even go so far as to dismiss them completely (as Keen does), seeing them as absolutely pernicious, debasing both language and thought.

One of the most common criticisms of the blogs is that they are too easy. Anyone can blog, and can begin doing so within minutes of getting online. The technology, though complex behind the screen, is simple enough for use even by those with minimal online experience. And there are no filters and no proctors, nothing to keep one from saying whatever one wants. This very ease has long bothered many, particularly those not involved with the Web, but also people who understand the real advantages of the editorial processes in other media in giving some sort of necessary order to discussion. Keen is one of these:

> In the digital world's never-ending stream of unfiltered, user-generated content, things are indeed often not what they seem. Without editors, fact-checkers, administrators, or regulators to monitor what is being posted, we have no one to vouch for the reliability or credibility of the content we read and see [on the Web].... There are no gatekeepers to filter truth from fiction, genuine content from advertising, legitimate information from errors or outright deceit. Who is to point out the lies on the blogosphere that attempt to rewrite our history and spread rumors as fact? When we are all authors, and some of us are writing fiction, whom can we trust?[2]

Keen begs the questions of the trustworthiness of the gatekeepers of the past and of whether or not we could ever tell fact from fiction, but he expresses a fear that many with little experience of the Web have been feeling.

By 2007, the dangers of a lack of control on the Web were beginning to convince even veteran *netizens* to agree. Some were simply throwing in the towel, seeing too many out-of-control emotions and too much stated without sufficient basis and envisioning no remedy. Others saw too much anarchy and incivility. A few began tossing around ideas for bringing about a little order.

Whether the anarchy of the Web is brought to order or not, however, the blogs have become important to many people's lives. Clearly, they are not going away. Meredith Farkas, writing in *American Libraries*, explains, in part, why:

> Many of us under the age of 40 grew up with a computer in our homes and were using it to communicate with other people by the time we were in our teens. People of my generation often didn't have access to a third place—a space where we could go to "hang out" outside of work and home. As a result, many have sought to make the online world their third place. The growth of social software (applications that enable the formation of online

communities at the grassroots level) has really facilitated this trend, allowing us to easily build online communities from the bottom up.[3]

Community, that is what lies at the heart of the blog—though that is not how the blogs have often been seen, too many envisioning them as a force weakening the very real-world communities they can—and often do—help strengthen.

The blogs, since their earliest days, have often seemed nothing more than individualism running rampant, each blogger doing what he or she wants with no regard for anyone else, no respect for process, expertise, sensibility, or for community. So strong has this image of the blogs been that its residues remain with us in 2007, though almost anyone who seriously looks at the blogs today recognizes that they are much more, that they actually have long been a *seeking out* of community and not a rejection of it.

Bloggers, of course, are aware of how they are seen. And it rankles. For the most part, they want to be taken seriously within the greater society, not dismissed as weirdo loners in their mothers' suburban basements. Though most will stoutly defend the right of anyone to say anything they wish on the blogs, they still want their own blogs, both personal and group, to reflect well on them. Some, including people involved in projects like Jay Rosen's Assignment Zero and the citizen-journalist group ePluribus Media, have been casting about for ways of showing those beyond the blogs how wrong they are in their negative depictions. Both of these groups want to prove that they care about careful research and fact checking, to show that bloggers do not simply babble. ePluribus Media has been developing a certification program that will alert the reader to a specific blog entry's adherence to good practice (as defined by ePMedia through an examination of traditional journalistic standards). Assignment Zero is putting into place its own formal vetting program as part of an attempt to bridge the gulf between amateur and professional journalism. Significantly, such programs are not really aimed inward at the blogs, but outward at the journalists whose territory the blogs are beginning to invade. Not yet do bloggers *as a group* have confidence in their own judgments of themselves; they need outside appreciation as much as any member of a society does.

There are plenty of other negative images of bloggers that various people are trying to address online, including some that have enough of an element of truth to represent a real danger, particularly to naïve or unwatchful bloggers but even to others as well. Given their wide-open nature, the blogs can become a venue of harassment and intimidation—and even of threat. To counter this from within, in early 2007 a number of bloggers and others with an interest in promoting online life began arguing for a "Blogging Code of Conduct." Among them was Jimmy Wales, the cofounder of Wikipedia, and Tim O'Reilly, an influential online activist and thinker (he is in large part responsible for the "Web 2.0" concept, the idea that Internet activity would move away from storage and programs on personal computers and onto the

Web itself, which would become the repository for everything with an online aspect, each individual tapping into even their personal data from whatever access point they happened to find available). As of this writing, O'Reilly's bloggingcode.org Web site was not yet up and running, but he had presented a proposed code[4] in response to a blogger named Kathy Sierra's revelation[5] that she had been threatened through anonymous comments on her blog:

> Her Web site, Creating Passionate Users, was about "the most fluffy and nice things," she [Sierra] said. Sierra occasionally got the random "comment troll," she said, but a little over a month ago, the posts became more threatening. Someone typed a comment on her blog about slitting her throat and ejaculating. The noose photo appeared next, on a site that sprang up to harass her. On the site, someone contributed this comment: "the only thing Kathy has to offer me is that noose in her neck size."[6]

Soon, Sierra decided to stop blogging (though she left her site online). The threats, while not likely to come to anything, had still knocked the joy out of what she had been doing. And, who knows? The threats could also be real, as sometimes threats are.

Not all in the blogosphere agree that a code would work or is even necessary. Markos Moulitsas, founder and proprietor of Daily Kos, wrote that "if you blog, and blog about controversial shit, you'll get idiotic emails. Most of the time, said 'death threats' don't even exist—evidenced by the fact that the crying bloggers and journalists always fail to produce said 'death threats.'"[7] However, many bloggers do feel that they have to take the threats seriously, that the venue of a threat has no impact on the danger it represents. Chris Clarke, whose Creek Running North is a popular nature and science blog, suspended his blog for a time in 2006 in response to threats against his dog Zeke. He recognized that the threats were likely meaningless, but weighed the possible harm to Zeke against the advantages of continued blogging and decided to stop.

Eventually, Clarke did start blogging again, but with a renewed sense of the connection between the blogosphere and the real world. When the "Code of Conduct" controversy arose, he responded to Moulitsas's comments with a post entitled "This just in: Markos Moulitsas is an idiot" in which he wrote, "Here's my take. Activists often get death threats when people who support the *status quo* find those activists effective. Kos does not believe death threats exist, never having seen one. Drawing of the obvious conclusions has been left as an exercise for the reader."[8] The implied insult is to Moulitasas's positioning himself as an effective political operant, but still an outsider.

Whether or not a Blogging Code of Conduct is desirable or would even be efficacious, the controversy points to several topics of serious interest to any consideration of the blogosphere, most of them pertaining to the image of the Web from the perspective of (and in relationship to) the "real" world, even by those who are deeply involved in blogging and other online activities. Moulitsas, consciously or not, posits a divide between online activity and that of the "real" world. This is consistent with his political philosophy, where he sees blogging as a means of creating a platform that can allow people to step easily from it and into "real" world politicking. To him, the worlds are not quite one and the same—the online world being something of a sandbox for trying out things that will later be built in the real world. Clarke, on the other hand, sees the Web as an expression of "real" world ideas and emotions, not as the birthplace of actions that have to be shepherded from the Web to the "real" world to "become" anything at all. Both views have certain validity, but Clarke's more than Moulitsas's reflects the growing recognition that the divide between the online world and the "real" one is not as great as once it may have seemed.

The two visions have nothing to do, really, with the intelligence of either (Clarke's post title notwithstanding). Instead, they reflect differing starting points. Moulitsas has become a brilliant political operative from a base within the Web—inside, looking out. Clarke brought his passion for his topics to the Web, moving from the outside in. Strangely enough, the Moulitsas view is that of the people who still know little of the sociology of the Web, yet it is also that of many old-time Web insiders, seeing what goes on there as removed from the "real" world in a way that Clarke, whose view of the Internet is as an extension of the "real" world, does not. The more technologically proficient and longest-term Web users tend to still be caught up in an old, romantic vision of cyberspace as a strange new world rather than simply an amplification of a world long with us.

Yet, at some underlying level and for all their squabbling, Clarke and Moulitsas remain members of a single community. They argue because they are linked, not because they have nothing in common. Their attitudes may be quite different, but many of their goals and concerns are similar. At some point, they may even come to a common understanding about how their community should act in response to the threats that are sometimes posted in blog comments. The reason for this is that both have learned the lesson Patrick Leary articulates in *Academe*:

> that the ecology of an active online community is surprisingly fragile. It can go wildly out of whack, and even self-destruct, in a very short time. I've seen any number of lists decline and die over the years. Some merely waste away through attrition and neglect until no one posts to them anymore; others become mere notice boards for calls for papers and the like, without any real interaction among subscribers. A few flame out spectacularly, bursting with so many nasty, off-topic messages that all the "lurkers" unsubscribe, leaving the disputants to fight among themselves until even they grow weary of it.[9]

What applies to the online listservs that Leary refers to also applies to blogs. The balances of the online world are precarious, for all the "freedom" proclaimed. For the online extension of the world to survive and thrive, it cannot be constantly clawing at its own throat. The freedom that facelessness provides (and one's online manifestation can be faceless, if one so desires) can bring down the entire structure.

For this reason, fewer and fewer serious bloggers hide behind anonymity. They may have started with pseudonymous screen names, but they eventually step out and admit who they really are. Recognizing that they are already bringing much of their offline life to the blogs, they want to bring in the rest, keeping their personalities and activities whole. Doing so also helps provide a solid base to the growing online communities, for the members become "real" individuals rather than faceless words that can be attacked at will. Growing community, also, can help forestall those, like Sierra's intimidators, who try to use the blogs for malicious purposes.

BlogHer, one of the many community blogs that are trying to build more than a "simple" online community and an example of blogs at their idealistic best, describes its mission as creation of:

- A do-ocracy where BlogHer doesn't serve women bloggers, but rather creates opportunities for all women bloggers to help ourselves and work together to voice and achieve our individual goals—professional, technical, social and/or personal;
- A robust BlogHer Network equipped with the tools we need to deliver on the education, exposure and community of women bloggers, branching out beyond a single blog to create a true community resource and meeting place;
- A community that regularly meets in person, at regional, local and specialized meet-ups, as well as at our annual conference, to continue our conversations. We are committed to extending our conversations and network even to those who cannot attend these meetings in person.[10]

Though the blogs are often depicted as isolating, many of the group blogs (at least) are reflections of desire to bring people together, physically as well as online. Bloggers can, and do, come together in many ways—as they did in order to discover just who was threatening Sierra and shutting them down.

David Riesman, author of *The Lonely Crowd*, a description of the American psyche of 1950 (as directed towards what others have and are doing), has also unintentionally provided us with a description of that aspect of the American personality that both repels us from the blogs and draws us to them:

What is feared as failure in American society is, above all, aloneness. And aloneness is terrifying because it means that there is no one, no group, no approved cause to submit to. Even success—the seeming opposite of failure—often becomes impossible to bear when it is not socially approved or known. This is perhaps why successful criminals often feel the need to confess, that is, to submit to the community's judgment, represented in the person to whom the confession is made.[11]

And this is another of the reasons why many bloggers, including the most successful among them, have abandoned their anonymity. They want community; they want to be known. They want to confess.

Yet there are dangers in giving up anonymity, even if one puts aside threats of the type that Sierra and Clarke have felt. But the dangers are no different than those of putting oneself on the line publicly anywhere. Yet many do believe that there is a qualitative difference in writing for a blog and other public activities. Writing in *School Library Journal*, Chris Harris listed five reasons for a librarian not to blog. The warnings he gives are worth considering, even if they are to be ultimately rejected. His reasons are as follows[12]:

1. Giving a "piece of your mind" is not always advisable.
2. The things one could say often should not be said.
3. Time at work cannot be justifiably used for a personal blog.
4. It is next to impossible to keep one's identity hidden.
5. Even a "private" blog is discoverable.

Though Harris is himself a blogger, his list sounds more like a warning for those who are not neterate at all (and not likely to become so) than a list of things that should be seriously considered by potential bloggers. More than anything else, this is a warning to the naïve, advice that blogging, though easy, is not something that should be taken on without a little preparation and consideration. Though the advice is well-meant, it buys into the idea that bloggers tend to act without thinking—and that people (especially potential bloggers) really do need something of a gatekeeper, or they will make fools of themselves. Harris writes, "If it's that deep, dark, secret bit that we try hard not to let slip out in public, then you would do well to avoid blogging about it."[13] The idea that bloggers may "accidentally" let slip something that might do them harm links to the fact that blogging in some ways resembles speech—and in speech our editing possibilities are much more limited than in any other verbal context. There is, of course, a quicker connection between the writing and the publication in blogging (a feature that does, indeed, making blogging a little more like speaking), but the admonition is ultimately no more useful than a warning to keep mum on certain topics at a cocktail party, where it may be alcohol that shortens the distance between brain and tongue.

About his second point, Harris writes, "Telling tales about colleagues or specific work situations may also land you in trouble."[14] This, too, is almost demeaning in its attitude towards bloggers and potential bloggers (it is almost as if Harris is saying to bloggers, "What are you, stupid?")—but it is fairly typical of the ways blogs and bloggers are viewed—and, unfortunately, of how they are sometimes used. It is as though Harris believes that many think the norms of propriety do not apply on the blogs. He may have a point: it is true, the blogosphere can seem a wild and dangerous place to those not familiar with it, but personal responsibility still applies. After all, the blogosphere is not an entirely new place with new sets of rules, but an expansion of an older public sphere, one with which most of us are at least familiar in passing.

Harris's third point is applied directly to school employees, but I am sure he would extend it to others: "Blogging takes time, but not during school hours, please. Use of school equipment for non-school activities likely violates board policy. Even if you are writing about professional practices on your personal blog, you should not do so using school equipment or the school's network access."[15] The assumption is that there is a distinct line between professional activities and personal blogs. Certainly, there is generally a supposition that blogging is a leisure-time activity, though that is changing. Harris says, essentially, that the wall between the personal and professional is so strong that no blogger should consider that he or she has broken through it, even if writing about professional activities—as long as it is on a personal, and not a professional blog.

As academic bloggers like Michael Bérubé and Juan Cole have shown, there can certainly be a professional aspect to blogging, and this will likely grow as others begin to see ways of using blogs to complement their professional lives. But the image, for now, remains: blogging cannot be part of one's career—unless called for in one's job description. This is an unfortunate limit that disallows the sort of serendipity that browsing in a library provides, the sort of exploration that can lead to new and startling ideas in any field. Of course, one has responsibilities other than blogging in most jobs and these must be attended, but people in many positions, especially in education, can make the case that their blogging is an aspect of their professional development.

"Once you go online, all expectations for privacy disappear. I'm not saying that you need to don a tinfoil hat, but with every click, understand that you are building a trail of evidence."[16] With less and less of what any American does being covered by privacy protections, this is not advice that should apply only to online activities. Everything one does, these days, should be treated as though it could become public. There's a good chance, after all, that it will.

Harris ends with this warning: "In the same way that teachers being arrested for driving while intoxicated receives unwelcome news coverage, educators' use of social technologies is subject to a higher level of scrutiny. This includes your personal, private use of these technologies that are, by their very nature, so public."[17] With athletes being fined for unbecoming behavior (often pictured on blogs), because they "represent" their sports, and people in other walks of life feeling pressure to conform in such a way as to not bring disrepute onto their employers, this, again, is not something that applies simply to bloggers or even to teachers.

Harris looks at blogging from a "real world" perspective, placing it within the matrix of quotidian life. But he is also imagining people donning masks to go blogging. Others from within the blogs also imagine masks, and seek to find who is "real" and who is simply masquerading. The real connection (and disconnections) between worlds virtual and real becomes quite important and even problematic. Sine Anahita, for example, writes:

> In an online world, where there are no spatial boundaries, a group is bounded by the virtual identities of the people who make up the group. For example, an online skinhead group ... is bounded by the virtual identities of its participants, by their virtual performance of a skinhead-appropriate sexuality, gender, race, and other markers of skinhead identity.... For an online social movement community, there are problems if virtual identities indeed mark the boundaries of online communities. First, virtual identities, like other postmodern identities, are continually being negotiated, and thus are in continual flux. How do virtual communities manage their borders if the virtual identities of the participants need to be regularly authenticated? Second, because virtual others are unseen and unheard, or are seen and heard only by easily manipulated digital photos or audio, online participants can never be sure that others' virtual identities are trustworthy. How do participants maintain a sense of trustworthiness of their online peers and the group boundaries they represent?[18]

This question only arises when one believes that the two worlds, virtual and "real," are distinct enough for a personality to be developed in one that has no relation to the other—while claiming just such a relationship (as opposed to the situation within Second Life, where there is no claim of real-world correspondence). Anahita examines a skinhead Web site to see how its users protect against this possibility, explaining, "Boundary maintenance is accomplished through blogging, which includes discussion of elements of an appropriate skinhead identity, exclusion of virtual identities found inappropriate, and reaffirmation of approved virtual identities. The boundaries of the group are thus located at the line between those virtual identities excluded from the group and those that are reaffirmed as belonging."[19] Something similar happens on most blogs, where small cues can alert users that their communicant is a ringer—ability to recognize them is, in fact, part of neteracy. In AOL chat rooms of the early 1990s, it was easier to make such distinctions. Rooms dedicated to women used questions such as "What is your panty size?" to weed out men posing as women. In most blogs, a real-world correlation to the online identity is an important part of entrée into the community. Today, most neterate bloggers can quickly pick out "newbies" and fakers quite quickly.

As a part of the "world" of the Internet, the blogs naturally have had to carry the baggage of popular perceptions of the Web. In fact, the cliché of blogger identity—someone in pajamas who has no ability to effectively negotiate the "real" world—comes more from images of the wider Internet than from any truth concerning bloggers. Going back as far as William Gibson's "cyberspace" from his 1984 novel *Neuromancer*, the most popular image of the online world has been of one divorced from quotidian reality, relating to it, but containing its own essence or being. Entry may come through the "real" world, but the Web world was thus commonly seen as having its own distinct existence. As we are seeing today, this view has very little utility, though it is still widely held.

Thanks to alarm about scams, hackers, and predators, to many who have not experienced it, the image of the Web is now that of an intimidating and dangerous place. But, as the millions who use it to their satisfaction will tell, it is also attractive—as well as increasingly useful, of course. Indeed, in the more optimistic aspect of any vision of the Web, the virtual world is seen as offering even greater possibilities than does the real one, for it encompasses the real one, widening it. The Internet is where people can overcome the limitations of their physical existence, becoming more powerful and versatile than they ever could in daily life. A person in a wheelchair can "walk" in cyberspace, and someone unable to physically get to another place (or space) can do so. Seen this way, the virtual world realizes possibilities that necessarily remain latent in the physical world. Ersatz as they remain, these can mean a great deal to people. As Sarah Holloway and Gil Valentine write, "This is a privileging of mind over body.... Some observers even claim that 'virtual' relationships are more intimate, richer and liberating than off-line friendships because they are based on genuine mutual interest rather than the coincidence of off-line proximity."[20] Many of the early enthusiasts of the blogs, following in the footsteps of earlier Web enthusiasts, used just this argument in promoting them. But the fact remains, the imagined driving of a car on the Web is distinct from driving on Interstate 80.

Just so, it rarely gives one the ability to remove oneself from the world that holds people to the Web. Even game playing may have certain correspondences to the world, but it is not the world, and most people using the Web do not want to use its game aspects for just that reason. They are interested in the Web *because* of the world, not in spite of it, and not to get away from it or to experience things on the Web that they cannot experience elsewhere.

Public perception aside, the idea of the Web as a cyberspace divorced from the world and with its own rules has never been the most common view of the Web among the people of the United States—among those who actually use it, that is. Such a view has come to be limited almost exclusively to science-fiction and game fans, to computer geeks, and to others who, for one reason or another, want to escape or expand away from the world of our daily existences. The majority of users, though, may have also (at times) viewed the Web as somehow divorced from the real world, but these have seen it (in this manifestation) as a pale imitation, a fantasy world for those unable to operate in the "real" one. As most Web users discover: "Disembodied identities are viewed as superficial and inauthentic compared with embodied identities."[21] Yet it is this perception of disembodiment that led to the early commonplace view of the blogs as places for complaint and commentary concerning a world that the people writing them have failed to negotiate successfully—though it has never had much reality in terms of the lives and purposes of bloggers, who have rarely imagined themselves as "living" on the Web.

Part of the reason for wide-spread acceptance of this view arises from the more common and generalized images of the usage of modern communications technology, some that have been with us for decades, but are more prevalent now than ever before. These include the vision of the person escaping into the headphones of an iPod (taking it simply as replacement for the Walkman of twenty-five years ago), shutting out the "real" world for a world of sound prepared by the listener herself or himself. Another is of the person so involved in a cell-phone conversation that he or she has almost no comprehension of the events occurring directly around them (though that person may even argue that the phone expands the world instead of contracting it). Included, also, is the even older idea of the "couch potato," the person whose passive life revolves around the images brought home through a television screen.

Though there is a great deal from mass media that passes to the Web, its use is intrinsically different from the passive receptivity associated with movies, radio, and television appreciation. The ability to *create* at the same "station" where one *receives* changes both perception and interaction, bringing the Web into a new realm of "massed media" where resources extend to all of the once-separate media and more, where the user can manipulate the multiplying available items in ever-increasing fashion. Fan fiction, for example, where people take characters, situations, and even stories from popular commercial products (films, television shows, and books, primarily) and create their own episodes, has now been a Web staple for more than a decade, showing people *acting on* media creations rather than simply absorbing them.

The very structure of the Web lends itself to manipulation by the individual from below and subverts attempts to control it from above, although

countries like China, not to mention the companies that do business there and supply governments with technology to censorship and monitor, have demonstrated that the Internet and its users can be brought to heel, mostly.

But social computing—blogging, commenting, messaging's movement beyond e-mail, and other group-oriented, collaborative systems—is emerging as a countervailing force. When everyone is an individual publisher, they are vulnerable as individuals. But when they band together in groups, when they form communities, when they connect, they become powerful, both politically and economically.[22]

This, of course, is one of the corollaries to "massed" media: not only are people more culturally influential through it, but they become more politically powerful. This is also the thinking behind Moulitsas's Daily Kos, probably the largest group blog in the world.

In some respects, it is only now, when mass media gain their interactive element and become "massed" media, that we can really start to understand what mass media have been in popular culture. Previously, there was a certain amount of truth to Irving Howe's assertion, made soon after World War II, that "the only people who can analyze the effects of mass culture on an audience are those who reject its uncritical acceptance of mass culture."[23] To many people, academic enthusiasms for aspects of mass (or popular) culture have always had a certain whiff of condescension. Today, it is more generally recognized that the only people who can analyze the effects of mass culture are those who have been a part of it. Asking someone outside (that is, someone from the older literacy culture) to comment on the Web today would be like asking someone from an orality culture to evaluate a literacy culture. Neteracy, quite simply, cannot be evaluated by those not neterate.

In keeping with his outsider attitude towards mass culture, Howe saw it as "oriented toward a central aspect of industrial society: the depersonalization of the individual."[24] By the 1960s, this had become the accepted view of mass culture, that technologically based dissemination was replacing Marx's "opiate of the masses," religion. Howe goes on to say:

> Mass culture elicits the most conservative responses from the audience. So long as the audience feels that it must continue to live as it does, it has little desire to see its passivity and deep-seated though hardly conscious boredom upset; it wants to be titillated and amused, but not disturbed. For those molded in the image of contemporary society, art has many dangers: its effects are unpredictable and its demands tremendous. Art demands effort, a creative response from the audience.[25]

And a "creative response from the audience" is just what we are seeing today. What Howe did not understand, what nobody at the time understood (for they did not yet have the examples of truly participatory "massed" culture to draw upon) is that people were not ever really satisfied in their roles as passive consumers. James Joyce, whom Howe refers to directly following the previous passage, was not ignored by mass audiences simply because he was difficult, but because he did not allow much room for their participation in the art through their own imaginings—something that more cartoonish "popular" arts have always done (through their lack of nuance and detail, if nothing else).

As soon as popular culture presented possibilities that common people felt they could follow upon, they stopped being passive and grasped their participatory possibilities. There is an old joke that the first album by the rock band Velvet Underground sold only 100 copies—but that each person who bought one went out and started a band of their own. The music (unlike Joyce's writing) hardly seemed professional or beyond what the average person could accomplish; it screamed to the listener, "you can do this, too." The formerly mass medium seemed handed to the individual for his or her own participation—on a platter.

Writing long before modern mass media, let alone "massed" media, pragmatist philosopher Charles Sanders Peirce posited a distinction between the individual and the mass in terms of ideas and the thought based on them:

> To know what we think, to be masters of our own meaning, will make a solid foundation for great and weighty thought. It is most easily learned by those whose ideas are meagre and restricted; and far happier they than such as wallow helplessly in a rich mud of conceptions. A nation, it is true, may, in the course of generations, overcome the disadvantage of an excessive wealth of language and its natural concomitant, a vast, unfathomable deep of ideas. We may see it in history, slowly perfecting its literary forms, sloughing at length its metaphysics, and, by virtue of the untirable patience which is often a compensation, attaining great excellence in every branch of mental acquirement. The page of history is not yet unrolled which is to tell us whether such a people will or will not in the long run prevail over one whose ideas (like the words of their language) are few, but which possesses a wonderful mastery over those it has. For an individual, however, there can be no question that a few clear ideas are worth more than many confused ones.[26]

In mass culture, the ideas are picked from the many and shaped—and only then are presented to "the people." In massed culture, the individuals, generally possessed of many fewer ideas, but with that clearer idea of them that Peirce argues can result, present those ideas individually. Yet they do so in significant enough numbers so that no one person's ideas or presentations are alone—and the aggregate can become something of great complexity and nuance. This is the idea behind Web sites such as Digg, which states on its front page that "Digg is all about user powered content. Everything is submitted and voted on by the Digg community. Share, discover, bookmark, and promote stuff that's important to you!" Though Digg has been accused of rigging its front page, even the fact of such accusations shows the power of the concept to many users of the Web.

"Mass Culture is imposed from above. It is fabricated by technicians hired by businessmen; its audiences are passive consumers, their participation limited to the choice between buying and not buying."[27] "Massed" culture, on the other hand, is an aggregate of individual effort from below, of personal manipulation of media possibilities.

The very seeds of the concept of "massed media" as opposed to "mass media" were planted, not surprisingly, by Marshall McLuhan in his distinction between "hot" and "cool" media:

> There is a basic principle that distinguishes a hot medium like radio from a cool one like the telephone, or a hot medium like the movie from a cool one like TV. A hot medium is one that extends one single sense in "high definition." High definition is the state of being well filled with data. A photograph is, visually, "high definition." A cartoon is "low definition," simply because very little visual information is provided. Telephone is a cool medium, or one of low definition, because the ear is given a meager amount of information. And speech is a cool medium of low definition, because so little is given and so much has to be filled in by the listener. On the other hand, hot media do not leave so much to be filled in or completed by the audience. Hot media are, therefore, low in participation, and cool media are high in participation or completion by the audience. Naturally, therefore, a hot medium like radio has very different effects on the user from a cool medium like the telephone.[28]

Though it provides more possible detail than any "hot" medium ever has, the Internet, is still "cool," for it offers possibilities for participation greater than any medium before it.

Yet the image of the passive "hot" medium absorber has been carried over into the Web, allowing many to see it, through the fact that both use screens, as analogous to television (which proved "hotter" than McLuhan imagined as technology "perfected" it):

> The scale and domestic place of the television prepared us for the screens of the "personal" computer. But computer "users" are not spectators, not viewers. The "interface" may retain some immobility (with focused attention on a cathode ray screen) but the computer "user" interacts with the framed image on a small screen, "using" a device—keyboard, mouse, or (in the case of touch-screens) the finger—to manipulate what is contained within the parameters of the screen. Software designers have worked to model "interface" to emulate the associative patterns of human thought, as we become dyadic partners in a cyber-metaphysical relationship.[29]

Partners and users—not viewers—that is what the contemporary netizen has become, in terms of the technology of the Web. So successful has been the interface that Internet users need be no more technically schooled in either hardware or software than a reader in the eighteenth century had to be in the processes of setting type, locking a chase, spreading the ink, and turning the screw of the press. In neither case was the cultural change connected to the technology, but to the uses of its products.

One of the errors many who see the Web in terms of mass media and passive consumption make when considering the blogs is to mistake them for part of what Neil Postman, in chapter 5 of *Amusing Ourselves to Death*, calls "'the peek-a-boo world"[30] of instant come and go. Because so many of the blogs are updated frequently (daily, in many cases), they can indeed seem ephemeral and fleeting, concentrating on the moment and not on anything weighty or long term. Certainly, "breaking" has become something of a blog cliché, especially on the group blogs dedicated to politics and contemporary issues. But, because of the search functions within many of them (not to mention the search engines of the Internet), much of the blogosphere has a lasting power much greater (and more easily accessed) than that of even those newspapers that still do not have Web presences of their own.

Most of the high-profile technological developments in communications of the twentieth century were one-directional—until the popularization of online possibilities and the cell phone. Though these are interactive and, thus, qualitatively different from movies, radio, television, and the rest (and cell phones are also qualitatively different from that nineteenth-century innovation, the telephone), the power of the images of the older technologies has been so strong that the popular idea of the customers for technology has generally remained, as I have said, one of passivity or, at least, of people cut off from their environment through technology. And it can certainly look that way: the image of someone gesticulating and shouting into a phone as they walk down the street is nothing if not the picture of someone unaware of their immediate environment. They are, however, actively engaged; there is nothing passive in what they are doing.

This negative depiction of the passive receiver, like the more positive images of the Internet (which are also based as much on myth and assumption as on reality), rises from a belief in an utter dichotomy when it comes to the Web and of the world. In this view, the two are different absolutely, though they have plenty of points of contact and may parallel each other to some degree. The evident rigidity and simplicity of such views, and their lack of ability to account for the significant interactions and influences between the "worlds," has led to the rejection of the idea of separation that we are seeing today, to people beginning to examine the two worlds in light of each other, seeing the online universe as simply an extension and amplification of the physical one.

Some people, coming from a technodeterminist as well as a separatist viewpoint, still focus almost exclusively on the impact of the Web (as a piece of technology) on culture. "Authors who take this approach commonly fall into the trap of assuming that the meanings of technology are stable and unproblematic."[31] Others take an opposite tack, and these are more popular, attempting to understand technology in cultural terms. To them, the real meanings of technology rest in their utilizations within human culture, where they are constantly used in varying and challenging ways.

Ultimately, both of these approaches have led to inadequate impressions of the blogs, at least in terms of understanding their impact, which has already been considerable. The blogs have been (and will continue to be) a dance between the virtual and the real—if a distance between the two must be posited or imagined. They are neither simply a social use of technology nor a necessary result of technology. The relationship between the virtual world and the real, in terms of the blogs, is quite a bit more complex and convoluted, because more than any other singular thing, it involves community.

The blogs cannot be understood as a part of technological developments leading to an online world any more than they can be simply analyzed as social manifestations taking advantage of technological possibilities (though these certainly are extensive, as I argue elsewhere[32]). The world of the blogs, undoubtedly, extends well beyond its physical expression through Web sites. It is a world that even rises above physical locality, at least to some degree, allowing like-minded people to find each other online, but it is also a world reflecting the needs and possibilities of specific physical localities, as the thousands of blogs dedicated to particular cities, towns, villages, and even neighborhoods make clear.

Yet, for all the evidence to the contrary, to many of those who are not actively involved in the blogosphere the blogs remain an aspect of an online world quite distinct from their "real" world. They fail to see the simple truth that the blogs are a real-world dynamic, though one housed in a technological realm.

Why the resistance?

One reason is that the blogs, though becoming commonplace in almost all American communities, retain many aspects of what one might call "genre," keeping many readers, unfamiliar with the conventions and unwilling to take the time to learn them, from being able to find a point of entry into the blogs. It takes a little bit of work to find real access into the blogs, more work than simply going to the Web sites and scanning them. In fact, to effectively "know" the blogs, one must participate in them—at least to the level of commenting. One does not have to become a real blogger, but experiencing the interactive aspect of the blogs is essential to knowing the blogosphere at all. Doing otherwise is akin to claiming to know a movie after looking at stills taken from it.

The complaints of many newcomers to the blogs begin to have a common sound to them: the blogs are sloppy, filled with anger, and are little more than commentary on what others have written. Those voicing such criticism generally are not looking at the blogs as conversation, as process—but as object. No one would make similar derision of informal discussion in speech. It is only that it is in writing (and, thus, creates a record) that the blog becomes a problem.

Those most aware of the blogs, and often most worried by them, are the people who make their living by the written word, or by writing the words spoken by others. Among these (though many have come to see the value of the blogs) are quite a few journalists, including luminaries such as Nicholas Lemann, who now heads the Columbia School of Journalism. Many skilled writers and incisive thinkers (in other areas) do not see the blogs as offering anything really new at all—other than simply an alternate venue:

> The more ambitious blogs, taken together, function as a form of fast-moving, densely cross-referential pamphleteering—an open forum for every conceivable opinion that can't make its way into the big media, or, in the case of the millions of purely personal blogs, simply an individual's take on life. The Internet is also a venue for press criticism ("We can fact-check your ass!" is one of the familiar rallying cries of the blogosphere) and a major research library of bloopers, outtakes, pranks, jokes, and embarrassing performances by big shots.[33]

Lemann sees the blogs primarily in terms of his own profession—and in terms of its print manifestation—and not in terms of the possibilities it may (or may not) realize. Imbued with "literacy" culture, he does not recognize the blogs as process rather than product or as a new manifestation of massed (as opposed to mass) media—and, in so doing, he personifies what Thorstein Veblen called "trained incapacity," described by Kenneth Burke through the example of businessmen "who, through long training in competitive finance, have so built their scheme of orientation about this kind of effort and ambition that they cannot see serious possibilities in any other system of production and distribution."[34] In the following passage Lemann uses an image appropriate to his viewpoint, unintentionally making the meagerness of his understanding of the blogs evident, for the opening of a fan implies a move to a two-dimensional model—not to the full three that blogging (the waving fan) actually represents:

> Citizen journalists bear a heavy theoretical load. They ought to be fanning out like a great army, covering not just what professional journalists cover, as well or better, but also much that they ignore. Great citizen journalism is like the imagined Northwest Passage—it has to exist in order to prove that citizens can learn about public life without the mediation of professionals.[35]

Perhaps the Northwest Passage did have to exist in the imagination of early explorers, impetus for their great voyages of discovery, but I do not think anyone involved in either citizen journalism or the blogs believes that it has not already been proven that professional mediation is not needed in the public sphere—for the very public sphere itself arose in the eighteenth century, *before* the mediators existed. Also, bloggers and citizen journalists do not spread out—they come together—a basic point about the Web and one that Lemann seems to miss.

The mistake of seeing the blogs *only* as a new venue for an old concept leads many to recognize little in the blogs that is different from what has gone before. Furthermore, given the breadth and variety of the blogs, it is easy to prove almost any assertion about the blogs through a sampling, or through a simple statement based on one's own experience, as Lemann does:

> In other words, the content of most citizen journalism will be familiar to anybody who has ever read a church or community newsletter—it's heart-warming and it probably adds to the store of good things in the world, but it does not mount the collective challenge to power which the traditional media are supposedly too timid to take up. Often the most journalistically impressive material on one of the "hyperlocal" citizen-journalism sites has links to professional journalism, as in the Northwest Voice, or Chi-Town Daily News, where much of the material is written by students at North-western University's Medill School of Journalism, who are in training to take up full-time jobs in news organizations. At the highest level of journalistic achievement, the reporting that revealed the civil-liberties encroachments of the war on terror, which has upset the Bush Administration, has come from old-fashioned big-city newspapers and television networks, not Internet journalists; day by day, most independent accounts of world events have come from the same traditional sources. Even at its best and most ambi-tious, citizen journalism reads like a decent Op-Ed page, and not one that offers daring, brilliant, forbidden opinions that would otherwise be unavail-able. Most citizen journalism reaches very small and specialized audiences and is proudly minor in its concerns.[36]

Here, once more, we see the problem with trying to comprehend something without understanding the differences between it and the older entities and concepts. Individual blogs may indeed reach small audiences and each some-times might be "proudly minor" in the stories it covers, but these blogs "mass," becoming something more. Lemann reminds me of a giraffe with wide sight due to its height disdaining the solitary, low-flying bee, never understanding the power of the hive.

David Cohn, a young journalist who also blogs and who is part of Rosen's New Assignment project, responded on his blog to an appearance by Lemann on PBS's *The News Hour*:

> Lemann's lament is one we've all heard from mainstream journalists. Yet, the argument is becoming increasingly superficial as hyper local citizen journal-ism projects continue to gain momentum. This notion that citizen journal-ism isn't "real journalism" is the argument of those watching the innovation train pass them by....

"What we see surfacing is a different form of usefulness, especially on a hyper local level," said [Jan] Schaffer [of J-Lab]. While it isn't the type of journalism professionals like Lemann are used to—Schaffer calls it "schmooze and news"—it's a new brand of journalism created out of discussion and forums, and is part of an ongoing conversation. "Take it or leave it, I don't think you can sniff at it," said Schaffer.

While I certainly don't think Lemann was scoffing at citizen journalism, I do think he is trying to point to some fundamental flaw that only professionals can fix in his mind—the ability to get organized and hone in on a subject. And that is where my real problem with Lemann's statement comes in.

Is he citing a flaw of citizen journalism or professional? In my mind, if citizen journalists aren't able to "conduct" the conversation, the fault lies with professional journalists—not the amateurs. Big media companies should be providing organization and tools to help start the process, as a recent report from Deloitte's Technology, Media and Telecommunications arm suggested. Or as Dan Gilmore says at the Center for Citizen Media, "one big question is whether the media will see this [organizing as] a cheap way to get 'free' content or help create an ecosystem that rewards people who are contributing the information."

Right now it seems they are doing neither. Instead of being trailblazers media organizations are waiting around for something to pop up that they can adopt.[37]

This type of conflict, between people who are the absolute masters of the older entity and its replacement, as the fact that Veblen identified it long ago indicates, is part of an ages-old process of coming to an understanding of new paradigms. I only wish it were easier to get the best of the old to understand the new.

One of the basics of a page-based mindset, one that sees words in terms of printed product and not as tools of verbal process, is the assumption that words, in their specific aggregates at least, can be owned. The tradition of copyright, three centuries old in Anglo-American legal history, is not likely to be weakened anytime soon, movements such as Creative Commons (which envisions a more flexible concept) notwithstanding. Yet the Web, where it is so easy to incorporate the words of another into one's own text, undermines copyright in a number of ways—even though there is constant pressure among bloggers to keep to "fair use" borrowing limits and to always provide appropriate citation. On iCommons, a Creative Commons site, is a blog piece on why bloggers should use Creative Commons licenses that includes this passage:

At the very least you must acknowledge your source when you reproduce some of that content. From there you must consider the proportionality of the copy. If you copy whole posts without attributing them and start impacting on the traffic to the other blog, you will likely run into problems. I still recommend seeking the permission of the publisher concerned before you reproduce content on your blog. It is also a good idea to check the terms and conditions on the site concerned, if they exist. Some sites prohibit any form of reproduction and this would likely negate the protection afforded by fair dealing. The end result is a blockage in the information flow and a pause in the conversation.

If your intention, as a blogger, is to have your content and your thoughts distributed as widely as possible, then reserving all your rights to your content is counterproductive. A more effective way of distributing your content and still retaining some control over how your content is distributed is using Creative Commons licenses.[38]

Even so, because of the ease of cut-and-paste on the Web, wholesale "borrowing" does take place, much of which is seen from outside as plagiarism. Little of it, however, is intended as outright deception. After all, even the most novice user of the Web quickly realizes just how easy it is to find the source of any set of words, making unmasking of the deceit likely for all but the most obscure blog. In fact, this is one of the first steps in becoming neterate. However, one also soon learns that *ideas* are not covered under copyright—only their expression. This distinction arose with the growth of the concept of word-as-thing that became so important to print culture. But it is not as obvious to those growing up with the Web as it is to those of us who grew up in a more completely literate, as opposed to neterate, culture where the word itself has a less exalted position. If, one might ask, the idea is fair game, what's so special about the specific words? Why are they protected by law in ways that the ideas may not be? Shouldn't the ideas, really, be more important than their expression?

Questions like these have no ready answer in a Web environment. When the word was seen as a product, it could carry the idea, allowing for the protection of the idea *through* the protection of the word. When the word becomes as easily malleable as it is on the Web, it can no longer be the sole vehicle for the idea it carries, nor can it be associated concretely with that idea—for the usage of the word has exploded out of all proportion to the growth of ideas behind it.

No use of words, of course, is entirely original. Though I did not know of an earlier coinage of *neteracy* when I first used it, a quick search of the Web showed it already had found its way (though not extensively) into the greater Internet conversation, sometimes not so differently defined. All of our words and our uses of them, like most of our ideas, are formed out of usages and ideas of the past. This is the basis of Harold Bloom's thesis in *The Anxiety of Influence*, though he wrote specifically of fledgling poets and their struggles with the great poets of the past looming over them. All creative work, in this view, is derivative, yet the struggle of the artist is to step out of that influence and into something original—an impossible-sounding task, but (Bloom would say) the basis for real creativity. Over the three decades and more since Bloom's book appeared, the importance of influence has been accepted as a natural part of any artistic development, though it was hardly ignored, even before.

Signs of influence were—and are—seen as something other than plagiarism. B. F. Skinner explains the distinction:

> Controlling variables are commonly overlooked in literary borrowing. A writer usually possesses extensive verbal repertoires generated by reading other writers. These are usually rejected or emitted only with appropriate ... [explanations] acknowledging the source. When it is inferred that the writer is aware of the source but, by not mentioning it, takes credit for the behavior, the result is called plagiarism.[39]

The writer can borrow, surely, and even *unconscious* borrowing, where there is no intent to deceive, can be accepted. But taking credit for the words of another knowing full well that one did not "create" the sequence oneself—that is still considered a crime, one serious enough to get the perpetrator kicked out of college, if that person happens to be a student, or to suffer professional disgrace, as has happened to scholars ranging from Stephen Ambrose and Doris Kearns Goodwin (whose plagiarism may, in fact, have been accidental) to Ward Churchill. Yet Pulitzer Prize winner Joseph Ellis, who used the stories of others when telling his Mount Holyoke students of Vietnam War experiences he never had, was accused simply of lying, not of plagiarism. Why? Because his borrowings did not appear in print.

Such a distinction may make little sense to tomorrow's neterate citizens, to whom "print" may not have the place of honor it retains even today.

Writing in the *Virginia Quarterly Review*, Erik Campbell tries to make sense of plagiarism (and the distinction between words and ideas) by dividing plagiarism into two types:

> most teachers are principally concerned with what I'll call Hard Plagiarism (HP)—line-by-line copying without attribution. Consequently, when teachers Google incongruously melodious extracts from suspected students' papers, they find that the words are ripped verbatim from an old Helen Vendler lecture, and subsequently let slip the hounds of comeuppance in the form of public embarrassment, failing grades, and phone calls home.
>
> And what of Soft Plagiarism (SP), pilfering another's *ideas*? Teachers don't have to worry overmuch about SP, largely—if not exclusively—because in order to borrow and slightly modify or paraphrase an idea, a student first has to engage in an act of *reading* ...[40]

Through *reading*, the ideas are incorporated rather than stolen. And that, we have decided, legitimizes (to some extent) use of extant word constructions. After all, as I have said, ideas do have their own, separate protection, for "ideas (as well as inventions, procedures, etc.) are protected by *patents*, but the actual *expression* of ideas is protected by *copyright law*."[41] And it is copyright that applies most directly to Web usage, where words still are the building blocks of almost all activity and "intellectual property" based on word order is the underpinning of possession and the law.

Writing in *Harper's*, the novelist Jonathan Lethem tried to loosen what he sees as an almost nefarious adherence to the use of copyright concepts to bring just about anything in the artistic or intellectual realm under control:

> The idea that culture can be property—*intellectual* property—is used to justify everything from attempts to force the Girl Scouts to pay royalties for singing songs around campfires to the infringement suit brought by the estate of Margaret Mitchell against the publishers of Alice Randall's *The Wind Done Gone*. Corporations like Celera Genomics have filed for patents for human genes, while the Recording Industry Association of America has sued music downloaders for copyright infringement, reaching out-of-court settlements for thousands of dollars with defendants as young as twelve. ASCAP bleeds fees from shop owners who play background music in their stores; students and scholars are shamed from placing texts facedown on photocopy machines. At the same time, copyright is revered by most established writers and artists as a birthright and bulwark, the source of nurture for their infinitely fragile practices in a rapacious world. Plagiarism and piracy, after all, are the monsters we working artists are taught to dread, as they roam the woods surrounding our tiny preserves of regard and remuneration.
>
> A time is marked not so much by ideas that are argued about as by ideas that are taken for granted. The character of an era hangs upon what needs no defense. In this regard, few of us question the contemporary construction of copyright. It is taken as a law, both in the sense of a universally recognizable moral absolute, like the law against murder, and as naturally inherent in our world, like the law of gravity. In fact, it is neither. Rather, copyright is an ongoing social negotiation, tenuously forged, endlessly revised, and imperfect in its every incarnation.[42]

Lethem is right, but he does not really extend his argument to the new world of the Web, where intellectual property is both being expanded and eroded. It is being expanded to cover ideas and artistic expression beyond "mere" words; it is being eroded by the very fact of Web culture, which sees little individual intellectual right—outside of that which the greater culture tries to impose through its laws, laws that (it sometimes appears) are meant to be broken through the very technologies they are meant to regulate.

Most of America—most of the world—still looks at the blogs and all of the rest of the Web from a "literary" standpoint, and try to both understand it and regulate it from that perspective. The trouble is that is inappropriate for neterate culture, where the needs are as different from the "literate" as the very building blocks. Eventually, our laws and customs will begin to reflect an understanding of neteracy, but that will not happen for some time. Culture, like cultural understanding, does not move fast.

Technology, unfortunately, now does. Human beings are pretty much the same as they were at the time of Gutenberg. We learn and change now at about the same rate we did then. Technology, though, is quite different—and it changes at a rate we could not imagine even a generation ago.

It took generations for humanity to adjust to a literacy climate.

How long will it take to adjust to neteracy?

We may be forced to adjust much more quickly than we would like. In fact, all that screaming against the Web and the blogs may be nothing more than resistance to change that is being forced on us faster than we can really even handle.

Chapter 3

THE BLOGS FROM WITHIN

Blogs and Other Online Entities Discussed in Chapter 3

Blog Time Passing, http://lancestrate.blogspot.com/search/label/on%20blogging
BoingBoing, http://boingboing.net
Burningbird, http://burningbird.net
Crooked Timber, http://www.crookedtimber.com
Daily Kos, http://www.dailykos.com
Democratic Underground, http://www.democraticunderground.com
Digg, http://digg.com
Electronic Frontier Foundation, http://www.eff.org
Facebook, Freedom to Tinker, http://www.freedom-to-tinker.com
Free Republic, http://www.freerepublic.com
Greenpoint Dog Log Blog, http://www.newyorkshitty.com
LanguageHat, http://www.languagehat.com
Language Log, http://itre.cis.upenn.edu/~myl/languagelog
MeFi Music, http://music.metafilter.com
MySpace, Things Magazine, http://www.thingsmagazine.net
TNL.net, http://tnl.net
TPM Café, http://www.tpmcafe.com
Waggish, http://www.waggish.org

Writing before the blogs had come into existence but after years of experience with the online community The WELL (the Whole Earth 'Lectronic Link), an important predecessor of the blogs, John Perry Barlow, former Grateful Dead lyricist and cofounder of the Electronic Frontier Foundation, predicted:

> When we are all together in Cyberspace then we will see what the human spirit, and the basic desire to connect, can create there. I am convinced that the result will be more benign if we go there open-minded, open-hearted, excited with the adventure, than if we are dragged into exile.

And we must remember that going to Cyberspace, unlike previous great emigrations to the frontier, hardly requires us to leave where we have been. Many will find, as I have, a much richer appreciation of physical reality for having spent so much time in virtuality.[1]

Even if the blogging world and the online world in general is nothing more than an extension of the world we consider "reality," it is still a frontier. It also, as John Perry Barlow indicates, mediates that world, much as eyeglasses do, or even mirrors. And that, though it has its advantages, can confuse things, even changing them through the change in the viewing they engender.

In many respects, the Web really is a mirror of the world, though never something as simple as a reflector. Those who fear the Web see it as a series of funhouse mirrors, distorting, and doing so with the willful connivance of both creator and customer. Those who relish John Perry Barlow's "new frontier" view it with all the relish of Alice contemplating the looking glass with one of her kittens in her arms:

> "Now, if you'll only attend, Kitty, and not talk so much, I'll tell you all my ideas about Looking-glass House. First, there's the room you can see through the glass—that's just the same as our drawing room, only the things go the other way. I can see all of it when I get upon a chair—all but the bit behind the fireplace. Oh! I do so wish I could see *that* bit! I want so much to know whether they've a fire in the winter: you never *can* tell, you know, unless our fire smokes, and then smoke comes up in that room too—but that may be only pretence, just to make it look as if they had a fire. Well then, the books are something like our books, only the words go the wrong way; I know that, because I've held up one of our books to the glass, and then they hold up one in the other room.
>
> "How would you like to live in Looking-glass House, Kitty? I wonder if they'd give you milk in there? Perhaps Looking-glass milk isn't good to drink— But oh, Kitty! now we come to the passage. You can just see a little *peep* of the passage in Looking-glass House, if you leave the door of our drawing-room wide open: and it's very like our passage as far as you can see, only you know it may be quite different on beyond. Oh, Kitty! how nice it would be if we could only get through into Looking-glass House! I'm sure it's got, oh! such beautiful things in it! Let's pretend there's a way of getting through into it, somehow, Kitty. Let's pretend the glass has got all soft like gauze, so that we can get through. Why, it's turning into a sort of mist now, I declare! It'll be easy enough to get through—" She was up on the chimney-piece while she said this, though she hardly knew how she had got there. And certainly the glass *was* beginning to melt away, just like a bright silvery mist.[2]

That, probably better than most anything else, captures the attitude of the proto-netizen towards the Web. And the books that Alice imagines are going the wrong way? In a sense, they actually do on the Web—in the blogs, at least.

One modern-day Alice, Lance Strate, a media studies specialist at Fordham University (who blogs at Blog Time Passing), ponders this mediation, in light of the fact that blogs are generally presented in a way that sometimes seems temporally backwards (more recent first):

> McLuhan was fond of that quote: *It's a poor sort of memory that only works backwards.* So blogs constitute a poor sort of memory, don't they?
>
> And blogs take us through the looking glass, or should I say, through the blogging glass. We find another world on the other side of the glass, the screen: it is a world that mirrors our own, yet moves in the opposite direction, where effects precede their own causes. It's a world with a magic ecology that reflects but also runs counter to our own.
>
> We *look through* the blogging glass and think we see others like ourselves, but maybe we just see reflections of ourselves, hear echoes of our own voices. We *go through* the blogging glass and become others to our own selves, spirits looking down at our own flesh. And like light through a prism, we are refracted from a unity to a multitude of identities and selves as we move through the blogging glass.[3]

If, as we saw in chapter 2, *outsiders* sometimes miss the aspect of community inherent in the blogs, is there a comparable part of the blogosphere that the *insiders* often refuse to address? Something they unconsciously distort? If so, perhaps it is that the blog communities tend to be much more narrow (even when numbering in the hundreds of thousands) and less expansive than their members—and John Perry Barlow—might imagine them to be. All the passion in the world can appear within a community, yet it still may have no impact outside. It stays on the other side of the looking glass. Sometimes, the blogosphere seems like that. "What blogging glass?" outsiders might ask. What interests the bloggers may be of little interest or effect elsewhere.

Ultimately, I don't think this is true. Why? Because the bloggers are not, as many who have not examined the blogs believe, simply mindless ranters, oblivious of the societies they inhabit. Jim Roeg, blogging on his personal Double Articulation, describes rather accurately what a blogger really does when trying to write: "I did what any sadistic yet conscientious blogger would do under the circumstances. I stalled for time. I procrastinated. I fed the fish. I blogged about other things. I watched TV. I even did the dishes and took out the garbage. Finally, after much avoidance, I plotted. I came back to it. I thought about it." Just like any writer, even one with a pencil and a pad.

Still, though there are more and more blogs presenting what might be described as mini-essays (or even full-blown ones), most of what one finds in the blogosphere, even in blogs specializing on a particular topic, are descriptions of the events of a personal life—with little attempt to do what good essayists do, to integrate their own tales into a greater point that becomes the focus of the essay. Much of what one reads on blogs tells little but of airport incidents of the sort one might relate over a beer, say, or upon chance meetings with old friends, or tells of the cute things one's pets have done. Sometimes, though the writing up of these things may be first rate, one is still left wondering, "So what?"

One of the corollaries to this major failing of the blogs is their tendency towards becoming platforms for self-promotion, with exaltation of one's friends a secondary topic. It is easy to do this: most blogs provide an "About Me" section that can lull one into thinking that the blog exists for no other reason than to show our individual merits to a thankful world. Not necessarily a bad thing, this is actually the core of what goes on at MySpace and Facebook, where the expressed purpose and success is social networking.

The trouble with all of this expression of personality on the blogs is that it hides a great deal of useful information—that someone sometimes preens does not mean that they do not also have something important to say or information to express that cannot be found elsewhere. There are, of course, blogs that try to make up for this by removing personality altogether and acting solely as aggregators of information on specific topics, from blogs, books, lectures, leaflets, Web sites, and ... wherever. Ironically, these blogs, though well meant (and often quite useful), can unfortunately get in the way of Web research, inserting themselves unwittingly as intermediate steps in Web searches, placing themselves between the search engine and the real target. Anyone who has done a Google search has seen this: many of the sites listed end up only directing the searcher to another.

The biggest problem with the blogs in this respect may be, however, that they speak only to the converted. Few of them are strong enough to be able to reach out to those not already inclined to agree, or who do not know the writer from previous experience. This limits the blogs in a way that Kenneth Burke wrote of more than seventy years ago, saying that even "if one speaks very clearly and simply on a subject of great moment to himself, for instance, one is hardly communicating in the desired sense if his auditor does not care in the least what he is saying.... Communication cannot be satisfactory unless the matter discussed bears in some notable respect upon the interests of the auditor."[4] Online excitement is extremely difficult to build on its own. It never amounts to much—unless it finds a way to spill over into the broader world that it has already pulled in—for it has little ability to convert. Bloggers have yet to really learn and understand the extent of their audience universe. As a result, they pull in their expectations, often writing to a small audience of friends, relatives, and colleagues, forgetting to formulate their addresses in ways making them accessible to the strangers who may stumble across their blogs.

As Burke says, one certainly cannot command the attention of those who have no interest in one's topic, especially in a venue such as the blogs, where there is nothing physical beyond the Web page itself to attract—or keep—attention. A blogger can even have difficulty getting people who do have a concern to listen, if they do not already make the connection: "the mere fact that something is to a man's interests is no guaranty that he will be interested in it."[5] This may be the greatest weakness of the blogs: in a nearly infinite universe, it is easy for one to turn away without regret from any one thing; in an "on demand" universe, there is very little incentive to turn to something one does not already know one will like. Entry into the blogosphere may be something of an experiment for most people. Once there, unfortunately, most of them simply allow their interests to fade back into their old patterns, just in a new venue. Few, so far, really take advantage of the full extent of neteracy possibilities.

There has always been a problem in preaching to the choir, as they say, for it rarely introduces anyone to anything new, though it can certainly whip the choir up into a frenzy. This, of course, has happened (and will continue to happen) any number of times in the blogosphere—and the results are rarely pretty. Yet, blog storms, for all of their silliness and ensuing embarrassment, *can* have an impact on broader issues. For example, in late April 2007, the consortium of media giants called Advanced Access Content System Licensing Administrator (AACS LA), the people who control the codes to copying HD-DVDs, sent a letter to Digg, one of the most popular news aggregators among the blogs, demanding that Digg take down stories revealing a numerical key unlocking certain of their controls. On May 1, upon the advice of lawyers, Digg complied.

Ed Felten, of the blog Freedom to Tinker, takes up the story: "Then Digg's users revolted. As word got around about what Digg was doing, users launched a deluge of submissions to Digg, all mentioning or linking to the key. Digg's administrators tried to keep up, but submissions showed up faster than the administrators could cancel them. For a while yesterday, the entire front page of Digg—the 'hottest' pages according to Digg's algorithms—consisted of links to the AACS key."[6] Digg, sensible enough to understand that its loyalty needs to remain with its users, threw in the towel, founder Kevin Rose writing:

> Today was an insane day. And as the founder of Digg, I just wanted to post my thoughts …
>
> In building and shaping the site I've always tried to stay as hands on as possible. We've always given site moderation (digging/burying) power to the community. Occasionally we step in to remove stories that violate our terms of use (e.g., linking to pornography, illegal downloads, racial hate sites, etc.). So today was a difficult day for us. We had to decide whether to

remove stories containing a single code based on a cease and desist declaration. We had to make a call, and in our desire to avoid a scenario where Digg would be interrupted or shut down, we decided to comply and remove the stories with the code.

But now, after seeing hundreds of stories and reading thousands of comments, you've made it clear. You'd rather see Digg go down fighting than bow down to a bigger company. We hear you, and effective immediately we won't delete stories or comments containing the code and will deal with whatever the consequences might be.

If we lose, then what the hell, at least we died trying.

Digg on, Kevin.[7]

Felten explains what sparked this "storm":

The first answer is that it's a reaction against censorship. Net users hate censorship and often respond by replicating the threatened content. When Web companies take down user-submitted content at the behest of big media companies, that looks like censorship. But censorship by itself is not the whole story.

The second part of the answer, and the one most often missed by non-techies, is the fact that the content in question is an integer—an ordinary number, in other words. The number is often written in geeky alphanumeric format, but it can be written equivalently in a more user-friendly form like 790,815,794,162,126,871,771,506,399,625. Giving a private party ownership of a number seems deeply wrong to people versed in mathematics and computer science. Letting a private group pick out many millions of numbers (like the AACS secret keys), and then simply declare ownership of them, seems even worse.

While it's obvious why the creator of a movie or a song might deserve some special claim over the use of their creation, it's hard to see why anyone should be able to pick a number at random and unilaterally declare ownership of it. There is nothing creative about this number—indeed, it was chosen by a method designed to ensure that the resulting number was in no way special. It's just a number they picked out of a hat. And now they own it?[8]

Whether "they" do or not will be determined by courts—both of law and of public opinion. But the question is now a part of debate within the public sphere.

Whatever the outcome may eventually be, this incident points to a growing power of the "mob" through technology, and to the way blogs can be used to make a point that the "powers that be" might not want to hear. The impact of this incident on debate far from the blogs may prove to be as extensive, for it points up much more clearly than ever before the difficulty of defining ownership under the umbrella of today's communications revolution, where information becomes more important than any physical thing. It also shows the effect of the blogs as spontaneous democracy or, if one does not like the result, as mob rule.

Just as the blogs were appearing at the end of the 1990s, MIT professor Henry Jenkins gave a talk at the University of Michigan entitled "The Poachers and the Stormtroopers: Cultural Convergence in the Digital Age." Towards the end, he said:

> The web contains enormous potentials for the creation of a more diverse and democratic popular culture—one which allows much broader opportunities for grassroots participation. We can point to many examples of the power of net communities to work around the centralizing authority of traditional gatekeepers. This is what makes the digital revolution a cultural revolution. But, we should not allow the utopian promise of cyberspace to blind us to the real struggles which will need to be fought if we are going to secure a place for all of us to participate in popular culture. We are going to be watching increasingly bloody fights about intellectual property rights in digital media over the coming decade and those fights are going to determine—in part—the cultural logic that will structure the 21st century.[9]

What happened at Digg could be the start of one of those fights. Even if not, the blogs will certainly be central to the struggles over ownership that are sure to come. Places that allow "anyone" to post—Digg, YouTube, and a variety of other venues—are going to run afoul of protective attitudes (if not of laws)—if not now, then later. And most of them have already.

In terms of the blogs themselves, it is incidents like the Digg one that strengthen their users' and creators' self-image, one that they are trying to establish by and for themselves, doing so against the pressure from what they see as the cultural arbiters who try to force them into categories chosen for them. David Riesman, writing long before the rise of the blogosphere, provides a description that applies well to bloggers as they saw themselves before they started to really come together: "All these people who do not fit, who do not hang together in the way that they are supposed to, who do not feel the identities they are supposed to feel, are unorganized. They have nobody to define them. They lack both the advantages and the dangers of the cultural compartmentalizers, who make their living by defining others' marginalities for them."[10] Ironically, the lack of definition by the "herd" is probably what led to the image of the bloggers as isolates.

They never were isolates (after all, as Willard Van Orman Quine wrote, "Language is a social art"[11])—they simply did not conform to recognizable patterns. Today, the bloggers now *do* have a means for creating their own definitions and have been learning how to use it effectively, breaking out from outside attempts to marginalize them. A hundred arrows shot at a blank target can create their own bull's eye at the center (even if many of the arrows miss the target completely, the trend will be toward the center); they do not need it painted on beforehand.

Not all blog "storms" carry the possibility of cultural impact as great as the one at Digg. One of the other notable blog frenzies (among the many) is known as Fitzmas, a portmanteau of *Fitzgerald* (as in Patrick, the investigator of the releasing of CIA agent Valerie Plame's name by people within the White House) and *Christmas*. It caused hardly a blink outside of the blogosphere— where it was, for a time, an overriding topic—at least among the liberal political blogs.

Mark Liberman's blog Language Log explains what happened while liberal bloggers awaited the indictment of Lewis "Scooter" Libby. According to the entry, by Benjamin Zimmer, the word *Fitzmas* first appeared in early October 2005, but didn't really hit the big time

> until Oct. 18 when the meme returned to Daily Kos, this time in a widely linked post by "georgia10" with the title "Dealing With Fitzmas." Anticipation about impending indictments was high at that point, and it would only increase as bloggers and the news media continued to speculate about the timing and nature of Fitzgerald's announcement. On her own blog, "georgia10" commented on Oct. 22 about the spread of *Fitzmas* (a term she credited to Democratic Underground), noting that a Google search just four days after her Daily Kos post already yielded a whopping 51,500 hits.[12]

Leftwing bloggers came close to dancing in the streets—or in front of their computers, at any rate. The excitement—on liberal blogs—was palpable, though negligible elsewhere. In fact, few aside from liberal bloggers would recognize the word today—and those liberal bloggers, soon enough embarrassed, would mostly prefer that they had never come across it.

Occasional forays into nuttiness aside, bloggers do see themselves as broadening conversation, not as simply talking to themselves, not as echoing each other to the point where they believe something significant is being said based simply on the volume of the sound. Even conservative bloggers would likely agree with their liberal counterparts that they are all trying to do something to expand the public sphere—and not only in terms of politics, but in all of their activities.

In fact, most bloggers would insist that blogging does not merely expand but heightens everything they do, online and off, and is enriched by them. In a way, they are all children of John Dewey, who wrote that "a good citizen finds his conduct as a member of a political group enriching and enriched by his participation in family life, industry, scientific and artistic associations. There is a free give-and-take: fullness of integrated personality is therefore possible of achievement, since the pulls and responses of different groups reënforce one another and their values accord."[13]

If Benjamin Franklin is the patron saint of the blogs (as I argue in *The Rise of the Blogosphere*), then Dewey must be at least their prophet. He understood something that has become the center of the success of the blogs, the power of association, especially in strengthening democracy and protecting liberty and equality in much the way that bloggers (especially politically oriented bloggers) do today: "Liberty is that secure release and fulfillment of personal potentialities which take place only in rich and manifold association with others: the power to be an individualized self making a distinctive contribution and enjoying in its own way the fruits of association. Equality denotes the unhampered share which each individual member of the community has in the consequences of associated action."[14]

The problem for bloggers is that an aggregate itself is not enough. Often, all aggregation results in is a variant of the Fitzmas hysteria, a lot of agitation but to no real purpose. People all yelling and demanding the same thing may sound good at the moment: "But no amount of aggregated collective action of itself constitutes a community. For beings who observe and think, and whose ideas are absorbed by impulses and become sentiments and interests, 'we' is as inevitable as 'I.' But 'we' and 'our' exist only when the consequences of combined action are perceived and become an object of desire and effort, just as 'I' and 'mine' appear on the scene only when a distinctive share in mutual action is consciously asserted or claimed."[15] This is just the perception of Dewey's that led Markos Moulitsas of Daily Kos to begin to reform his liberal political blog from a forum for comment and complaint into an instrument for change, allying himself concretely with Democratic Party political ends and moving his activities from simply online and into to the broader society where the Web is but one of many avenues for community activity.

For a Deweyesque vision to prevail, bloggers are going to have to seek new possibilities frequently—and many of them are, arranging "meet ups" with other bloggers, even setting up and attending national conventions stemming from their online activities. Their blogs, however, are going to have to become more aggressively pointed if the movement as a whole is to be more than just social networking. Simply reflecting on life does not move the conversation forward or move people to reach out from their own lives.

The idea is not simply to use the blogs to develop a community of the like-minded, or the blogs do end up as no more than Nicholas Lemann's "church newsletters." For one thing, without outreach, such narrowly focused communities end up diminishing; they tend to toss people out more than they bring them in. For another, most bloggers do learn that disagreement is not necessarily a bad thing and that they have to work through (and with) disagreement in order to succeed. Those writing on group blogs (in particular) can (and do) fight, and fight viciously—even with their friends—and they learn to discourage what they call "concern trolls," those who judge everything through a single issue. Also, the bloggers generally recognize the value of alliance for the particular goal of any of the blogging communities they may join. Most would nod in agreement with Riesman as he writes:

> I believe it is a fallacy to assume that people can co-operate only if they understand each other (this is the illusion of many semanticists), or if they like each other, or if they share certain preconceptions. The glory of modern large-scale democratically-tending society is that it has developed the social inventions—such as the market, the practices and skills of negotiation, and the many other devices which allow us to put forward in a given situation only part of ourselves—which allow us to get along and, usually, not to kill each other while retaining the privilege of private conscience and of veto over many requests made of us by our fellow men.[16]

And, since Riesman's time, society has developed other "social inventions," such as the blogs, that take the motion he describes even further. It is not only for the "glory," as Riesman puts it, but, it can be argued, the very success and progress of modern societies is based on utilization of "social inventions."

For the moment, it remains true that the blogs have yet to find a way to be much more than reflective, becoming formative. They have proven to be an avenue for effective fundraising (a result of their congregations of the like-minded), giving bloggers collectively much more power and visibility than they have ever had, but they have yet to show themselves as useful tools towards conversion.

Given their predilection towards the similar or agreeable and the fact of linkage and aggregation, it is no surprise that the blogs are criticized for not providing much that is original, acting almost exclusively as amplifiers for things created elsewhere. Being as the world of the blogs itself is not "new" but (like the Web itself) is an extension of cultural and technological forces in play elsewhere, this should surprise no one.

Paradoxically, originality—that much vaunted myth of print culture—needs other thought, construction, and presentation in order to be defined as "original." It needs them, in fact, to be created at all. An understanding of this may be what provides the energy behind the blogs, for the impact is closer to the surface there, where links take us more directly and quickly back, than ever before. For all of our worship of originality (somewhat misplaced, in my view), it remains true, as Karl Popper writes, that:

> The sociology of knowledge argues that scientific thought, and especially thought on social and political matters, does not proceed in a vacuum, but in a socially conditioned atmosphere. It is influenced largely by unconscious or subconscious elements. These elements remain hidden from the thinker's

observing eye because they form, as it were, the very place where he inhabits, his *social habitat*. The social habitat of the thinker determines a whole system of opinions and theories which appear to him as unquestionably true or self-evident. They appear to him as if they were logically and trivially true, such as, for example, the sentence "all tables are tables." This is why he is not even aware of having made any assumptions at all. But that he has made assumptions can be seen if we compare him with a thinker who lives in a very different social habitat; for he too will proceed from a system of apparently unquestionable assumptions, but from a very different one; and it may be so different that no intellectual bridge may exist and no compromise be possible between these two systems.[17]

The blogs are bringing those "hidden elements" into the light. And the "social habitat" can now be spread out like the evening in T. S. Eliot's "The Love Song of J. Alfred Prufrock," "like a patient etherized upon a table." In fact, the notes to his "The Wasteland," today, would be presented as a series of links—and would hardly raise an eyebrow, not even if not composed by Eliot alone.

Original thought never comes from a questioning of *everything*, but does arise from assuming a great deal and limiting the questioning to a few simple topics. An original idea or movement, then, builds on a system of agreement or (at least) of acceptance or willingness not to contest—*outside* of the arena of originality. Springing into general consciousness so quickly, the blogs and blog communities are often examined in all aspects of their manifestation, and then are criticized for not doing *everything* in a new way. Their real success, however, will be in doing only one or two things in a new way, co-opting the rest from the general assumptions of modern societies. It may be true that the blogs have yet to provide anything really original, but they are a growing and changing phenomenon. Their real originality may only become apparent some years down the road.

It will probably be in the area of community where the blogs do finally prove to have their greatest impact and originality. The annual blog conventions that have been springing up, for example, do not resemble those centering on television shows or serial movies, where the intent is simply to revel for a few days amongst the like-minded before returning to a more mundane (less costumed, at least) existence. Meant to build community, the blog conventions do provide possibilities for socializing, but they are heavy on information and planning sessions, taking advantage of convergence to plan future activities as well as building the "we" that Dewey speaks of.

The movement is toward connection, not division. Speaking of the 2007 Brooklyn Blogfest, blogger "Miss Heather" wrote, "More often than not, the comments I read of the above nature [complaints about the blogfest] were worded in *ahem* a very hostile and belligerent manner. Although I *disagree* with the *way* these people chose to air their grievances, I *agree* with the point they were trying to make. Being someone who is friendly to what the Blogfest is trying to do (but has some very serious concerns) I feel compelled to give my two cents."[18] The attitude she expresses, of wishing to point out problems but to do so constructively, is really the standard (her comment on other complaints aside) of the "meet ups" of bloggers.

An academic blogger (a medievalist) who uses the name "Dr. Virago" wrote of a breakfast "meet up" in Michigan:

> I was really pleased that this year there was a real mix of people in different stages of their careers, and also a better gender mix. I think it says something about the status of blogging that we had such a mix, and that bloggers from all those stages of career were willing to come and meet other bloggers. In other words, blogging is becoming less of a sub-culture and more of a mainstream culture. It also says something that there was also a mix of pseudonymous and non-pseudonymous bloggers, and that if asked, people generally revealed their pseudonymous blogs. Somewhere someone noted that when rounds of introductions were made, we didn't identify our blogs, but I think in my case it was more a worry about our voices carrying to tables of non-bloggers. I still worry about non-bloggers' attitudes towards blogs. Who knows if we have an Ivan Tribble among the medieval crowd. But one-on-one I don't think people cared that much.[19]

"Ivan Tribble," mentioned in chapter 1, has warned against blogging by academics. This group of academic bloggers wants to do more than express, but to expand, taking their discussion beyond their departments, helping create Brad DeLong's "invisible college."

The conventions are meant as loci for focus on aspects of agreement, points on which all of the particular group can act as one. Through the seeming cacophony of the blogosphere, those who want to use blog communities for greater ends have learned that, to develop group effectiveness, they must find ways for the group to speak with a single voice. Moulitsas addresses this need by insisting that his Kossacks agree on just one simple idea, that it is better to elect Democrats to public office than Republicans. Beyond that, he demands very little of those who use his group blog. As a result, Yearly Kos, the annual convention that has grown out of Daily Kos, operates with a sense of cohesion and purpose that the diversity of attendees might seem to belie.

Yet there do need to be demands on members of any community if it is going to become a "we" rather than an aggregate of "I." The individualism inherent in a PC-based network with no centralized control and no gatekeeper makes any community structure fragile, and leaves the blogs open to charges of anarchy and narcissism. And then there is, as Ron Rosenbaum writes in *The Atlantic*, "cyber-disinformation. Something about the lonely void in which online interactions are conducted seems to encourage the tendency toward the extreme or abusive mode in communication—because you're not face-to-face with the person you are berating or baiting."[20] The question, then, for community organizers in the blogosphere, becomes how to get people to cooperate and toe lines of *netiquette* when there is very little possibility of a stick effective on the recalcitrant. This is extremely important today, when the blogosphere is growing at such a phenomenal rate and the problem of incivility with it. Michael Froomkin writes:

> The Internet community is aware of the problem—almost hysterical about it at times. The community is responding to the influx with a massive education effort, producing FAQs [Frequently Asked Questions], books, web pages, and of course, flaming away at violators of netiquette. Whether these efforts will suffice to preserve the Internet's norms remains unclear.
>
> Some de facto Internet standards are set by a combination of peer pressure and socialization. The main channels by which this is communicated, other than one-to-one education, is through "FAQs." These documents, prepared by self-selected volunteers, attempt to distill some Internet wisdom, or Internet norms, for newcomers.... Many of these attempt to set out the basic rules of Internet conduct, or "netiquette." Basic rules of netiquette include asking permission before forwarding a private message, respecting copyrights, reading the FAQ before asking silly questions, and remembering not to send messages in all capital letters except for emphasis.[21]

Other means of enforcing netiquette include pointed comments and use of the "troll rating" systems on various group blogs, where comments can be made to disappear if a certain number of community members find them offensive. Still, most attempts at netiquette work because *most* people *want* to cooperate and try to be considerate of the feelings of others. Something about the particular online community has attracted them—and this is where most group-builders in the blogosphere concentrate their effort, on giving individuals communal reason to come back to their Web sites and to cooperate when contributing to it.

A problem with this is the very immediacy of the blogs, the ease of publishing or commenting on the spur of the moment. If one is feeling annoyed, a hasty comment can put readers off one's blog forever. Blogger Shelly Powers writes about what this means: "I realize that to succeed in this medium, I should focus on the bright, lightsome qualities of weblogging—make a call for hands, tell you how much I *love* you and such, but frankly, poor impulse control comes to my mind more often than not when I think of 'weblogging.' The poor impulse control that leads us to write in haste, repent at very long leisure. The same poor impulse control that tempts cooler and more calculating heads, who seek to use this medium more as weapon than means of communication."[22] She is right: a successful blogger manages not to alienate, but even to find ways of disagreeing without seeming oppositional. The danger she points out is not specific to blogs, but is one that Kenneth Boulding described fifty years ago when writing about "image":

> If I think that Mr. A is a mean and surly individual I will treat him in such a way that he will become meaner and more surly. If I think he is a good fellow I will treat him in such a way as to increase his affability. So there is opportunity here for fantastic dynamic series of misinterpretation, misunderstanding, frustrations, and breakdowns. We must reckon with the fact that in passing from one person to another messages become strangely transformed. My friend lets fall an innocent remark which I interpret falsely as being hostile and before we know where we are my action and his reaction and my reaction have made us enemies. We are dealing here with a world of mirrors and it is often hard to see what is being reflected.[23]

The importance of netiquette is not far removed from that of etiquette in our other interactions: the dangers of misinterpretation, of the world of self-created funhouse mirrors, have been with us since long before the advent of the Internet.

One of the ways people try to attract readers is through reciprocal links, adding to one's *blogroll*, a list of recommended blogs—those one reads regularly or finds particularly sympathetic—created, in part, with the hope that the other bloggers will return the favor (a hope often amplified through an email alerting the other to the link). The blogroll is part of the active aspect of the blogosphere, for each blog (properly executed) should constantly grow and change, given the evolving interests of the individual bloggers. However, the blogroll remains a phenomenon limited to the more active and out-reaching blogs: "only about one-quarter of all initially randomly-generated blogs were found to have any outbound links to other blogs. Including inbound links raises the percentage of random blogs connected in some way to other blogs to 58%, but that still leaves 42% of the blogs tracked by blogs that appear to be social isolates, neither linking to nor being linked to by others."[24]

But are these linkless bloggers really "social isolates"? If so, why are they blogging at all? If one really wants to isolate, one does not blog. A more likely explanation is that many blogs never "take off," even in the creator's mind. Most blogs quickly become moribund; the concentrated activity necessary for successful blogging proving more than the particular individual wants to engage upon.

The quote below, from a post on her own blog On the Left Tip, is by RenaRF, who is also an important and popular blogger on Daily Kos. Significantly (as with all of her blog entries), it is filled with internal links and surrounded by others. RenaRF is a political activist who sees her blogging as part and parcel of her "real world" political work:

Last week, I got an invitation to attend a fundraiser hosted in the home of a prominent Arlington-area couple (Arlington, Virginia). The invitation said that both Tim Roemer and James Carville would be the guest speakers at the event, and they were. I'm fortunate enough that I had the money to attend what would be considered a pricey event. I had always intended to make a sizable donation to add to my other donations, and what the hey—this way I could make the donation *and* get to stargaze a bit....

I had a small, purse sized notebook with me, and when we had a break in our conversation, I pulled it out and readied myself for the high-visibility speakers. I can't remember who asked me if I was a reporter—but I told them that I wasn't, but that I was a blogger and had every intention of writing up the evening. This turned us to the subject of blogs, and I was asked where I would post this—I told them I hoped to post it at Daily Kos and Raising Kaine, time permitting. Everyone knew Raising Kaine—lowkell has done an outstanding job of bringing in those who are not especially in the blogosphere. Some had heard of Daily Kos, but you could tell it was not a place where any (that I could identify) spend their time....

Now—let me say that I was taking copious notes during the remarks by the speakers generated interest. I caught sideways glances, not unfriendly ones, that looked askance. I was amused with the idea that someone might have thought I was "legitimate" press....

I can't remember who said it, but earlier in the evening this point was made: "We have to out-work them. We have to want this more than they do."

At this point I chimed into the conversation talking about the Netroots and the blogosphere and how much emphasis they are placing on the GOTV [Get Out The Vote] effort. That's when I got "the comment".... I want each of you to understand, however, that this was in no way said scornfully—rather, it was just put out there as common knowledge:

> "Bloggers just sit on their butts behind their computer screens. They spend their time just talking to each other and that's fine—but they're talking to a small audience."

Not this time. *HELP ME* prove this guy wrong. If you've given money, do more. Google your candidate and find the address and phone number for the campaign office. Call it. Show up there if possible. *Demand* that they put you to work.[25]

This passage impressed me when I read it last fall, for RenaRF was taking up the challenge of the clichéd image of the blogger and using it to raise money for campaigns that really had little to do with the blogs. I asked RenaRF, via email, what had brought this about:

I fully expected that blogging my real life activities would be a good thing. What I saw even on Daily Kos, which is a "motivated" community, was repeated comments from people over time that indicated to me that they were behind their computer screens and not doing what they could and should do to return Congress to the Democrats. Given that I already felt I had a chance at a platform that would be widely read, I decided to do what I would have done anyway (e.g., volunteering for Webb; attending events for Webb) and then write about it to help allay any fears and/or heighten awareness of the critical need for people to get up out of their chairs and do whatever they could. I tried to provide, literally, no excuses. For people who had "safe" Dems and weren't in close physical proximity to candidates needing feet on the street, I referred them to MoveOn's Calls For Change (where they could call into swing districts regardless of where they lived). I also had as a goal to pull some money out of those in "safe" districts. My ultimate goal was to direct those funds to Webb, but generally I just wanted to share the wealth with Democratic candidates who had a chance at challenging to overtake a seat and/or those who were in seats that were considered threatened....

What struck me was how few people at the fundraiser, who were obviously committed Democrats, realized that the Netroots could push someone over the line. For example, when I checked ActBlue contributions for Webb, they came in at slightly under 10% of the total funds raised to put him in the Senate. That's a powerful message. Of the people at the event who knew about and further had an opinion about the Netroots, the responses were VERY either/or. Either they wanted to court the blogs and leverage that power OR they felt that the Netroots spent too much time attacking Democrats when they should have been supporting them. I understand the latter sentiment, and I think it's imperative that so-called "establishment" Democrats engage with the Netroots. We're a very forgiving bunch when we are engaged, I said to the person who made the comment.

I guess I felt like I was living that intersection. I was on the street, dedicated, and committing my time and money (along with MANY others) and then writing about it—about my feeling of involvement, about how invested that level of commitment made me feel to push Webb to victory, and about how I believed each and every blogger at Daily Kos should and could have the same type of experience. The goal was absolutely to get people engaged, and while I likely only reached a small percentage of those who were on the fence or to whom it hadn't occurred there were things they could be doing, it WAS a small percentage who got out there when they otherwise would not have. I felt like my reputation and relative visibility at Daily Kos would aid in that regard.[26]

The gist of RenaRF's comments is that the blogs are not the end-all, but simply a tool. They aren't community themselves, but they can be used to further community concerns.

What, then, makes a blog successful? What brings readers to them, if not simply a desire for community—and if the blogs themselves aren't really the community? David Benjamin Auerbach, who blogs as "Waggish" on his blog of the same name, provides a list for building readership:

1. **The Short Horizon:** Tristan Louis [of TNL.net] speculates that what makes big blogs popular are lots of short entries. Well, this blog doesn't provide any evidence to the contrary. But it underscores a major aspect of blogs, which is the brutally short horizon for content. Between RSS [Really Simple Syndication] aggregators and how rarely people go through archives of blogs, a given entry has prominent existence for a week at most, and far less on many blogs. Consequently, most readers will only read each entry of a blog they're following once, and may often miss entries.

2. **Quantity:** Following from the short horizon, bloggers do best when they post early and post often, and most of them follow this model. There is little harm from overposting; the worst that will happen is that people skip an entry. There is great harm from underposting: people will forget about you. Having taken some sabbaticals myself from Waggish, I've seen the downside to leaving your blog in a static state for too long. Yet the emphasis on quantity leads inevitably to more redundancy and less originality in content, on average.

3. **The Gestalt:** There is much less of a focus on discrete work in blogs than there is in most other media. Individual posts may be called out for brief (or occasionally permanent) fame, but in the stream of work being published by an individual, quickly fading into the horizon, blogs are identified by gestalt characteristics rather than by discrete posts. To draw the literary analogy, bloggers are much more Balzac than Joyce.

4. **Specialization:** How many blogs do you know that wander all over the place, topic-wise? (Answer: "My friends'.") Someone like language hat establishes themselves and attracts interest by focusing resolutely and consistently on a core set of topics. Again, with the lack of attention on discrete entries, blogs do best when they have a definable gestalt. (This applies to aggregators as well—the best ones stick to their areas of interest.)

5. **Instant Feedback:** What with the short horizon, most responses to a blog entry are received within hours or days. Not only does this provide a huge amount of feedback to authors before they distance themselves from the work, but it encourages collaboration and argument, as well as nudging authors to work with their audience's reactions in mind and address them. (Okay, this one is pretty obvious/unarguable, though someone should write a more thorough piece on the difference between political single-voice vs. community blogs. Freepers [people who post

on Free Republic, one of the premier rightwing blogs] scare me; it
would be interesting!)

6. **Need for Triage:** Between the short horizon and the sheer quantity of
   blogs and content out there, a role for aggregators/gatekeepers to point
   people to selected pieces of content was inevitable. Whether MeFi,
   BoingBoing, or Things, many of these are more popular than most
   blogs consisting of original content.[27]

Auerbach's short guide to how to succeed in the blogosphere addresses only
the practical side of blogging, but this is what most people first think about
when starting to blog, and Auerbach certainly is not trying to write to the
experienced and successful blogger (who would not need the advice), but to
the fairly new blogger, the person who has gotten their feet wet, but has not
felt that their efforts are leading to the results they want. Auerbach assumes
that his audience has answered for themselves the question "Why blog?"—at
least for the moment, but have not yet gotten to the place of wondering just
where their blogging will take them or imagining just what this community is
that they want to see attracted to their blog.

For the purposes of his list and of his advice, Auerbach is positing the blog
itself as static, its change (in posts and comments) as the dynamic. In a way, he
is crossing the divide between the older vision of a creation as a "thing" and the
net-centric view of a creation as a process, a divide described by Luis Arata:

> Like a statue on a pedestal or a frozen oracle, the object of creation has been
> defined classically as something to contemplate. From an interactive perspec-
> tive, this leaves most of the creation out of the picture. A first quality of an
> interactive perspective is that it opens multiple points of view through the
> blurring of boundaries of realities and objects once conveniently fixed. This
> shifts the emphasis away from the object and tilts it more toward the subject
> who perceives. Viewers interact with objects in a way that celebrates subjec-
> tivity and diversity. Multiple views of a common phenomenon can coexist
> even if they are mutually exclusive. Objects themselves can remain fuzzy and
> metamorphic.[28]

Any blog, different from one day to the next, fits this new vision of "object."

Of necessity constantly watching reactions to particular posts and changing
their approaches, successful bloggers might be said to be looking *around* their
own works (and those of others) instead of simply *at* them. When I first read
Arata's words, I was reminded of Roland Barthes's essay "From Word to Text,"
where he, too, addresses this divide between the static and the active, but from
a time before the advent of the World Wide Web.

Barthes details what he saw as an "epistemological slide"[29] from discrete
"work" to "Text," something with a broader set of boundaries than those of a

physical object. His view presages a move from print culture, with its deifica-
tion of the work, to net culture, where all objects are malleable, clay for the
creation of the next piece and never holy in their manifestation, where no
object is central for there is no static object in the first place. In many ways,
the blogs (like Dada collage or pastiche) fit well his conception of "Text," so it
is worthwhile to stop here to review his seven "propositions" (or "enuncia-
tions") about "Text," for they can add a different dimension of understanding
to Auerbach's advice to bloggers, providing a philosophical basis for understanding of the "what" to go with the "how."

First, Text "is experienced only in an activity of production."[30] It is not the
"thing" that a work (a book) is, but is a process, a demonstration: "its consti-
tutive movement is that of cutting across (in particular, it can cut across the
work, several works)."[31] Though Barthes died almost two decades before the
advent of the blogs, his conception of "Text" fits them well, for they are
defiantly process, not static items. Their very form, generally with the most
recent entry appearing first, keeps them from appearing simply as works with
new appendages ... and no single entry or diary can really be construed as a
work in itself.

Second, Text "cannot be contained in a hierarchy, even in a simple division
of genres. What constitutes the Text is, on the contrary (or precisely), its
subversive force in respect of the old classifications."[32] The boundaries of a
work (its covers, perhaps) cannot contain a Text, which operates in a manner
more like conversation or Skinner's "verbal behavior," as a dynamic. Though I
would argue that the blogs themselves do constitute a genre, it is not in the
old sense of classification or delineation. One of the more significant aspects
of blogs is that they constantly subvert classification: an academic blog, for
example, can easily encompass humor or political invective, for there are no
editorial constraints forcing any to be any one thing.

Third, the field of the Text "is that of the signifier and the signifier must
not be conceived of as 'the first stage of meaning,' its material vestibule, but,
in complete opposition to this, as its *deferred action*."[33] There is no closure in
Text, no contained meaning, no expectation of answer, no determined signi-
fied to go with the signifier. Though there are plenty of bloggers who believe
that they have the "answers" and are blogging merely to share them, the aggregate of the blogs creates a Text not of knowledge but of exploration, something that drives those who believe in truth as a concrete entity crazy. "How
can you trust the blogs?" they ask, never realizing that they pose exactly the
wrong question, for the blogs aren't claiming to provide anything trustworthy
at all. Instead, they *come from* concepts of meaning that may or may not have
validity, and *go to* points that are left up to the reader (and new writer) to
determine. The core of Barthes' point is that the reader (and the writer, too,
as a reader) *comes to* the blog most often not for meaning but for verification
within another ongoing conversation. The Text, after all, is laid out for

someone coming to it later, not for conversation to arise from it, but to be brought in, almost as an artifact for examination. In this sense, it does not originate, but signifies what might best be conceived of as an older conversation.

Fourth, "The Text is not a co-existence of meanings but a passage, an over-crossing; thus it answers not to an interpretation, even a liberal one, but to an explosion, a dissemination."[34] The being of the Text is such that it cannot be reduced to "meaning" or any other static thing. Put coarsely, Kurt Gödel's famous proof demonstrates that no system can be both complete and consistent. Just so, the blogs (together as Text) do not even *purport* to provide a closed and complete system or even a consistent one—and certainly not both. The blogs cannot be looked to for answers, but for questioning, or for a conversation that stretches over all the works of the past to a conclusion that is nothing more than a "work" to be used in the next conversation, as the next point indicates.

Fifth, the work "refers to the image of an *organism* which grows by vital expansion, by 'development' ...; the metaphor of the Text is that of the *network*; if the Text extends itself, it is as a result of a combinatory systematic."[35] Barthes was struggling to encapsulate an idea with no idea that it would soon become a reality. In many ways, and with few bloggers ever realizing it, his concept of "network" has become both the physical and metaphorical basis for the blogs.

Sixth, the Text "decants the work (the work permitting) from its consumption and gathers it up as play, activity, production, practice."[36] Through it, the distance between writing and reading is diminished if not extinguished. The importance of comment on the blogs, and of linkage (which is also used for comment, though in the context of another blog) shows the reduction from separate, almost deified "work" to "Text" with all its implied interactivity and plasticity.

Seventh, the "Text is that space where no language has a hold over any other, where languages circulate (keeping the circular sense of the term)."[37] For a long time, focus has been on the work, leading to an emphasis on the details of the work and its construction. Grammar, for example, had superseded conversation, presentation replacing discussion. By contrast, the details of language itself become less important on the blogs than the continuum each conversationalist enters into.

Auerbach's suggestions are certainly advice on what to do with a "Text" in Barthes' sense of the word, and not a "work," though the "Text," the blog, is made up of individual works, the diaries (and even the comments).

Writing in another context (and, as do most, using "text" in the sense that Barthes applies to "work"), media scholar Jonathan Gray sums up what Barthes is trying to supercede: "The attempt to understand the text has taken the form of examining it as a singular, autonomous entity, and as a sealed packet of meaning. Another tradition of research has examined the interrelation between this packet of meaning and its audiences, seeing how an audience interacts with its contents after opening the packet."[38] This last, "reader response," moves towards Barthes's position, but it still does, as Gray indicates, rely on package and not on the dynamic. The "work" is still the thing.

One of the processes occurring through the blogs is that what had been physical and conceptual barriers between *creator*, *text*, and *audience* are breaking down. None of the three is a distinct entity or even packet any longer, not when the text itself becomes malleable. The most extreme example of this breakdown is, of course, the wiki, where there is no defining barrier creating authority, but it exists in blogs as well, where the comment function can become an important part of the text—the text essentially emasculated if presented or discussed without its comments.

For community blogs, in fact, it is the comment that carries the diary. The text (the screen, the page) is only the common marker for something that includes a great deal more, and that can only be examined as a totality dominated by comment and comment volume. Those people, and they are legion, who see the blogs (and bloggers) as divorced from the world, mistake a part (the initial text, the post or diary) for the whole, seeing a synecdoche as in fact the whole that it simply represents.

Even so, the comments, too, are just one aspect of the dynamics of the blogs. Another, as we have seen, is the link. Michael Bérubé, whose leadership in the blogosphere through his own extremely popular, though rather academic, blog earned him the nickname "Choirmaster" over the two years before he retired his blog in early 2007, writes about his own experiences in blogging:

> One of the joys and challenges of blog writing—and one of the things that distinguishes it from every other kind of writing—is the plasticity of the hyperlink: on one hand, the hyperlink works as a kind of hyperfootnote, providing not merely the reference to a secondary text but access to the text in its entirety; on the other hand, there is no reason why hyperlinks should always be used so "transparently," and, as I have found in my career as a blogger, they can also be deployed in a more Borgesian or Nabokovian vein to undercut, ironize, or otherwise trouble the protocols of textual reference. Those postmodern intertextual high jinks are impossible to reproduce in print, as is the metonymic skid involved in leaping across Web sites from hyperlink to hyperlink.[39]

When I teach writing for the Web, I stress the link and its importance—and not simply because it is a sign of a networking and community, but because it can add quite a bit to the act and art of writing. One of the things the link does is keep the writer aware not only of audience but of sources, in ways of immediacy never before practical. Writing with links, one has to think how a reader might or might not use them, and then has to manipulate one's own text with that in mind. This, as Bérubé hints, can lead to new types of play, but it can also make the writer ask (for both play and serious purposes), "OK, are they following the link, or not? And what do I do if the answer is 'both'?" One has to make sure that the link does not provide a piece of the puzzle unavailable in the present work, but that the present work does not cover the material linked too closely—allowing the reader who has followed the link to drift away through boredom at perceived repetition.

The successful dynamic of the blog is dependent on more than following Auerbach's points with Barthes's in mind. In fact, the *physical* dynamic depends more on these two factors discussed, the links and the comments. The links pull from the past and the comments drag the story into the future present (that is, they keep the story from receding too quickly into the past itself). Bérubé notes that, "the best, most thought-provoking blogs are renowned not only for the quality of their writing but for the quality of writing they stimulate in response. It is in the daily give-and-take between bloggers and commenters—many of whom, of course, have their own blogs as well— that discursive communities are formed online, and it is in such give-and-take that blogs create the taste by which they are to be enjoyed."[40] Carried with many comments is a link to the commenter's own blog, facilitating the discussion and taking it beyond the immediate venue. Link and comment become inextricably intertwined, stimulus, response, and reinforcement embodied on the screen.

Not all is always well in the comment section, however, for control is necessarily ceded—at least to some extent—to the commenter. And the commenter is not always polite or willing to stick to the conversation outlined by the diary. Some of these responders simply want to further their own agendas, but others have somewhat more pernicious (in terms of the ethics of the blogosphere) purposes in mind. Shirley Duglin Kennedy writes about them:

> Yeah, it's hard not to feel violated when the comment function of your blog (which is supposed to facilitate the free exchange of ideas among your readers) is hijacked by ne'er-do-wells. Comment spammers take advantage of the open comment forums on blogs (which usually let posters use HTML) to try to raise their Google rankings by posting links to sites that sell the same sorts of goods and services being flogged in email spam (e.g., porn, pills, poker, pirated software) or are "link farms" (pages that are nothing more than a bunch of ads and links to other sites).... Since comment spammers often use scripts or other automated methods of posting their swill, incorporating a so-called "Turing test" ensures that all comments are posted by humans and not machines. You've undoubtedly encountered versions of this in your online travels, where you are required to type in a series of numbers

and/or letters before you could log in or post something. (For those who are interested, this has its own acronym—CAPTCHA, which stands for Completely Automated Public Turing test to tell Computers and Humans Apart.)[41]

CAPTCHA became the basis for something of a word game on Bérubé's blog in the months before he closed it. On his blog, the CAPTCHA letters always created a word and commenters added the CAPTCHA word to the end of their comment, somehow relating it to what they were saying. But CAPTCHA has become a necessary, if not always completely unwanted, aspect of online life.

The best bloggers are never satisfied to blog at just one site, even their own. All of them blog for a reason—to communicate. They are driven, like Coleridge's Ancient Mariner, to grab hold of the nearest "wedding guest," gasping "There was a ship…." Even Bérubé, who had shut down his blog, found it hard to stay away, his posts now popping up on Crooked Timber and TPM Café. A teacher, lecturer, and prolific writer even offline, Bérubé felt he no longer had the time for the intensive focus successful individual blogging demands. On group sites, he does not have the pressure to constantly produce, so can turn his attention back to his other tasks.

Still, as his inability to let go completely shows, there is a real attraction to blogging. One blogger, who calls herself "Digby" of Digby's Hullabaloo, expresses it well:

> There is also freedom in this kind of writing and an intellectual challenge. Writing as a genderless entity, without history or corporeal identity and without (usually) allowing myself to resort to personal anecdote or appeals to authority, I think my arguments became sharper, more tightly reasoned. The blogging ethic (driven by the technology that allows it) requires that one not only make a logical and consistent argument, but one must document and substantiate one's work by linking to source material. These demands that bloggers "show their work" and the feedback from our highly intelligent audience of pedants and political junkies served as a kind of diffuse editorial check that lends credibility over time to any blogger but especially to pseudonymous writers like me—at least among my readers.[42]

Even if only a few people are "listening," one can create an elegance in prose on the Web with responsibility only to oneself—and there can be a real satisfaction in doing so.

Glenn Greenwald, a lawyer who became a blogger and then a best-selling author (*How Would a Patriot Act?*), also changed his blogging in 2007, moving his blog to *Salon*, an online magazine with closer ties to the mainstream news media than to the blogosphere. His move and rationale were different from

Bérubé's, for he still sees the blogs as his primary venue and his books (success notwithstanding) as the adjunct. He provided this explanation for his move and tried to allay the fears of the community that had grown up around him:

1. Other than some design changes (actually, design improvements), the content of this blog will remain exactly the same. The first term I negotiated with *Salon* was complete editorial freedom—no editorial interventions, no topic "assignments," and no content, length or topic restrictions. I can post when and how frequently I want, and I have access to post 24 hours a day, 7 days a week, and posting is immediate. In essence, *Salon* wants to publish *this* blog, not some modified or constrained version, and so I have exactly the same freedom to post there that I have here.

2. The principal motivation in moving is that the move will immediately result in a substantially increased readership for the blog, along with enhanced visibility generally. As easy as it is to forget, there are still substantial numbers of politically engaged people who do not read blogs, or who read them only periodically.

   The influence of the blogosphere is growing inexorably, and I think it is still in its incipient stages, but blog readers are still a subset of political readers generally. While the *Salon* readership overlaps to some extent with the blogosphere, there are large numbers of *Salon* readers (as is true for most magazines) who don't read blogs, and blogging there will simply enable me to be read by more people.

   There is also still some lingering (albeit diminishing) bias against people who are "just bloggers." In some eyes—myopic ones—writing principally for your own blog is credibility-limiting. That is changing and should change more rapidly (since, as I've said before, I think the best and most reliable political writing and analysis is found, with rare exception, in the blogosphere), but that bias persists and can still be somewhat limiting.

   Anyone who expends the substantial amounts of time and energy required for daily political blogging believes, I'd say almost by definition, that the more people who are exposed to what they write, the better. I think that objective will be fulfilled in multiple ways from this move.

3. A significant factor in moving to *Salon* was how positive my previous experiences have been in writing there. I have guest blogged for Tim Grieve on two occasions and written numerous articles over the last few months. The editors there are excellent and the suggestions they make are always intended to improve, not dilute, what one writes. And they are committed to publishing unique and consequential content which many other media outlets probably would be too timid to publish.[43]

Greenwald sees blogging as a tool, not as an end in itself. His attitude is probably that of most successful bloggers today. Their commitment to the blogosphere only extends to its use towards their goals in communities whose presence on the Web may only be tangential.

Ultimately, however, what the blogs are will be determined not by "premier" bloggers like Bérubé and Greenwald but by the masses of relatively unknown bloggers. Recently, on taking a childcare leave from Daily Kos, Moulitsas saw "his" community continue on without missing a beat. He then wrote:

> I like to talk about this being a "leaderless" movement, and that no single individual is really all that important to it. No one individual was indispensable for the rise of the netroots. Subtract any of us now, and the movement would continue to chug along with barely a bat of the eye. And what better example of that is there than the fact this site actually has had its best April ever despite the general absence of the guy whose name is on the site's masthead?
>
> At the end of the day, this isn't a movement based on personalities or individuals, but on our collective action and influence. We're all expendable. None of us are essential. And it's wonderful.
>
> **Update:** A corollary, from the comments:
> **or rather**
> we're all essential.
> just no more essential than the next person.
> and it's not a leaderless movement. It's a movement with so many leaders, so many different ones on any given issue or … day, that it's the quintessential "leaderfull" movement.
> I like that.[44]

And that, in essence, is the heart of the success of the blogs in the eyes of bloggers themselves.

Chapter 4

THE BLOGS, POLITICAL
ISSUES, AND THE PRESS

Blogs and Other Online Entities Discussed in Chapter 4

AMERICAblog, http://www.americablog.com

Assignment Zero, http://zero.newassignment.net

Crooked Timber, http://www.crookedtimber.org

Daily Kos, http://www.dailykos.com

Digby's Hullabaloo, http://digbysblog.blogspot.com/2007/05/i-love-my-navel-so-much-by-digby.html

Digital Universe, http://www.dufoundation.org

Earth Portal, http://www.earthportal.org

ePluribus Media, http://www.epluribusmedia.org

FireDogLake, http://www.firedoglake.com

Free Exchange on Campus, http://www.freeexchangeoncampus.org

Greg Palast: Journalism and Film, http://www.gregpalast.com

The Houston Chronicle, http://www.chron.com

iBrattleboro, http://www.ibrattleboro.com

ManyOne, http://www.manyone.net

Media Matters for America, http://www.mediamatters.org

MyDD, http://www.mydd.com

Talking Points Memo, http://www.talkingpointsmemo.com

TPMmuckraker, http://tpmmuckraker.com

The Valve, http://www.thevalve.org

In considering the Web, Darren Cambridge, a professor of Internet studies and information literacy at George Mason University, makes a useful distinction between what he calls the "network self" and the "symphonic self."[1] The former values play and entrepreneurialism, the latter integrity and balance. The former is a process of continual learning, the latter of mastery. The former is atomized and aggregate, the latter holistic and systemic. The former celebrates the network, the latter the individual.

This distinction is significant to any study of Web cultures and their utilizations, for it addresses an essential difference in attitude between those trying to utilize Internet possibilities, those who approach it through a horizontal perspective and those who want to see it vertically. It also explains why the Web, for all of the attempts to bring it under vertical control, seems to gravitate back to a more horizontal position, for it was *designed* as a horizontal platform. As creator Tim Berners-Lee asserts, "There is no 'top' to the World-Wide Web. You can look at it from many points of view."[2] And look at it (and use it) from many angles is just what people do.

Even earlier than Berners-Lee's creation of the Web were other decisions that also ended up leading to a Web with a decidedly nonhierarchical bent. Of these was one initially promoted by Paul Baran of the RAND Corporation in the early 1960s. He "and his colleagues advocated 'packet switching,' by which messages to be transmitted were broken down into a number of separate bundles that were then sent along any free and operational communications lines, switching from one to another until they were finally reassembled at their destination. In this way messages could pick their own way through the maze of surviving lines, so no single break into the system could stop them."[3] Such a system subverts attempts to place barriers anywhere on the Web, for the information, backed up in any one pathway, simply finds other avenues—and the number of avenues, today, is beyond count.

Many organizations, be they for-profit, governmental, or altruistic, operate on a traditional model of command, generally running vertically from the top down. There is a certain efficiency to this: decisions, when needed quickly, can be made quickly. Channels of responsibility can be clearly defined—"the buck stops here." Yet this model does not always work, of course, for the assumption that the *ability* to make effective decisions will rest with those at the top is not always warranted. As Laurence Peter so elegantly demonstrates in his 1969 book *The Peter Principle: Why Things Always Go Wrong* (coauthored with Raymond Hull), people tend to rise in vertical organizations until they reach their level of incompetence—where they stay. One gets promoted if one does a good job but, as soon as one starts to mess up, one stays put. So, the efficiency promised by the vertical model is often subverted by those very people who must put it into operation. Still, if you want to get something done, and quickly, a vertical model will generally prove more useful than any other we humans have yet to develop. "In the ideal type of the authoritarian system we have a strict hierarchy of roles, each role-image containing the expectation of subordination to higher roles and authority over lower roles. Decisions originate with the higher roles and are transmitted to the lower roles as orders. The lower roles are expected to execute the orders without any back-talk."[4] When this works, it is extremely efficient.

Because a vertical structure can be easily abused by those at the top, few organizations use it purely. Most have developed systems of protection for those on the lower rungs of the ladder, providing "voice" or empowerment that the decision-makers at the top cannot ignore. Representative democracies, of course, operate this way, as do industries with strong union presence. In such instances, authority "is now supposed to proceed from below. The higher roles are supposed to act on behalf of and to be responsible to the lower roles. What this means in practice is that the decisions of the higher roles have to be made by discussion.... In the authoritarian model the feedback is indirect and is to a considerable extent under the control of the higher roles themselves. In the democratic model the feedback is much more direct and has a more powerful influence in the modification of decisions."[5]

At the other organizational extreme from the purely vertical is the completely horizontal structure, one where there is no command pathway at all and decisions come through the group as a whole. Town-meeting governance, for example, works this way. Quakers, with no clergy and no formal creed, also struggle to use this sort of decision-making. The most obvious drawback of a horizontal structure is that its very nature can impede resolution. The only way it works absolutely is through consensus, something human beings rarely are able to reach.

Neither of these models is morally preferable to the other. Horizontal structures can lead to tyranny as deadly as any fostered through vertical structures, as the old Chinese communist concept of "mass-line leadership" demonstrates. Through a need to come to consensus quickly, those who resist are either exiled from the organization or forced to endure a process for bringing their ideas into line with the majority. Ideally (though the actuality was quite different), leaders come out of the mass and reflect the will of the mass, but are also given the task of making sure that the will of the mass is universal. Here, just as in vertical organizations, a protection for minority opinion is needed—as well as a way around blocks to consensus. Unfortunately, the means used by the Chinese communists were overly draconian, to put it mildly, nearly destroying the nation and ruining millions of lives.

A horizontal structure works best, then, when there is no *need* for consensus, when activities can be initiated and executed by individuals or groups within the whole without impinging upon the rest. This requires a massive universe, one where there is always room for execution of another approach—where one activity does not end up imperiling another. Few "real world" arenas offer such a possibility. In some societies (such as that of the United States), religious bodies have it, for there are both generally minimal pressures for moving quickly and myriad religious choices. Educational institutions, on the other hand, do not—the demands of time as students grow make speedy decisions mandatory.

Different people, of course, are drawn to the vertical or the horizontal, but rarely is anyone indifferent. With the rise of conservative talk radio in the eighties and nineties came complaint that there was no liberal counterpart. Oh, here and there was one, but no one could touch the conservatives, who dominated the airwaves absolutely—and still do, though there are concerted liberal attempts to break in, including Air America radio. The problem is that talk radio contains an essentially vertical structure—with just enough of a horizontal aspect to keep listeners feeling that they are participating. The host controls almost everything that goes on.

The blogs, on the other hand, with their essential horizontal nature, have proven a much more comfortable venue for liberals—though there are, of course, extremely successful conservative bloggers, they cannot compare, either in numbers or in impact, with their liberal brethren. The problem is that the blogs provide little direction, little sense of how things "should" be. The webmaster controls surprisingly little.

The tensions between vertical and horizontal structures have been around for a long time, of course. In American history, they have been at the heart of the conflicting world views of Alexander Hamilton and Thomas Jefferson and, more than a century later, between Walter Lippmann and John Dewey. Contemporary "neo-conservatives" trace their own desire for a vertical predominance all the way back to Plato. The dynamics of the struggle between the two motivate the American political system; they are not likely to find resolution, nor should they, for they are what makes representative democracy possible.

Though they like to imagine a horizontal base, on most levels commercial and professional news organizations must operate on a vertical model. Associations of entities within the profession, such as the Associated Press, can have horizontal aspects, and no news operation would be effective if the top did not listen to the bottom—but the fact remains: decisions are made from the top. Limitations of time and space make no other model practical.

Like most industries established before the arrival of the Internet, the commercial news media have tried to impose the models that led to their early successes onto the Web, not really understanding that it takes an entirely different perspective and a completely *new* model for Web success. Barnes & Noble, in the retail field, had a premonition of this, which is why the company initially established an independent arm, bn.com, for its Web presence; the company did not want to hinder its Web operations with "bricks-and-mortar" thinking. However, by the time it established bn.com, it was already too late for it to compete head-to-head with Amazon.com. What Barnes & Noble needed, and what it has since found, was a way of using online and physical retail together, each bolstering the other. *The Washington Post*, when it first went online, followed the early Barnes & Noble pattern—its online operation was even physically separated from its print headquarters. Unfortunately, like Barnes & Noble, the *Post* and most other news-media entities moving online saw the Web as simply offering new means of distribution of product already offered elsewhere. At first, they did not understand that the Internet was going to be much more than that—and quickly. They did not know how to take control of the situation, and so they lost their early opportunity to dominate journalism in the expanding universe that includes the Web. Continuing tensions between old-line journalists and the new, Web-based kind have been the result.

One of the most vexing problems facing professional journalism in relation to the Web, the blogs, and citizen journalism is that journalism, in American society, cannot set itself aside as the exclusive purview of the certified. Yes, as Andrew Keen writes, "Becoming a doctor, a lawyer, a musician, a journalist, or an engineer requires a significant investment of one's life in education and training, countless auditions or entrance and certifying exams, and commitment to a career of hard work and long hours. A professional writer spends years mastering or refining his or her craft in an effort to be recognized by a seasoned universe of editors, agents, critics, and consumers, as someone worth reading and paying attention to."[6] But, condescension aside, there are flaws to this argument. For one thing, lumping together disparate professions this way and then picking out aspects of individual ones as though they (or something like them) apply to all is a little disingenuous. Doctors, lawyers, and engineers have passed over educational and regulatory hurdles that musicians, journalists, and writers do not face. For another, some of the greatest examples of success in these last three fields came to their high status *despite* Keen's "seasoned universe." Finally, a journalist faces a different situation from other professional writers and artists in general, for the journalist plays a role relating to Constitutional American rights, something the others do not, and something that makes it impossible for there to be barriers to entry into the field. "Freedom of the press" is a freedom for people to use the press unhindered by government oversight (there was no distinct profession called "the press" when the Bill of Rights was written). That means anyone with the means can enter into journalism; they do not need to prove themselves first. Though the same is true of music and other forms of writing, there is not such a close connection, in those fields, to the political needs of the society.

Musicians and writers, aside from journalists, are not dealing with information in quite the way journalists do (to say the least) and are not directly or necessarily involved in the political life of the nation. The fact that journalists *are* puts them apart from the others, and from doctors, lawyers, and engineers, completely. As a result, journalists have to work more concretely in the intersection between the horizontal and the vertical than do members of any other profession.

One of the causes of the tensions faced by the news media in moving to the Internet is best described through Thorstein Veblen's "trained incapacity" or, as Kenneth Burke describes it, "that state of affairs whereby one's very abilities can function as blindnesses."[7] Burke gives the example of chickens trained to come running for food at the sound of a bell that will eventually find themselves arriving not to eat, but to be slaughtered. Their "education" serves them ill in the new situation. Significant to journalism and the Internet, one "adopts measures in keeping with his past training—and the very soundness of this training may lead him to adopt the wrong measures."[8] This is not to say that there is no longer room from traditional journalism—there is—simply that the older journalists have to understand that the universe of their profession has grown, and that their particular training may not transfer well into all of the new areas (though I doubt it will get them slaughtered, as some do seem to fear).

Without boundaries but with plenty of opportunity, that "newer" sort of journalism quickly began to appear on the Web, filling in the space the commercial news media had ignored. Appalling many of the older professional journalists through their apparent lack of both ethics and skill, the new journalists (bloggers, citizen journalists, and more) and their output resembled nothing so much as the press of the early days of the American republic, when those very rules and ethics now seemingly missing had yet to be established within the profession. These new amateur journalists are expansive and noisy (just as their forbearers in the early years of the Republic were), and their work, according to Keen, "has been peddled [with] the promise of bringing more truth to more people—more depth of information, more global perspective, more unbiased opinion from unbiased observers. But this is all a smokescreen. What the Web 2.0 revolution is really delivering is superficial observations of the world around us rather than deep analysis, shrill opinion rather than considered judgment."[9] Oddly enough, this makes it sound like the Web is simply bringing to journalism more of the same! The fact is, there has been a lot of junk in journalism for a long, long time—it, too, is subject to what has come to be known as Sturgeon's Law, after science-fiction writer Theodore Sturgeon's supposed response to a comment about ninety percent of science fiction being crud. "So what?" he reportedly responded, "ninety percent of everything is crud."[10]

Tense relations or not, the two journalisms will ultimately make each other better, each helping the other separate the wheat from the chaff. As Henry Jenkins writes: "The new political culture—just like the new popular culture—reflects the pull and tug of these two media systems: one broadcast and commercial, the other narrowcast and grassroots. New ideas and alternative perspectives are more likely to emerge in the digital environment, but the mainstream media will be monitoring those channels, looking for content to co-opt and circulate."[11] Given the reinvigoration of professional journalism going on today in response, in part, to the challenges of the Web, I expect to see more of what Jenkins predicts than the devolution Keen fears.

By the Civil War, American journalism had developed into something not so far distant from what we in America knew up to the time of the Web; the new Web-based journalism is already heading in directions that have never before been explored. The reason for this is more the very structure of the Web, its horizontal emphasis, than it is anything particular to journalism itself—although the desire for a reinvigorated and broadened public sphere does provide motivation. The threat to this, and the threat to the Web generally, is the threat to the concept of Web Neutrality posed by corporations that want to bring the Internet within vertical control structures. The new forms of journalism on the Web neither threaten traditional journalism nor are threatened by it. The old and the new can, and probably will (if Net Neutrality is maintained), coexist peacefully.

Unlike "traditional" journalists, the newer journalists, especially those who have come up through the Web, do not see things in vertical fashion, each chain rising independently. Vertical thinking, however, still controls a lot of what is done by traditional journalistic entities, even on the Web. Each item, be it a blog, a story, a Web site, a newspaper, a newscast, or any other "thing," is seen independently and as part of a hierarchy. Recognizing that a new type of thinking needs to be involved, some of those who grew up within the older journalistic entities are trying to develop new paradigms for journalism on the Web, but these are few and far between. One example of just such an attempt is NewAssignment.net, the project of journalism professor Jay Rosen, which attempts to integrate vertical and horizontal structures as well as Web and "traditional" journalists into what is hoped will be a new journalism dynamic. Most, however, do not see the need of a new type of interconnectivity—and these will fall behind as surely as Barnes & Noble did, before it recognized that its Web operations did not need to be separate from its bricks-and-mortar stores—that, indeed, the two can support each other.

The vertically minded see a blog simply as a blog and not as just one piece of a network of activities and technological utilization. The clichéd image of a blogger in pajamas all alone, spilling out his heart or her opinions becomes the entirety of blogging—and the idea that it might just be a small part of a greater interactive whole is never considered. Knowing the popularity of blogs, such people bow to the necessity of incorporating a blog into their news sites (assuming that is appropriate to the business they are in), but they keep them as isolated pieces. They are not even surprised, then, when their blogs become nothing more than glorified "letters to the editor" columns, or venues for complaint and diatribe. And they are confused by the continued popularity of the blogs, which, they have proven to their own satisfaction, are "nothing, really nothing at all."

A "pie fight" on Daily Kos in mid 2007 highlighted the divide between the professional journalist and the amateur blogger—even when they are on the same side politically. Greg Palast, a popular journalist, author, and media personality, found himself attacked by a blogger using the name "drational." The upshot of "drational's" diary[12] was that Palast, rather than just reporting the news, was manipulating information for his personal aggrandizement. The seven hundred comments that followed ranged from virulent attacks on Palast to defenses just as passionate.

The next day, Palast posted a response on his own blog and on Daily Kos, writing in a hurt and confrontational manner with this, towards the end: "My conversation with the Drats of this world must end here. If you want to debate me, first read my book. If you want to criticize my methods, make sure your method includes some on-the-ground investigative work."[13] Though Palast was writing out of anger and frustration, early on calling "drational" "illiterate" and using the tired stereotype of bloggers: "get out of your PJs," he overreacted and let his attitude towards amateurs take over. Like many from the world of professional journalism, Palast resents that he must now "answer" to amateurs, whom he feels do not have the expertise to question him or the other professionals in the field.

Not surprisingly, Palast's response brought on one of its own on Daily Kos, by "DHinMI," titled "Does Greg Palast View You With Contempt?" Included is this passage:

> What's great about DKos is that everyone who registers has a voice, and other than a handful of people who Markos [Moulitsas] has made contributing editors, everyone's voice is innately equal. The community may over time give more respect to some community members because of the force of their arguments, the wit and style they use in diaries and comments, the passion and care with which they compile and present evidence, or the empathy with which they understand and convey other people's stories. There are plenty of reasons why people are liked and read with interest and respect at DKos. But the important thing is, it's mostly a meritocracy. Every one of the contributing editors started out as just another commenter. And everyone here, regardless of UID [User ID], has an equal opportunity to employ reason, skill and critical thought to make cogent points and compelling arguments.[14]

Palast, in the eyes of this blogger, was arguing that he, as a professional journalist with the skills and access of his trade, deserves special treatment by those whose cause he champions.

A diarist named "xaxnar" soon came back with a defense or (at least) an explanation for Palast's reaction to the first diary:

> Imagine you are someone who has dedicated their life to fighting the good fight. You've been doing it for years. You ask tough questions, you dig hard for the truth, you do the hard work of building a solid case.
>
> You've been threatened repeatedly; you've moved because a town decides it doesn't care to have you living around there. You develop an attitude because you discover being deferential and polite just makes you easier to ignore—and you see plenty of "journalists" making a really good living by sucking up to power instead of speaking truth to it....

You sweat blood, shortchange your family and friends and yourself, to follow up stories and document your work. You put out reports on TV and write books knowing there are people who are determined to keep your work from being heard, people who will work to discredit it and lie about you—and they'll get a respectful hearing because of who they are. You keep doing it anyway.

THEN someone you don't know, writing in a forum that's still in its infancy, one you'd expect to be sympathetic, raises serious charges about your work and calls you dangerous to all that is right and holy. What kind of credibility do they have? How much research and fact checking have they done? Are they sincere—or are they a stalking horse for those who want to silence you? Have they even read the books you've written or gone to the sources to verify them? At best this is friendly fire—at worst, well....[15]

That pretty well sums up the views of many professional journalists, most of whom do not really know what may have been going on elsewhere, what the "amateurs" may or may not have been doing, reading and learning—so focused have they been on their own activities. They were raised with the idea of a passive audience waiting for them to provide the information: "read my book; then we can talk." They forget that the book is not the thing, or even the topic, that it is but one avenue into the topic. To them, the blogs are an annoyance, gnats getting in the way of the "real" work and discussion.

In the hands of the new breed of journalists, however, including the "citizen journalists" whose appearance and activity on the Web has shown that the nonprofessional can match the professional journalist almost every step of the way, the blog becomes an entry into a fascinating and fruitful new world of research, data management, discussion, and writing—all open to anyone for either participation or observation, or both.

That openness provides an aspect of the new journalism that had not before been present. In the past, stories were meant to be complete when ink hit paper—a correction was something of a failure. On the Web, when constant revision is simple and, indeed, expected, the *process* of journalism can become much more open to the reader, inviting the reader to participate, even. This is a much more radical change than at first it might seem, for it removes the barrier between professional and consumer, showing the latter how the former works and allowing the latter to actually contribute immediately to the work of the former. What it does, of course, is add a new and horizontal aspect to the journalist's craft.

Certainly, and this is what scares the professionals, one of those few universes of human activity where a real horizontal structure is actually possible is the World Wide Web of the bloggers and amateur journalists. On the Web, horizontal groups can form, operate, split, and re-form without materially affecting other groups or individuals. Thanks to Web creator Berners-Lee, the tyrannies over so much of human existence just are not threatening on the

Web (and are not insisted upon, not yet at least)—because Web "publication" is not tied to any cycle, time pressures are less, and the virtual space involved is, to all practical purposes, infinite.

By providing tools and not structure, and then by freely distributing the tools (the codes), Berners-Lee insured that the universe of the Web would resist, at least, any impulse to impose a vertical structure upon it. The credo of dissatisfied users of any particular site on the Web might be, as e. e. cummings writes in his poem, "pity this busy monster, manunkind," "there's a hell of a good universe next door; let's go"—on the Web, one does not have to put up with much, for one can always move on, creating new Web sites and "worlds" at will.

Oddly enough, it is this, the ability to move on, that scares people used to operating within the confines of vertical organizations. Though always part of the American psyche (best expressed, probably, in the mythical personality of Daniel Boone), it seems anarchic to a mindset used to structure and hierarchy—and dangerous. In early 2007, I listened to a professor from a "distinguished" university speak about the news media, a professor who worries that no one is setting the agenda anymore, who feels that discussion and focus should never be completely free-ranging; if it is, he fears, it will never produce results. Gatekeepers, to his mind, are an absolute necessity, or discussion will lack all direction. Many who are invested within vertical organizations feel the same way—and a good number of journalists are among that group. They fear the chaos that might result from a lack of formal process.

One person so concerned by the chaos of the Web that he has initiated a complex and ambitious project to tame it is Joe Firmage, founder of Many-One Networks and Digital Universe Foundation. Seeing no one to trust as the guides to the Web, Firmage has set out to provide just such advisors—along with a system that can inspire confidence. ManyOne describes itself as an organization that, along with "leading institutions," is

> catalyzing a new "high quality" web—a digital commons called the Digital Universe.... As part of this effort, hundreds of the world's science and education leaders have joined together to create an authoritative, comprehensive, non-commercial source for environmental news, education and debate online....
>
> Around this high quality of information, people will soon be able to create communities that reflect issues, opinions, projects or other needs related to the information. These communities will increasingly have access to multimedia tools that will change the way people view the Web, informing, educating, engaging and involving people worldwide.[16]

Firmage is trying to meld the vertical ("leaders; authoritative") with the horizontal ("communities; people"), providing something that people can come to and use with confidence from the very first. He is also trying to address the problem identified by Bill Bradley, that the "blogosphere has enabled the free expression of ideas more broadly, rapidly, and cheaply than ever before, but when tens of millions all speak at once, brilliant ideas get lost in the cacophony."[17] Digital Universe describes its mission as "to organize the sum total of human knowledge and make it available to everyone. It is an ever-growing array of commercial-free portals mapping the highest-quality Internet destinations, as recommended by experts recognized in their fields. These experts review public contributions, create context and attest to the reliability, integrity, and accuracy of the portals."[18] One ambitious portion of the project is Earth Portal, something of a carefully vetted Wikipedia.

The problem with this, from a horizontal viewpoint, is that important work that really should be part of the education of the individual is moved to the "experts" who provide the gatekeeping. A *neterate* person should know how to negotiate the Web for accurate information without need of a guide; providing guides may only keep people from being fully able to manage the Web for themselves.

There are aspects of *neteracy* that will never be learned except through the doing, just as there are with "literacy"—which is really quite a bit more than simply learning to read and write. A truly literate person, when they pick up a book, turns immediately to the publication information: when was the book published? By whom? Where? What edition is it? Having done this thousands of times, the literate person can quickly prejudge the work—not completely, but with reasonable accuracy. There are many other clues that the literate person uses almost unconsciously in deciding what avenues to pursue when presented with an array of written works. These clues can only be understood through experience; no amount of memorization will work. And that experience cannot be gained by someone who, for example, has only used a card catalogue, allowing the librarian to fetch the selected book.

The really literate person does not spend all their time in the library, of course, but examines books and other written material everywhere, constantly making decisions about it—from advertisements on a bus to used copies of, say, the bowdlerized Armed Forces edition of Dashiell Hammett's *The Maltese Falcon* from World War II.

Just so, the neterate person will be encountering the Web just as often as the literate person has print. They cannot be expected to use only the "library" of Earth Portal—certainly not as more than a starting point. The neterate person will have to learn to evaluate all sorts of information on the Web, in just the same ways that the literate person has learned. The question is not to protect citizens from the chaos of the Web, no more than it is to protect them from "bad" books (though people try, and have tried, to do both). It is to teach them to be able to evaluate. Instead of looking from a vertical mindset and doing "for" the people, Firmage might do better to consider the Web from a horizontal perspective and then help educate the people instead.

Horizontal efforts centered on the Web are beginning to show that they can be effective or, at least, that they may one day be effective. After the Coast Guard had called off its search for the missing boat of Silicon Valley researcher James Gray, his peers, and not just at Microsoft (where he worked), set up their own search network, using Google Earth and other tools to try to determine where he was. They did not set up an organization or establish a hierarchy, but fell into the pattern now beginning to seem natural to those who structure their work through the Web—they developed themselves into a network. They understood one of the basic premises of the Web universe, that a broad, loosely connected horizontal network can often come up with solutions that a hierarchical, traditionally vertical organization, no matter how competent, might miss. The result was what a "veteran deputy of the Coast Guard called ... 'the largest strictly civilian, privately sponsored search effort I have ever seen.'"[19] Though not successful, this search did point out just how powerful individuals equipped with Web tools can be when they start to reach out to each other and cooperate as a network on a specific task.

Though the new horizontal Web models, as in the case of the search for James Gray, have yet to realize their full potential, the signs are there that they will. In terms of journalism, they are perhaps closer to this realization than in other areas, for two of the major tools of the profession—words themselves and sources for research—lie at the heart of the Web as it has developed to date. Though many journalists still do not see how a story can generate "spontaneously" from the thousands of bloggers exploring the Web, the work of the professionals, and the fast-growing document base available, it is beginning to happen—and some people, most notably Jay Rosen, are exploring ways of harnessing it into effective and professional journalism.

Rosen's New Assignment and its first major project, Assignment Zero, are attempts at bridging the gap between amateur and professional journalists while still accenting the enthusiasms of the former and the skills of the latter. Assignment Zero experiments with the concept of *crowdsourcing* (as Jeff Howe had named it in *Wired*[20]) as a means of generating stories, working from professionals to amateurs and back again. An explanation accompanies the project's first story for *Wired* magazine:

> Inspired by the open-source movement in programming, which has produced world-class software like Firefox, Assignment Zero allows citizen journalists to work with professional editors on a story.
>
> "This is an attempt to bring journalists together with people in the public who can help cover a story," says project founder Jay Rosen....
>
> In keeping with this new and untested approach to journalism, the team's research and reporting are up on the Assignment Zero site for you to see—or even use to write your own article, if you don't like this one—in the [Assignment Zero website's] Citizendium reporters' notebook.

There you can get a sense of how much good material doesn't make it into an article, as well as the amount of research required to pen a statement as simple as "a random sampling of the unapproved articles revealed content that was generally inferior to what's available at Wikipedia."[21]

This last is a reference to the topic of the article, Wikipedia.

The Assignment Zero site explains: "Crowdsourced journalism is a term that certainly sounds like a fully developed practice, but it's in its nascent stage. We want to explore the particulars to better understand when crowd-sourced journalism occurs, how it occurs, why it occurs … yeah, you get the idea."[22] The points of Assignment Zero are to provide a base for future stories related to this first one by keeping the raw material behind the story available to future researchers, to show amateur researchers and writers a means for involvement in professional journalism, to teach amateurs the needs of accurate fact checking and ethical journalism, and to involve professionals in the work of amateurs to insure that the professionals keep in mind the value of amateur work and continue to involve the amateur in their work.

Though without the formal "pro-am" structure of New Assignment and Assignment Zero, a number of national stories have arisen where both amateur (horizontal) and professional (vertical) involvement have been of importance. One of these stories of 2007 that grew, in part, out of a horizontal Web model concerned the scandal surrounding the firings of a number of U.S. Attorneys in December 2006. On January 12, 2007, Justin Rood posted a blog diary on TPMmuckraker (one of the sites in Josh Micah Marshall's Talking Points Memo network) called "Cunningham Prosecutor Forced Out."[23] Drawing on a story in *The San Diego Union-Tribune*,[24] it concerned the resignation of the U.S. Attorney for San Diego, Carol Lam. Twenty-five comments were added. Three days later, Rood, who works for TPMmuckraker, posted news that another U.S. Attorney, Nevada's Daniel Bogden, had also been forced out.[25] This time, there were twenty-two comments. The next day, Rood increased the list of resignees to seven, with a probable eighth.[26] The number of comments increased to sixty-five.

By the end of the month, Rood and fellow TPM investigator Paul Kiel had produced fifteen more posts on the topic, comments sometimes numbering in the hundreds. Much of what they were doing was taking the stories from regional newspapers and putting them together to show a national pattern (and more). They were aided by Senator Diane Feinstein's statement on the firings mid-month, but much of the impetus keeping the story alive came from them and from the amateur bloggers who soon started joining in. Between the politicians in Washington who were pressing the Attorney General for explanation and the bloggers, they managed to keep story building.

Where was the national mainstream news media on this?

Marisa Taylor and Greg Gordon of McClatchy's Washington bureau were about the only professional journalists from a "recognized" national news organization who were on the story.[27] They became a primary source for the bloggers, who reached out to examine the implications in the McClatchy stories. By the middle of March, lack of real interest by much of the commercial news media notwithstanding, the scandal had become the biggest on-going story in the nation outside of the continuing occupation of Iraq. As it was the work of McClatchy reporters, in fact, along with local stories, that probably alerted the bloggers that something more was going on in the Justice Department than simply a shuffling of positions, it never could have been the case that other members of the professional press were unaware of the story. They just did not react to it, did not see it as important, or could not see a way of framing it in manners appropriate to their publications.

Eric Boehlert, of the liberal media-watchdog group Media Matters for America, wrote in mid-May that this had "morphed into arguably the most important Beltway news story of the year…. The media man at the middle of the story is clearly Josh Marshall, owner and founder of Talking Points Memo and its offshoot, TPMmuckraker. Collecting string, working the phones, and relying on the collective wisdom of his dedicated readers, Marshall and his small staff helped piece together the scandal long before most mainstream media outlets were even paying attention."[28] Though McClatchy deserves at least as much credit, as do all of the other bloggers who worked on the case, the leadership of Marshall's crew was certainly critical.

Following the lead of TPMmuckraker but lacking the resources of large news media entities, the citizen-journalist group ePluribus Media began calling on volunteers to help put together its own stories on the scandal, introducing crowdsourcing into the investigations. This was not the first time ePMedia had been involved in crowdsourcing. In fact, one of the first major examples of crowdsourcing involving the blogs had actually led to the creation of this citizen-journalism organization. It was the Jeff Gannon affair,[29] where "SusanG," a blogger on Daily Kos, put out a call for others to help her discover Gannon's background. Through work of the individuals who responded, along with that of bloggers on other sites led by John Aravosis of AMERICAblog, Gannon's background soon came to light. It was quickly established that Gannon, whose real name is James Guckert, was not only a "ringer" in the White House Press Corps (he had no background in journalism and no affiliation with an established news media organization), but that he had recently advertised himself (along with nude photographs) as an "escort"—things the members of the press who had rubbed elbows with him for over a year had not bothered to look for, let alone discover.

Though a new term, the concept of crowdsourcing, like so much else, has old roots, growing out of the newsgathering situation that Walter Lippmann described soon after World War I:

> All the reporters in the world working all the hours of the day could not witness all the happenings in the world. There are not a great many reporters.

And none of them has the power to be in more than one place at a time. Reporters are not clairvoyant, they do not gaze into a crystal ball and see the world at will, they are not assisted by thought-transference.... The point is that before a series of events become news they have usually to make themselves noticeable in some more or less overt act. Generally too, in a crudely overt act.... There must be a manifestation. The course of events must assume a certain definable shape, and until it is in a place where some aspect is an accomplished fact, news does not separate itself from the ocean of possible truth.[30]

No matter how much they would like to, the press cannot find every story on their own—they have to let many come to them, so to speak. Crowdsourcing, rather than constituting a threat to professional journalism, is but one recent means for encouraging that.

No matter how one views the commercial news media, this fact remains: no story is going to gather sustained national attention in America unless the big news-media entities carry it. For them to do so, the story has to be "newsworthy," having attained that "certain definable shape" Lippmann refers to. The problem for the commercial news media with the U.S. Attorneys story seems to have been in determining a molded form that could be quickly presented, encapsulating something that had no single, clear-cut "event" associated with it.

The virtue of crowdsourcing, from a citizen-journalist or blogger point of view, is that it forces the commercial news media to find a way to present the story—if the crowdsourcing is successful, that is. The story is not only advocated by numerous entities, but is added to (even if just in little ways) by information gathered from the diverse researchers, each working on their own. Before the Internet, it was difficult (though not impossible) for most individuals to get hold of the raw material behind a story. Now, with material released frequently by governmental (and other entities) directly to the Web, and often in great volume, location and traditional forms of access become quite a bit less important. That object of derision and cliché, the blogger at home in pajamas, therefore, can now do actual primary research, combing through emails, for example, released by the White House and the Justice Department, trying to recreate the narrative of events surrounding the story.

In a media-saturated world, it is hard to sustain a story to the point where the commercial news media *have* to pick it up, but the persistence of a crowdsourced story can make that happen much more often and more quickly now than ever before—even when the media feel the story is trivial or just plain wrong. Initial opposition to the Iraq war seemed wrong-headed and unimportant to many in the news media,* so coverage of the opposition to it tended to be dilatory, at best. Yet, by the 2006 election, it was opposition to the war

---

*See *Bill Moyers' Journal: Selling the War*, http://www.pbs.org/moyers/journal/btw/transcript1.html.

that was fueling the national debate. A corollary to crowdsourcing, individual concern, had snowballed, forcing the commercial news media to both reexamine the assumptions it had accepted (and reported) as truth and to expand its universe of inquiry regarding the war.

The crowdsourcing of the U.S. Attorneys story at ePluribus Media began when one member emailed two others in late January 2007. "Something is sticking in my craw" about this, she wrote. Building on what this group had discovered and had presented to each other through email, that citizen journalist, who uses the name AvaHome, put up a query on the group's research site along with the data she had found already stored there. Two days later, the three decided that more information was needed, so they, and others who were becoming interested in what they were finding, published a rough crowdsourcing call on the ePMedia community site as well as on the vastly larger Daily Kos, hoping to get further information and spark involvement by people beyond the immediate ePMedia community.

Over the next ten days, four further calls for information (along with recaps of the information so far gathered) culminated in a story, "The Gonzales Seven,"[31] on the group's vetted site. Since that publication on January 29, 2007, a number of further *Journal* articles have appeared, under the names of a variety of members of the organization but all reflecting work done by up to a dozen different volunteers. By May, the story the ePMedia citizen journalists were following had been expanded to include the Voting Rights section of the Justice Department and the citizen journalists were developing actual sources within the Department.[32]

Though the story had started elsewhere, had been picked up by many others, commented on and linked to, the purpose was not to gain exposure or fame for ePluribus Media by horning in on a story but to provide knowledge of an unfolding narrative in a form the volunteers felt would be useful to American citizens. This fact led to several changes in focus. Soon into this project, for example, the people working on it realized that neither they nor the people who were discussing it on the various blog sites had solid knowledge of the duties of the U.S. Attorneys, the differences between them and the Assistant U.S. Attorneys who work for them, the extent of the staffing of each office, or the process of selection. Discovering and presenting more about the offices, and not just the holders, soon became an important part of the discussion and research.

No one person dominated this process and there has been no single, all-encompassing story. Like the method, the results are a network of stories that refer to each other and work off of each other—from a number of venues, including professional journalism sites, citizen journalism ones, group blogs, and individual ones. As is the standard on the Web, nothing stands alone. Each piece is dependent on many others, though perhaps not necessitated by any particular other.

The point? Journalism itself, in quite a number of situations, does not need a vertical organization to work. ePluribus Media is a relatively small organization working on a miniscule budget (compared to commercial news organizations). Yet it can put together a network of stories and information (timelines, for example) that can be useful even to professional journalists as a story continues to unfold and, more importantly, to a citizenry hungry for the information that can make it more able to participate effectively in the public sphere—as actor and not simply observer.

Few traditional news media organizations have been willing to work the open fashion of crowdsourcing, as Rosen found in the 1990s when his "civic journalism" movement met intense resistance from the professional journalists—but they can, if they are willing to give up some of their vertical control, allowing their journalists to directly work with and for their readers and not simply at the behest of their editors—who could also become involved in direct communication with readers in development of stories. In this way, they will be crossing that boundary between the older organizations and the new, Web-influenced ones. This will be hard for the commercial journalistic entities to accept and to do, but newfound recognition of the demands of the Web may just make them more open to a new way of broadening journalism without weakening it, of bringing the community more directly into the story, thereby strengthening the public sphere, finally really following the advice of John Dewey and helping *really* create an informed populace.

After all, one learns by doing much more than by watching—a truism that can apply to journalists as much as to the people they "serve."

Of course, the U.S. Attorneys story was not the first time that a story had to trickle up for the commercial media to really get hold of it. When David Halberstam died in 2007, he was remembered by some for having created the antiwar movement through his reporting. According to Richard Holbrooke, "In the decades since [the Vietnam War], Halberstam and his colleagues often have been blamed by right-wing commentators and some military officers for the loss in Vietnam, on the grounds that their reporting undermined domestic support for the war. This is, of course, nonsense; in war, success speaks for itself. Spin may delude the public for a while, but not indefinitely—and meanwhile people die. The basic truth is simple: Halberstam's reporting was right, and the official version was not."[33] Halberstam was lauded, in much the same way as he was criticized, by those who opposed the war—and it is just as much nonsense, for the news media were not the only sources of information about Vietnam. Halberstam was a reporter, and not an advocate. It was the antiwar activists who took his reportage (among many other things) and created a movement. Still, the romanticization of the intrepid reporter that hit full swing through Halberstam and his generation of talented journalists has led to quite a different impression.

If Halberstam was anything specifically unusual or original (and he was), it was in the way he worked. As George Packer writes:

Halberstam's wartime work will last not just because of its quality and its importance but because it established a new mode of journalism, one with which Americans are now so familiar that it's difficult to remember that someone had to invent it. The notion of the reporter as fearless truthteller has become a narcissistic cliché that fits fewer practitioners than would like to claim it. "David changed war reporting forever," Richard Holbrooke, who had known him in Vietnam, said last week. "He made it not only possible but even romantic to write that your own side was misleading the public about how the war was going. But everything depended on David getting it right, and he did."[34]

Packer is right, though Holbrooke is probably overstating the case. Halberstam was only able to succeed, in part, because there was already a receptive audience in place, Americans who were bothered by pictures of self-immolating Buddhist monks, or who were not comfortable with the very concept of U.S. involvement in another ground war in Asia, or who, like my family and me, had actually lived in Southeast Asia themselves during the war's early years. Instead of trying to change the people (using his position in a way similar to the presidential "bully pulpit"), Halberstam credited his audience with a capacity to listen and to recognize the truth of his reporting, even if some of them might be inclined not to accept what he was writing, even if he might get into trouble with the powers-that-be. This, as opposed to the shallowness and deliberate blindness of reporters in the early stages of the Iraq war, was certainly a part of his genius. By the Iraq war, it was not romantic but tantamount to treason to oppose the popular sentiment for an unnecessary war—just as it had been in the mid-sixties, before the nation turned against the war. However, the trust in the intelligence of his audience to read and even change their opinions that Halberstam displayed had been replaced by trust in the sources of "information" within the government and a fear that opinions, now believed to be set in stone, could never be challenged, let alone changed.

When there is no Halberstam, no national media presence to carry a story, it is up to the people to do it themselves, as was happening with the U.S. Attorneys scandal, even after Congress had begun to look into the situation. In this case, however, the politicians and the blogosphere soon were able to present information damning enough so that the commercial news media had to begin to take real notice. Even as they began to cover the story, however, many would have agreed with Howard Kurtz of *The Washington Post* who wrote that "I don't have the sense that people are standing around the water cooler arguing over whether Carol Lam and David Iglesias [two of the fired attorneys] should have been let go."[35] Not quite understanding that the blogs had replaced the water cooler, thus allowing himself to discount the discussions there, Kurtz had it quite wrong.

Even months after the start of Congressional investigations, there were others, like *The Chicago Tribune*'s Douglas Kmeic, who could, while recognizing the brouhaha, deny its substance: "There's been a steady drumbeat of allegations of scandal and impropriety in the anticipated sacking of Atty. Gen. Alberto Gonzales. There's only one problem. There is no scandal or impropriety."[36] He could not know this with any certainty—but he could see that the story was not one that could be easily identified—and it was this, perhaps, that made him discount the story. Whatever the reason, he certainly could not go as far as *The New York Times* did in an editorial in May: "At best, the firing of eight United States attorneys, most of them highly respected, is an example of such profound incompetence that it should cost Mr. Gonzales his job. At worst, it was a political purge followed by a cover-up. In either case, the scandal is only getting bigger and more disturbing."[37] Finally, nearly five months after the firings, at least part of the commercial news media had taken serious notice.

Whatever the outcome of the U.S. Attorneys scandal, it has shown the benefits of integrating the vertical model of the professional new media organizations with the horizontal model of citizen journalism, for that is basically what happened during the process of this becoming a major national story. It should also allay a few of the fears harbored by many older journalists who see the blogs as competition, as a threat, when they really should be viewed as an opportunity. As Robert Kuttner writes:

> Defenders of print insist that nothing on the Web can match the assemblage of reportorial talent, professionalism, and public mission of a serious print daily. The 2006 State of the News Media Report by the Project for Excellence in Journalism found that just 5 percent of blog postings included "what would be considered journalistic reporting." Nicholas Lemann, dean of Columbia's Graduate School of Journalism, wrote a skeptical piece about Web journalism in *The New Yorker* last July, concluding that not much of the blogosphere "yet rises to the level of a journalistic culture rich enough to compete in a serious way with the old media—to function as a replacement rather than an addendum." John Carroll, the former editor of the Los Angeles Times, says, "Take any story in a blog and trace its origins, about eighty-five percent of it can be traceable to newspapers. They break nearly all of the important stories. Who's going to do the reporting if these institutions fade away?"[38]

The mainstream media, aware that its future lies in involvement online to some degree at least, may actually find, through stories such as the U.S. Attorneys one, a way of ensuring its survival with its sense of pride, self, and mission intact. As Kuttner also writes in his *Columbia Journalism Review* article, "a far more hopeful picture is emerging. In this scenario the mainstream press, though late to the party, figures out how to make serious money from the Internet, uses the Web to enrich traditional journalistic forms, and retains its professionalism—along with a readership that is part print, part Web. Newspapers stay alive as hybrids. The culture and civic mission of daily print journalism endure."[39] Those who understand this "are embracing the Web with the manic enthusiasm of a convert. The Internet revenue of newspaper Web sites is increasing at 20 percent to 30 percent a year, and publishers are doing everything they can to boost Web traffic. Publishers know they are in a race against time, they are suddenly doing many things that their Internet competitors do, and often better."[40] He continues: "The irony is that in their haste both to cut newsroom costs and ramp up Web operations, some newspapers are slashing newsroom staff and running the survivors ragged. At many dailies, today's reporter is often pressed into Web service: writing frequent updates on breaking stories, wire-service fashion; posting blog items; and conducting interviews with a video camera. If journalism is degraded into mere bloggery, newspapers will lose their competitive advantage, not to mention their journalistic calling."[41]

On a more positive note, journalists can take comfort in these words from John Dewey: "We have every reason to think that whatever changes may take place in existing democratic machinery, they will be of a sort to make the interest of the public a more supreme guide and criterion of governmental activity, and to enable the public to form and manifest its purposes still more authoritatively. In this sense the cure for the ailments of democracy is more democracy. The prime difficulty, as we have seen, is that of discovering the means by which a scattered, mobile and manifold public may so recognize itself as to define and express its interests."[42] Crowdsourcing, blogging, and citizen journalism could actually be the curative for the malaise that commercial journalism had fallen into by the start of the 1990s, a malaise that led to such ready acceptance of government propaganda at the start of the Iraq war, turning even journalists who should have known better into what amounted to administration mouthpieces or, as comedian Stephen Colbert called them to their faces during the 2006 White House Correspondents Association annual dinner, "stenographers."

One of the areas where many have been expecting to see the public "define and express its interests" is community news coverage. In fact, one of the definitions of "citizen journalism" concerns community affairs—and there has been a movement on the Web towards development of sites devoted to specific localities. Former reporter Dan Gillmor was responsible for one of the most ambitious of the early sites of this nature, Bayosphere.com, about which he wrote as the experiment was coming to a close:

> Although citizen media, broadly defined, was taking the world by storm, the
> experiment with Bayosphere didn't turn out the way I had hoped. Many

fewer citizens participated, they were less interested in collaborating with one another, and the response to our initiatives was underwhelming....

We envisioned Bayosphere as a place where people in the San Francisco Bay Area community could learn about and discuss the regional scene, with a focus on technology, the main economic driver. My tech and policy blogging would be an anchor, hopefully attracting some readers and, crucially, some self-selected citizen journalists who'd join a wider conversation....

Bayosphere attracted quite a bit of traffic, and some heartening effort on the part of some citizen journalists.... But as is obvious to anyone who's paid attention, the site didn't take off.... Here are some of the lessons:

- Citizen journalism is, in a significant way, about owning your own words. That implies responsibilities as well as freedom. We asked people to read and agree to a "pledge" that briefly explained what we believed it meant to be a citizen journalist—including principles such as thoroughness, fairness, accuracy and transparency.
- Limiting participation is not necessarily a bad idea. By asking for a valid email address simply in order to post comments, you reduce the pool of commenters considerably, but you increase the quality of the postings.
- Citizen journalists need and deserve active collaboration and assistance. They want some direction and a framework, including a clear understanding of what the site's purpose is and what tasks are required.
- A framework doesn't mean a rigid structure, where the citizen journalist is only doing rote work such as filling in boxes.
- The tools available today are interesting and surprisingly robust. But they remain largely aimed at people with serious technical skills.
- Tools matter, but they're no substitute for community building.
- Though not so much a lesson—we were very clear on this going in—it bears repeating that a business model can't say, "You do all the work and we'll take all the money, thank you very much." There must be clear incentives for participation, and genuine incentives require resources.
- On several occasions, PR people offered to brief me on upcoming products or events that they hoped I'd cover in my capacity as a tech journalist, but were happy to give the slot to our citizen journalists. This testifies to a growing recognition among more clued-in PR folks that citizen journalism is here to stay.
- Although the participants—citizen journalists and commenters—are essential, it's even more important to remember that publishing is about the audience in the end.
- If you don't already have a thick skin, grow one.[43]

Six months after Gillmor presented this open letter on the Bayosphere site, in June 2006, Bayosphere became part of a larger operation to provide community Web sites, Backfence.com, which styles itself as "Do It Yourself Local News" with more than a dozen sites for cities in four states.

Both Bayosphere and Backfence are for-profit operations coming into communities rather than rising from those communities. In other words, their approach (or structure) is essentially vertical in nature, though their intent is to encourage horizontal activity. Like Rosen, with his New Assignment, they want to provide the opportunity for "citizen journalists" to get involved in "real" journalistic activities, but they still want to keep control in the hands of the professionals and those who fund the projects. This, I believe, is their greatest weakness.

Speaking to *Business Week*, one of the principal investors in Backfence, Josh Grotstein said, "Whoever can get this thing right—there's a lot of money there."[44] Maybe. But that presupposes a successful integration of the vertical and the horizontal—for there will be little money in any single and horizontal citizen-journalism site of this nature. The money would come in replication, and replication does not lend itself so easily to local initiative. As a "former Backfencer says explaining the site to potential users left them feeling they were being sold something, as opposed to being given something."[45] Local initiative, sponsored from outside, always makes people suspicious.

One "citizen journalism" site focusing on a single physical community that *has* managed to achieve success is iBrattleboro in Vermont, which may have the advantage of not having been started by journalists steeped in a tradition of vertical editorial control. Founders Chris Grotke and Lise LePage explain that they really had very little plan or idea of how to control what they were creating: "We launched iBrattleboro.com in February of 2003. It wasn't called Citizen Journalism at that point. What we were doing didn't really have a name that we knew of and was hard to describe—it's an online news thingie that the readers write."[46] The informality and lack of clarified vision probably helped iBrattleboro at the start, for a user could come onto the site without feeling directed or manipulated in the way they might by Backfence. As time passed and the site grew, it proved necessary to institute formal guidelines, but users had, by then, developed a sense of "ownership" that was able to continue to be passed to new users as the online community around the site grew even amid new restrictions and necessary (though loose) editorial control. It is this, the sense of joining a real community, that has been the cornerstone of the success of many group blogs, including the huge Daily Kos, with its 120,000 registered users and several times that many additional and regular readers.

Today, iBrattleboro does have a help page with its own guidelines presented through a Frequently Asked Questions (FAQ) section. These provide a good picture of just how a local citizen journalism site styles itself:

What is this?
 iBrattleboro.com is an online community news website written by and for the people of Brattleboro and surrounding towns. It is a place to share

the "talk of the town," a virtual meeting place to write about local stories, comments, announcements, events, news, and creative work.

Why?

All people need to have a voice in their community.

Can anyone submit something?

If you have a local story to tell, this is the place. Anyone can submit a story, events, or links. We ask that it be of interest to Brattleboro and southern Vermont, of course, and we hope everyone is polite.

How do I contribute to iBrattleboro?

It's quite simple, really. Click on the above link that says "Submit Story" and write away.

What section should I put it in?

Take your best guess, based on the topic of your story. (We might change it, of course.)

What can I contribute?

That depends on you. We'd like to see stories about subjects that interest you. Share your expertise. You can write a story or a poem. You can review movies, concerts, and plays. Tell everyone about a recipe you made or book you read. Spread the word about an event. Contribute wit or opinions.

You can also add your comments to what has already been written.

It may sound corny, but you put the "i" in iBrattleboro.

I submitted something, but I didn't show up right away. Where is it?

We take a quick look at everything before it goes up. Most items will be viewable within 24 hours.

Are there editors?

Brattleboro web developers, MuseArts, Inc., own the site and acts as moderators, as well as contributors. Authors should assume there are no editors, so check your spelling and facts, or someone may comment and correct you!

Where can I buy a copy?

You can't. We don't have a print version. It's part of our way to save trees, and we're really only good at web publishing. iBrattleboro is online only.

Who is responsible for what I read?

Ultimately, you are responsible for what you read. The submissions and comments are the property and responsibility of the person who wrote it.

I'm having trouble with iBrattleboro ...

We don't want that to happen, so please let us know what we can do to make it better.

Do you edit things we send in?

We look things over, and sometimes correct spelling and spacing so it displays nicely. We do reserve the right to NOT publish something, or to delete things that have already been posted. We may add an editor's note.

Are you a big out of town company collecting local email addresses?
Hardly. MuseArts is two people who live in Brattleboro, and we promise
we aren't collecting or selling email addresses. We make web sites. You probably know us. If you don't, we'd be happy to meet you someday.[47]

Even when presenting the rules for their site, Grotke and LePage keep their
tone conversational and informal, keeping away from presentation of plan or
formula and deliberately making it clear that, though they design Web sites,
the purpose of this site is not eventual creation of (say) a citizen-journalism
empire.

Though it has not yet proven financially viable to create a centrally owned
network of local citizen-journalism sites, certain older commercial news entities have successfully melded the citizen-journalism approach with their own
online presences, creating a model that may prove to be that for the future of
online professional journalism. One of these is Chron.com of *The Houston
Chronicle*. The site strives for something of universality, presenting what is
essentially a contemporary online newspaper that builds on the older print version as well as Chron.Commons, which it describes as "your words, your pho-
tos, your life."

Though *The Houston Chronicle* is owned by the Hearst Corporation, it is
an established local entity, recognized and supported by a substantial percentage of the Houston population. This gives it an advantage that Backfence
lacks, a local presence and the confidence built through that, allowing it to
establish a horizontal entity within its vertical commercial structure without
raising alarms in potential customers the way Backfence did. In a sense, the
success of Chron.Commons rests on the same principle that has allowed iBrattleboro to work: both come *from* the community, rather than *to* it. That one
was a two-person start-up and the other a creature of a major commercial
institution does not matter: both *belong*. In this, as in many other of its
aspects, the Web is tied to localities.

The basis of Chron.Commons is recognition of the fact that, as Henry Jenkins
says, people who identify with and participate in "a net community build upon
each others' ideas and contributions, often literally incorporating other people's
words into their new text. Fans respond to the mass produced texts of film and
television in this same collaborative fashion."[48] Furthermore, this can work most
efficiently when the fans have a prior connection and confidence in the venue.
Building on the former, Chron.Commons tries to provide the latter, facilitating
discussions on movies, politics, sports, almost anything at all—with a disclaimer
about responsibility for content, but allowing users to say anything they want. In
this, Chron.Commons allows users even more freedom than iBrattleboro—and a
broader range of discussion than a merely political blog like Daily Kos.

Other types of communities have also come onto the blogs in attempts to
circumvent the commercial press, though not at all from the perspective of the

citizen journalist. One of these is an organization explicitly created for a Web presence by a consortium of education-related groups (and others), including the American Association of University Professors, the American Federation of Teachers, the National Education Association, and the United States Student Association. The organization was established to counter what the member organizations see as attacks on universities by the likes of David Horowitz and the Association of College Trustees and Alumni. I asked Craig Smith of the American Federation of Teachers to answer a few questions about it:

What led to the creation of Free Exchange on Campus as a blog, and why did you choose a blog over other possible forums?

I would say that our decision was driven by two main factors: flexibility and community. We wanted to establish an online presence to give our coalition a certain identity, but we also knew that identity would change over time as our coalition grew and matured. The blog format provided an opportunity to start a conversation that would evolve over time as our coalition did.

At the same time, we wanted to start to build a community of people who were concerned about our issues and could be part of a discussion about those issues. The blog let us easily involve multiple people from within as well as outside of the coalition in the discussion and start creating that sense of community. The blogs more informal character contributed to people being willing to participate and test out ideas. It also allowed people to come and go as contributors, while at the same time the discussion created a certain narrative history that any newcomer could track and enter quite easily. That ongoing conversation has served as a centerpiece around which to add on other pieces of our work.

Has Free Exchange fulfilled its expectations?

I think the answer to that is a definite "yes," and "it is yet to be seen." We formed Free Exchange and started the blog to counter the negative attack messages that David Horowitz and other right-wing pundits and organizations were aiming at higher education faculty and students and to protect the free exchange of ideas on campus (as our name suggests). In particular, we wanted to correct the misrepresentations and fabrications about colleges and universities (and their faculties and students) that were going unchecked. Clearly, the attention we gained both from the media and other blogs as well as the response from those we were "fact checking" suggests that we were successful in that goal.

While we continue to serve that function, we are also hoping to expand the discussion about academic freedom to examine that topic from multiple perspectives and engage a wider community in that exploration. Whether we can do that or not successfully, remains to be seen.

What do you see as the future of projects like FEOC?

If by "projects like Free Exchange" you mean collaborative blogs around academic or political issues, I think the future is bright. There are plenty of examples of powerful group blogs ranging from the big political blogs (e.g., MyDD or FireDogLake) to smaller, but clearly engaging academic blogs (e.g., Crooked Timber or The Valve). I think that the blog format lends itself extremely well to both groups. We have obviously seen that on the big political blogs that there are many, many people looking to engage in a discussion (or at least be able to put their opinion out there). On the other hand, academics have traditionally valued discussion as a means of sharing and learning and blogs simply become another outlet for that creative work.

When you have a project such as Free Exchange that crosses over between academic topics and political debates, you have the potential of pulling in people from both interest groups. That is both our advantage, and our challenge. Some readers might see the blog as overly political while others might see the topic as too academic. That said, I think that the development of the blogosphere has created a really wonderful public space for discussion and debate (among other things). In particular, I think that in the political and academic arena, we will continue to see groups like Free Exchange take advantage of that space to promote their issues and engage a wider community.

Any other thoughts about Free Exchange or blogging would be more than appreciated.

One thing that those of us involved in Free Exchange keep thinking about and talking with others in the blogosphere about is how to use the blog as more of an organizing opportunity. Most of the groups in Free Exchange have an organizing orientation—organizing members, affiliates, or individuals around advocating on political issues. Anyone who has been involved with organizing knows that typically we try to get people out talking face-to-face with each other since that is the most effective type of organizing (rather than sitting behind a computer anonymously commenting on blogs or simply lurking about).

However, there does seem to be a connection between on-line activity and organizing opportunities. Specifically, the blog has provided us not only with a way to get information out, but also with a mechanism to find individuals who identify with our cause and engage them. For instance, we have had readers who have shifted from sending us a message, to suggesting a topic or idea that might be pursued, to actively working to gather information or get others involved in their local situation. This is a slow process and certainly cannot be the center of an organizing effort, but clearly the interactive nature of the blog provides us an opportunity to actively involve more people in our work—much more so than a static Web site or email.

    This idea is certainly nothing new, but it does represent what I think
is the most interesting part of a discussion of blogs, politics, coalitions,
activism and the public sphere. We are doing what we are doing at www.
freeexchangeoncampus.org because we ultimately hope to create a more
public conversation about an issue, academic freedom, that has traditionally
been limited to the higher education community. We believe that public
work is necessary if we are to protect academic freedom and the free
exchange of ideas on campus and beyond. The blogosphere offers a real
opportunity to put that conversation into a public forum.[49]

It is not surprising that a coalition that includes the American Association of
University Professors would end up sounding a little like John Dewey, one of
the AAUP's founders.

For Free Exchange on Campus, as for citizen journalists, both issue and
community oriented, the very idea of "journalism" goes beyond reporting the
news to community. In America, the idea of "community" carries within it a
horizontal sense of people coming together, with the iconic image being one
of Amish folk coming together almost spontaneously to rebuild a burnt barn.
We have often accepted vertical structures, but generally with the proviso that
there be a protected public sphere where the hierarchy can be discussed and, if
need be, changed.

Chapter 5

THE BLOG IN
POPULAR CULTURE

Blogs and Other Online Entities Discussed in Chapter 5

The Blog of Henry David Thoreau, http://blogthoreau.blogspot.com
Confessions of an Aca-Fan, http://www.henryjenkins.org
Ghostfooting, http://ghostfeet.wordpress.com
I, Walt Whitman, a Blogger, http://blogwaltwhitman.blogspot.com
kNOw Future Inc., http://knowfuture.wordpress.com
Passport, http://blog.foreignpolicy.com
Prelinger Library Blog, http://prelingerlibrary.blogspot.com
Snakes on a Blog, http://www.snakesonablog.com
With Hands Held High, http://whhh.blogspot.com

Writing almost half a century before the advent of the blogs, Bernard Rosenberg noted that there "can be no doubt that the mass media present a major threat to man's autonomy. To know that they might also contain some small seeds of freedom only makes a bad situation nearly desperate. No art form, no body of knowledge, no system of ethics is strong enough to withstand vulgarization. A kind of cultural alchemy transforms them all into the same soft currency. Never before have the sacred and the profane, the genuine and the specious, the exalted and the debased, been so thoroughly mixed that they are all but indistinguishable."[1] Today, we are seeing the results of that "vulgarization," and are learning that those "small seeds of freedom" have indeed been present—and have sprouted. As a result, what has come to pass is far less cataclysmic than Rosenberg's words might have led one to believe. "Vulgarization" there is, but there has also been an ingesting of both art and knowledge that has created new art and knowledge, much of it bad, but some of it of a quality on par with anything of the past. Certainly, what we are seeing is not just a grey glob, that "same soft currency"; surprisingly, the alchemy has served a positive purpose—there is surely at least a little gold created. "Most of what the amateurs create is gosh-awful bad," writes present-day media scholar Henry Jenkins (who blogs at Confessions of an Aca-Fan), "yet a thriving culture needs spaces where people can do bad art, get feedback, and get better."[2] And it has—and is. For that space has now been provided, in part, through downloadable files and even by the very existence of Web pages themselves. And Rosenberg's "seeds of freedom"? They have sprouted into (among other things) the blogs, this participatory platform allowing people to bypass cultural gatekeepers of all sorts, helping loosen control of the content of communication pathways that has for so long rested in the hands of commercial entities—even though, as librarian Woody Evans, who blogs in Ghostfooting (and many of us forget as we use the Web), warns, companies like Google, for example, though they assist the bloggers, are "out to make money. If they were really interested *primarily* in 'organizing the world's info' above and beyond profit, they'd be some kind of NGO. But they're a publicly traded corporation beholden to their shareholders. Anybody who organizes 'the world's' info is a cultural gatekeeper—and … your profit motive will skew your impartiality when it comes to selling access to cultural artifacts."[3] Possibly, we are even seeing an uneasy truce developing between the corporations of the metropole and the people, the rest of us, who are on the periphery (as the corporations see it).

One of the tensions on the Web, of course, is just that one between the commercial and the amateur. Though neither side likes it, each needs the other. The commercial wants results and the control that will ensure future results; the amateur wants the freedom to play. So, these two remain often at odds, but in ways quite removed from what was envisioned fifty years ago, when it was believed that technology would give the commercial the complete upper hand, when it was often imagined that the only recourse for individualism would be a new Luddism, a smashing of the machines.

Occasionally, even in the 1950s, there were hints in popular entertainments that people understood that technology could be turned against the rulers, be they corporate or otherwise. Generally, though, this was seen as happening through the inside, through what was often a temporary usurping of the centralized control that helped the people begin to question their authorities. In Philip K. Dick's early novel *The Man Who Japed*, the main character is able to strike a blow against the hierarchy by broadcasting "information" that the long-dead founder of the system ruling Earth was a cannibal:

> "It was clearly an art," Professor Sugermann said. "Properly prepared, boiled enemy was a gourmet's delight. We have the Major's own words on this subject." Professor Sugermann, again visible, unfolded his notes. "Toward the end of his life the Major ate only, or nearly only, boiled enemy. It was a great favorite of his wife's, and, as we've said, her recipes are regarded as among the finest extant. E. B. Erickson once estimated that Major Streiter and his immediate family must have personally assimilated at least six hundred fully-grown 'impossibles.' So there you have the more or less official opinion."

Whamp! The TV screen went, and again the image died. A kaleidoscopic procession of colors, patterns, dots pass rapidly; from the speaker emerged squawks of protest, whines, squeals.[4]

The only thing, it seems, that the system is unable to respond to is satire, resorting instead to random sounds and images. But success, in this form, was predicated on taking control, even if just for a moment, of the centralized communications system—something that, today (as so much becomes further decentralized so quickly), seems quaint or retro, as in the film *V for Vendetta* (James McTeigue, 2005) and the Alan Moore comics that inspired it, where the vision of the "future" is a deliberate (or perhaps not—the first of the comics was published in 1982, before the newer visions of technology were coming online) throwback to older dystopian conceptions.

For all the changes in perception over the last half century, to understand the current revolution in communications and its impact on American culture it is useful to first look back those fifty years. During the 1950s, the discussions on mass culture and popular culture resulting from the post-machine-age communications revolution, the one following on the heels of World War II and bringing television into a central role in the American home, were approaching their height, spearheaded by the likes of Marshall McLuhan, who would become something of an icon during the next decade. It was the time of the first blossoming of what would become "cultural studies" as a specific field of inquiry and of the commencement of directed study on the impact of technology on human activities.

Though the study may be fairly new, its subject (as an independent entity) goes back much further, beginning, really, 150 years earlier. As another scholar from the fifties, Dwight MacDonald points out, "The historical reasons for the growth of Mass Culture since the early 1800's are well known. Political democracy and popular education broke down the old upper-class monopoly of culture. Business enterprise found a profitable market in the cultural demands of the newly awakened masses, and the advance of technology made possible the cheap production of books, periodicals, pictures, music, and furniture, in sufficient quantities to satisfy this market. Modern technology also created new media such as the movies and television which are specially well adapted to mass manufacture and distribution."[5] MacDonald preferred the term "Mass Culture" over "Popular Culture" because it suggested "mass consumption" more directly. Today, however, we are seeing a popular culture that, though tied to consumption, is fracturing the "mass," making even that distinct from MacDonald's view of it: "Mass Culture is imposed from above. It is fabricated by technicians hired by businessmen; its audiences are passive consumers, their participation limited to the choice between buying and not buying."[6] Though that is still an aspect of mass culture, it is no longer true that it both presumes and creates a passive consumer (if it ever really did).

In fairness, it needs to be pointed out that, at the time MacDonald was writing, communications technologies had established "face-to-face contact through the mass media, between the communicator and millions of other persons.... It is important, however, to notice that with all the developments of mass communications such communication is still 'one way.' In two-way communication there is still no substitute for face-to-face contact. Even letters and telephones are poor substitutes for the living presence."[7] We have come far from the situation Kenneth Boulding was describing in that passage, contemporaneously to MacDonald. Today, there are those who would even argue that communications possibilities through the Internet are becoming so nuanced that they may soon and effectively replace "the living presence." Indeed, "feedback" has become so powerful that it now has an accepted place in the creative process, much to the distress of those who wax nostalgic for an era of the independent and solitary artist.

Though possibilities for participation were more limited fifty years ago, the fact that the consumer has a more active role in consumption than once was assumed has long been apparent, if not popularly recognized. The creators of mass-culture products have always known this, explained Herbert Gans in the 1950s:

> The general feedback hypothesis suggests that there is active, although indirect interaction between the audience and the creators, and that both affect the makeup of the final product. This is in contrast to earlier models of the relationship, in which one or the other of the participants were pictured as passive. Thus some critics have suggested that Hollywood products are so similar that the audience has no real choice, but must passively accept what is offered. Others have argued the opposite, that the movie makers are virtually passive, and give the people "what they want." Neither statement is accurate, but each has some truth. The audience is obviously limited by what is offered, but what is offered to it depends a good deal on what it has accepted previously. The movie-makers try to create pictures good enough to attract the audience, but at the same time they try to make sure that people will be satisfied with the movie they have chosen, by guessing and anticipating what will please them. Here, they use audience research to find out what people want, and make inferences from the choices people have previously expressed at the box office.[8]

Today, we recognize, and almost without question, that there is a constant negotiation between product (representing, of course, the producer) and consumer, with the consumer never simply accepting but ever commenting through perceptions of the product and through resulting actions. We have to: that negotiation, once it has been removed from the research universe of Hollywood (and of most cultural-studies writers), has been forced to the center of popular culture through the revolution in communications technologies that we are currently experiencing, a revolution that allows the consumers to "talk back" with a force and form never before even imaginable.

This is quite a change from the world half a century ago, one where it was not imagined that control (of any sort) over technology, especially communications technology, would fall in the hands of its consumers. Indeed, at the beginning of his book *1984*, George Orwell describes Winston Smith's living situation:

> Behind Winston's back the voice from the telescreen was still babbling away about pig-iron and the overfulfilment of the Ninth Three-Year Plan. The telescreen received and transmitted simultaneously. Any sound that Winston made, above the level of a very low whisper, would be picked up by it, moreover, so long as he remained within the field of vision which the metal plaque commanded, he could be seen as well as heard. There was of course no way of knowing whether you were being watched at any given moment. How often, or on what system, the Thought Police plugged in on any individual wire was guesswork. It was even conceivable that they watched everybody all the time. But at any rate they could plug in your wire whenever they wanted to. You had to live—did live, from habit that became instinct—in the assumption that every sound you made was overheard, and, except in darkness, every movement scrutinized.[9]

There is no sense, here, that the two-way aspect of the technology can be used by Smith, not in any way that expresses his own power (which really does not exist). It, too, becomes part of the control from afar. In no way is it part of what Smith can use for his own purposes. At best, he can avoid it, but can do even that only in small ways.

Indeed, even after all the changes of the last decade and a half, many still see the uses of technology primarily from a centralized focus, and there certainly are worries on that front, for the battle for decentralization and parity of power certainly has not yet been decided. A blogger called "Nicole" writing on With Hands Held High, says this, in regards to *1984* and contemporary society:

> It is a warning of what our race is doing to ourselves, and what can and quite possibly will happen.... If the government can *legally* listen to your phone conversations, search your things without a warrant, spy on you, monitor your purchases and even what you check out of the library, what does that say about this so-called "democracy?" How is that any better than Orwell's depiction of a similar society?... What's next? Feds are already wiretapping us and listening to our phone conversations, maybe they'll start watching us too. Reading our thoughts, controlling what we know and what we think we know. Wait, this is starting to sound like Orwell's book....[10]

The difference, however, is that, today, "Nicole" is able to use the technology, too. The very idea of a hacker is of one who not only burrows into the center, but of one who forces a diffusion of control.

In *The Man Who Japed*, human cultural attitudes are formed by a central agency, called Telemedia, the one that is briefly taken over, but people are watched by mechanical devices:

> His attention fixed itself on the pack of juveniles. They were here, the earwig-like sleuths. Each juvenile was a foot and a half long. The species scuttled close to the ground—or up vertical surfaces—at ferocious speed, and they noticed everything. These juveniles were inactive. The wardens had unlocked the metal hulls and dug out the report tapes. The juveniles remained inert during the meeting, and then they were put back into service.
>
> There was something sinister in these metal informers, but there was also something heartening. The juveniles did not accuse; they only reported what they heard and saw. They couldn't color their information and they couldn't make it up. Since the victim was indicted mechanically he was safe from hysterical hearsay, from malice and paranoia. There could be no question of guilt; the evidence was already in.[11]

Here, the technology supposedly *for* justice only can be used *against* the humans. There can be no arguing with it, nor (or so it seems) manipulation of it. These "juveniles" are one of the nightmare visions of the fifties, the implacable watching machine. Today, we are more comfortable with the machines themselves, transferring our fears to the people who run them—for there are always (Dick's vision here notwithstanding) people behind them.

If the era between the two world wars can be called the machine age,[12] when mechanical devices became prevalent in American culture, then the post–World War II era might be named the first era of technology. The ideas and inventions that had begun even before World War I came to a first ubiquity during the machine age, but they exploded in possibility and utilization in the aftermath of Hiroshima and Nagasaki. The progression from the machine age, however, was foreseen, was almost a natural progression, a logical movement into new possibilities. What is now happening, what began happening with the introduction of the World Wide Web in the early 1990s, was *not* predicted—at least, not generally. The models for future technology that were posited in the fifties, as we have seen, usually assumed centralization. What we are seeing now, though it does have aspects of centralized control, is also a determined decentralization, needing another model completely if this seeming contradiction is to be easily understood.

In the film *Forbidden Planet* (Fred Wilcox, 1956), Dr. Morbius protects the alien technology he discovers from fellow humans, not believing that it could be used for good, seeing only a centralized control of it (by him) as safe. The point, as he sees it, is that technology can destroy humans, if not carefully overseen.

Technology, in this view, has a life of its own. Indeed, the technology Morbius protects has long outlasted its creators. What we are experiencing today is a different view of technology completely (though an evolving one—the older image is still alive and kicking within it), one that ties much more closely into culture and the ability to utilize the technology—and the goal of that utilization.

One lesson *not* learned from World War II that should have been learned was that technology alone has little impact. In most areas, the Germans were well ahead of the Americans they were fighting. Their tanks were better, so were their submarines, and they had developed deployable jet aircraft. The Americans, though, had two real advantages. First, they could produce their slightly worse tanks, subs, and planes in such numbers that the technological advantage the Germans enjoyed became irrelevant. Second, and much more important to the discussion here, American soldiers were comfortable with their technology. Common soldiers found themselves repairing broken-down weapons and vehicles—and even improving them (hooking up telephones on the rears of tanks, for example, so that the infantry could communicate with those inside). Troops of few other countries could do the same. American technology succeeded not because it was advanced, but because it could be used, manipulated, repaired, and improved in the field.

The point is that technology alone has no impact. It needs understanding, acceptance, and a place in a plan towards a goal.

It almost seemed, though, that the nation came to believe after the war that technology alone could solve any problem. But many, even in the fifties, of course, did recognize the weaknesses of this view, and understood that industrial might alone would not prove sufficient (something else many Americans *had* come to believe in the wake of World War II) to improve the world. Among these was Philip K. Dick, whose 1963 novel *The Man in the High Castle* contains within it pieces of a science-fiction novel by a character created by Dick. One of those passages goes like this:

Only Yankee know-how and the mass-production system—Detroit, Chicago, Cleveland, the magic names!—could have done the trick, sent that ceaseless and almost witlessly noble flood of cheap one-dollar (the China Dollar, the trade dollar) television kits to every village and backwater of the Orient. And when the kit had been assembled by some gaunt, feverish-minded youth in the village, starved for a chance, of that which the generous Americans held out to him, that tinny little instrument with its built-in power supply no larger than a marble began to receive. And what did it receive? Crouching before the screen, the youths of the village—and often the elders as well—saw words. Instructions. How to read, first. Then the rest. How to dig a deeper well. Plow a deeper furrow. How to purify their water, heal their sick. Overhead, the American artificial moon wheeled, distributing the signal, carrying it everywhere … to all the waiting, avid masses of the East.[13]

Today, there are still people who have such idealistic visions … such as Nicholas Negroponte, with his One Laptop Per Child project. They forget that it is not technology alone that drives cultural change or creates new worlds, but the interaction between the old and the new—or between, to use the image created by Henry Adams, the dynamo and the virgin. As Adams wrote, "whatever the mechanicians might think, both energies acted as interchangeable force on man, and by action on man all known force may be measured."[14] Like the old and the new, the machine and belief (culture) are inextricably linked. It is foolhardy, therefore, to imagine that Negroponte's $100 (now $200) laptop will be grasped to the bosom of Africa (say) with the passion that the continent has embraced the cell phone. Negroponte's machine is being presented as the discrete answer—something it never has been and never will be. It will likely be superseded by a version of the iPhone before it ever gets off the ground.

The African writer and editor Binyavanga Wainaina wrote an article for *Bidoun* in which he explains quite clearly the problems with the Negroponte vision. His take on the subject dovetails perfectly with my own, one built during my four years in West Africa, and he makes me understand an incident that happened while I was teaching at the University of Ouagadougou in the mid-1980s.

A Dutch physics professor at the university developed a seminar for secondary-school science teachers to show them how to make use of available items for experiments in their physics classrooms. Though the experiments he had designed were ingenious and could have been quite effective, the teachers rejected them unanimously. "What, we don't deserve equipment of the quality found in your schools in the Netherlands?" they cried. "Aren't you, this way, condemning us to a perpetual second class?" The Dutchman was devastated—but the African teachers had a point. The things made for the poor by the rich carry with them a slightly repellant odor.

Wainaina writes about the wind-up radios, rarely seen today in Africa, that were once all the rage in the developed world for the underdeveloped:

> But Trevor Baylis's Freeplay Radios still exist. You will find them among new age fisherfolk in Oregon; neoblue collar sculptors working out of lofts in postindustrial cities; backtoearthers in Alberta; Social Forum activists and neoGrizzly Adams types everywhere. Angstridden victims, all. But the enthusiasts of the windup radio suffer not from poverty or lack of

information but from wealth, vague guilt, and too much information. They are the only people who can find nobility in a product that communicates to its intended owner: you are fucked.[15]

Later in his article, Wainaina explains:

A windup radio. A magic laptop. These pure products are meant to solve everything.

They almost always fail, but they satisfy the giver. To the recipients, the things have no context, no relationship to their ideas of themselves or their possibilities. A great salesman can spark a dialogue with you; in a matter of minutes, you come to make your own sense of his product, fitting it into your imagination, your life. You lead, the salesman follows. Whereas a pure product presents itself as a complete solution; a product built to serve the needs of the needy assumes the needy have measured themselves exactly as the product has measured them....

There are few useful "development models" for genuinely selfstarting people. I am sure the One Laptop per Child initiative will bring glory to its architects. The IMF will smile. Mr. Negroponte will win a prize or two or ten. There will be key successes in Rwanda; in a village in Cambodia; in a small, groundbreaking initiative in Palestine, where Israeli children and Palestinian children will come together to play minesweeper. There will be many laptops in small, perfect, NGO-funded schools for AIDS orphans in Nairobi, and many earnest expatriates working in Sudan will swear by them.

And there will be many laptops in the homes of homeschooling, goat-tending parents in North Dakota who wear hemp (another wonderproduct for the developing world). They will fall in love with the idea of this frugal, noble laptop, available for a mere $100. Me, I would love to buy one. I would carry it with me on trips to remote Kenyan places, where I seek to find myself and live a simpler, earthier life, for two weeks a year.[16]

Wainaina's point deserves reiteration: much of the technology developed in the metropole for the people on the "fringes" (in the view from the metropole) fails simply because it was developed more for the image of the "simple fringe life" contained in the metropole and not for the life as it actually exists on those fringes. Only in following the desires of the people living that life can one develop products for them—not by deciding what they *should* want.

This is exactly the disconnect that has caught the commercial news media and some in the entertainment media by surprise over the last few years: they had thought they knew what products to "give" the people. They have not been able to see that their audience studies have been too narrow, that they have been tailored to one view of the world, to a view from the center reaching out, of a hierarchy reaching down. Once other possibilities showed themselves, people took them, blindsiding those in the media asleep in their confidence in an essentially captive audience. One of the things African farmers showed me as I struggled to be the interface between them and the metropole as a Peace Corps Volunteer working in agriculture is that you cannot "give" technology to people and expect results—they have to want it. It has to fit in with their understanding of their needs and of the world, and with their desires. The blogs, we are seeing, certainly do that, in America.

One point of contention the blogs have brought to the fore, as we have seen, is that between amateur writers and professionals online. Like the African teachers who did not want to feel that they were relegated to taking scraps from the table, amateur writers on the Web have not wanted to accept second place to the professionals. This has led to contentious situations, such as the one surrounding the concept of Net Neutrality, which argues that the means of distribution on the Web should be the same for everyone, that corporations, for example, should not be able to pay for a special, faster rate of "delivery" of their pages or downloads.

In all of these instances, we are seeing conflicts between hierarchical, vertical models and horizontal ones. Only today are we really seeing resistance to the idea that technology and its benefits flow outwards and downwards from a center, replacing that with a model of decentralized manipulation of technological developments (and of manufactured items), making them responsive not to "central planning" but to the actual end users. This is a difficult shift to make, and we are in the midst of it.

It was not until the 1970s that the earlier and naïve attitudes towards technology really began to change in any large way, in part because of the first glimmerings of understanding of the limitations of resources through the first oil crisis and through E. F. Schumaker's book *Small Is Beautiful*. Still, the U.S. and Europe poured—and are still pouring—billions of techno dollars into developing countries, comfortable in the assurance that technology, all by itself, was the answer. Still, people like Baylis and Negroponte have not made the final link: the "appropriate" in "appropriate technology" has to be determined by the user, the outsider it is brought to, and not by the insider from the metropole, no matter how noble his or her intentions.

Again, it may sound naïve to say, but when people, even poor people, want something (that is available) badly enough, they find ways of getting it. And Africans, recently, have proven that point. As Christine Bowers, writing on the *Foreign Policy* magazine blog Passport, says, "mobile phone penetration is through the roof, especially in Africa. In 2000, fewer than 8 million Africans had a mobile phone—now over 100 million do. That's one in nine."[17] Considering that telephones of any sort were not even *available* twenty-five years ago over much of the continent, that is amazing. In terms of culture, it may be even more astonishing than the rise of the blogs in somewhat more developed countries over the same period of time. And its impact may be as great.

In fact, it is possible to imagine that Africans will bypass the laptop completely, turning instead to something like the iPhone.

It may remain to be established just why cell phones have taken off so in Africa while a myriad of other gee-whiz technologies have not (though others, including bicycles and battery-powered transistor radios, also once did—as will future ones), but it will prove to be the result of cultural forces dating back decades, if not longer, and not *simply* because of availability. Clearly, and anyone dealing with Africa should be able to see it, if Africans are going to come onto the Web, they are going to do it in their own way, and that will probably be through the cell phone rather than, as happened in the United States, through the PC (personal computer). The implications of this are hard to see, but it may develop into an entirely different conception of the blog, making it (for Africans, at least) a more individual communications platform than it is for Americans.

Of course, the differences in attitude towards communications technologies fifty years ago and today do have a basis in the technologies themselves. Because it is tied to a mouse and a keyboard, the relationship between the user and a computer connected to the Internet is quite distinct from that between a television viewer connected to standard cable. The former demands a great deal more interactivity than the latter. Surfing the Web, then, becomes something quite distinct from channel surfing.

The dance between American culture and technology began much, much earlier than the 1950s—as did the bifurcated view of "the world" in opposition to "technology" that can still be seen today in discussion of culture, a bifurcation that colors absolutely our vision of the Web. Even before the Civil War, Henry David Thoreau made note of this duality, comparing technology to a ranging predator: "The whistle of the locomotive penetrates my woods summer and winter, sounding like the scream of a hawk sailing over some farmer's yard."[18] Outside his idyll, huge changes *were* going on, too, significant enough to intrude upon him, as he said. [Significantly, Greg Perry has made Thoreau's journal into a blog, The Blog of Henry David Thoreau (http://blogthoreau.blogspot.com). He has also created I, Walt Whitman, A Blogger (http://blogwaltwhitman.blogspot.com). These are attempts to make the work of the writers more accessible through presentation in a contemporary context.] As Leo Marx, yet another scholar of the fifties, explains, "By 1844 the machine had captured the public imagination. The invention of the steamboat had been exciting, but it was nothing compared to the railroad. In the 1830s the locomotive, an iron horse or fire-Titan, is becoming a kind of national obsession. It is the embodiment of the age, an instrument of power, speed, noise, fire, iron, smoke—at once a testament to the will of many rising over natural obstacles, and, yet, confined by its iron rails to a predetermined path, it suggested a new sort of fate."[19] Since then, other technological advances have caught the public imagination, each one of them embodying its new age, suggesting a world distinct from the old. So powerful is our current obses-sion, communications technology, that it hardly even needs' to be identified as a continuation of this tradition.

The pattern of the obsessions continues, with many now positing a brave new online world (whatever *that* may mean) that has already reached into our older and comfortable world in much the way the train whistle was stretching towards Thoreau, whether he (or we) would want it or not. There is an obvious nostalgia in such attitudes, making the dichotomy as much future/past as technology/pastoral. The golden age is always behind us, never ahead.

There has always been, in America, a tension between the idealized vision of the past and the equally idealized perception of a technologically driven future where the golden possibilities always lie ahead. Ultimately, this dichot-omy is no more useful, however, than that dividing the "real" and the "virtual" into separate "worlds." In neither of these cases is there a simple either/or, one or the other.

Fortunately, many people (Walt Whitman may have been one such) have always rejected the certainty of the dichotomy in this, seeing one whole. They, too, have their contemporary followers, more and more of them as the com-munications revolution continues:

> Just as the emperor's new clothes turned out to be an agreed-upon fiction, so is American technology clothed in a black box more imagined than actual. It is a part of our material condition and is of our own making....
>
> By saying that technology is a part of our material condition and is of our own making, I merely mean to assert that the tools and processes we use are a part of our lives, not simply instruments of our purpose.... The usual way to put this notion is to say that technology is not autonomous.... We might say that ... technologies are socially constructed for certain pur-poses. The impact they have on any one of us is the result of a complex calculus of class, race, gender, luck, and other similar variables.[20]

Technology is part and parcel of the cultural whole, not something that can be separated out either as threat or promise. As Bill Bradley says, "it must be remembered that Web sites are only tools. The values of those who use them will determine to what end they apply the tools. Thoreau once said about the telegraph, 'It's an improved means to an unimproved end.' The same applies to information technology, unless our values shape its impact. Being able to transmit massive amounts of information in nanoseconds will mean nothing if we lose our humanity in the process."[21]

The people who understand this are not, of course, simply technological optimists (often, they are believers in appropriate technology, not simply technology), but are people like outsider librarians "Rick Prelinger and Megan Shaw Prelinger [... who] think the conflict between a so-called digital culture and a so-called print culture is fake; they think we should stop celebrating or lamenting, the discontinuous story of how the circuits will displace the shelves, and start telling a continuous story about how the two might fit together."[22] To me, they may have it right. Change there is, but it may be evolutionary, these two so-called sides working together, integrated, creating a new whole. The city of gold may be neither past nor future, existing only in the process, the connecting of the two—in the here and now, if we choose to see it. This fitting together is the likely future of the Web and the world, yet it is one that does require a change in our vision of technology and culture.

It would be wrong to dismiss or simply underestimate the power of the sense of invasion felt by many (and not just by Africans) as new technologies make their presences felt—or are imposed. Certainly, the type of intrusion by technology that Thoreau saw was still uppermost in many minds as television developed its place in American culture. In a famous screed against TV in 1956, Gunther Anders wrote:

> In actual fact, the type of mass consumption discussed here threatens to dissolve the family under the guise of fostering the intimacy of family life. For what now dominates in the home, thanks to television, is the outside world—real or fictional; and this outside world is so unrestrictedly dominant that the reality of the home—not only the four walls and furniture, but precisely the shared family life—becomes inoperative and phantom-like. When that which is remote becomes familiar, that which is familiar becomes remote. When the phantom becomes real, reality becomes a phantom. The home tends to become a container, its function to be reduced to containing a video for the outside world. The realm of the phantoms is victorious over the realm of the home without even the chance of a contest between the two; it triumphs the moment the television set enters the home: it comes, it is seen, it conquers. At once the ceiling is full of leaks, the walls become transparent, the cement uniting the members of the family crumbles away, the shared privacy disintegrates.[23]

In other words, technology is destroying our most basic structures. It does not express, but invades and rips apart. Anders saw the impact of technology as so overwhelming that it was eventually going to rid audiences of their voices: "Since the receiving sets speak in our place, they progressively rob us of our ability to speak, of our opportunities for speaking, and finally even of our pleasure in expressing ourselves."[24] Yet, what we were seeing, it has turned out, was not a loss of voice but simply a technology that did not have the ability to accommodate that voice. Clearly, as the current communications revolution is showing, the ability and desire to speak was always with us amid the silence; people were just awaiting the means.

Anders provides a list of the consequences of the "new" technologies, consequences many still hold as truths, but that are being demolished as the public
embraces the new interactive and participatory technologies:

1. The invasion via technology leaves us "only listless, passive consumers
   of the world."[25] This goes far beyond even Thoreau's vision of technology. Just before his line on the whistle, Thoreau wrote, "The men on
   the freight trains, who go over the whole length of the road, bow to me
   as to an old acquaintance, they pass me so often, and apparently they
   take me for an employee; and so I am. I too would fain be a track-
   repairer somewhere in the orbit of the earth."[26] The railroad may be
   intrusive, but it is also much more, as Thoreau recognized, for it
   includes the capacity for taking even its human creators and main-
   tainers to as yet unimagined places. Certainly, by carrying people, it
   does not make them passive. Neither does communications technology.
2. Because the images we watch are not real, "we too are like phan-
   toms."[27] There's something of creation of a dichotomy and yet a subse-
   quent blurring of it, here, taking Victor Lindlahr's "you are what you
   eat" to a metaphysical extreme. The conceit of jumping into a phantom
   world has amused artists for a long time, but the idea has rarely been
   that the "real" world becomes less "real" by virtue of the interaction
   and participation.
3. The robbing of speech represented by the technologies is also a robbing
   of freedom. There may be a modicum of truth, here. Certainly, though,
   once they had found the new avenues of technological speech, people
   have taken to them, perhaps reclaiming both speech and freedom.
4. Our lack of ability to act on the world perceived through technology
   has made us voyeurs. Perhaps this, too, is true. But we are now seeing
   that many had also yearned to be spied upon. In fact, one of the driving forces behind the blogs may just be that desire to be noticed.
5. An event is no longer tied to place when broadcast, "it becomes a
   movable, indeed, almost ubiquitous object."[28] This is another expression of dichotomy, providing a separate "reality" to the broadcast world
   that, I believe, we are now seeing the end of.
6. Events, when replicated and distributed for a price, become commod-
   ities. True again, and this is at the heart of the problems faced by the
   commercial news media. However, when individuals, bloggers and citizen journalists, become the ones replicating the events, they take the
   "sale" out of it, returning the event (to some extent, at least) to the real
   public sphere.
7. The result of numbers five and six is that "the difference between being
   and appearance, between reality and image of reality, is abolished."[29] If
   the dichotomy that had been established is accurate, then the "real"

world begins to disappear and the "virtual" world takes over. There are many who have actually embraced this concept (the proponents of venues such as Second Life, for example), but the experience seems to be that the image remains simply a tool for understanding and negotiating the real.

8. The new ascendancy of the reproduction reshapes the original, for it is now made for reproduction, becoming "merely a master matrix, or a mold for casting its own reproductions."[30] Yes, technological possibilities for replication certainly do change the original, but is that change necessarily a reduction?

9. The last point also depends on acceptance of the dichotomy between virtual and real, for the upshot of the technological invasion is that "the concept of 'the world' is abolished in so far as it denotes that *in which* we live. The real world is forfeited."[31] It is certainly true that technology tempers our views of the "real" world, but the vision it produces does not *replace* the real world.

The problem with Anders's view is that it is predicated on acceptance of that dichotomy of worlds, the real and the virtual. Today, as I have pointed out, we are much more aware of the weakness of this model (though its popularity continues), yet there were even people pointing it out in the fifties. Henry Rabassiere, writing in the very issue of *Dissent* where Anders's piece first appeared in English, fingered what many now see as the obvious, that the "truth is that at all times most public events are experienced vicariously and that each society has its special means of communicating to its citizens the preferred picture of reality; at all times did people rely on teachers, travelers, pictures and other second-hand information to form their view of the world. Today's mass media and extreme mobility potentially increase our sources of information to the point of universality, where cross-checking has become easy and willful distortion has become difficult."[32] In other words, rather than presenting a new world, technology does little more than present the societal image of the real world *writ large*. The last statement of Rabassiere's, about cross-checking and distortion, now seems to have been particularly prophetic, for it presages what have become very real activities on the blogs.

Furthermore, it is Rabassiere's view, that the technology itself should not be the central consideration in examination of technology vis-à-vis culture, that can be seen today reflected in the work of Henry Jenkins, whose concept of *convergence* shies away from associating societal change with specifics of technology. He writes, "In the world of media convergence, every important story gets told, every brand gets sold, and every consumer gets courted across multiple media platforms.... This circulation of media content—across different media systems, competing media economies, and national borders—depends heavily on consumers' active participation.... Convergence does not occur through media appliances, however sophisticated they may become. Convergence occurs within the brains of individual consumers and through their social interactions with others."[33] This convergence, in Jenkins view, is more useful for describing what is going on through our current communications revolution than other terms, for it focuses on the user:

> "cultural convergence," a term I have coined to reflect the fact that the technological convergences being discussed in the information and entertainment industries, the bringing together of all existing media technologies within the same black box in our living room, actually build upon a complex series of cultural and social shifts which are redefining how we relate to media and popular culture. Anyone who wants to see what convergence looks like should visit my house and watch my adolescent son, sprawled on the living room rug, watching a baseball game on our big-screen television, listening to techno on his cd-player, and writing e-mail to his friends or doing homework on his laptop. At the moment, the technologies aren't talking to each other. They're on different sides of the room. But, it doesn't really matter very much in cultural terms, since as consumers, we are already using different media and their contents in relation to each other. Sociologists are starting to refer to the "N Generation," the "Net Generation," or "Gen.Com" children who have come of age in relation to interactive technologies and digital media and who operate under the rather bold assumption that they can be active participants shaping, creating, critiquing and circulating popular culture. "Cultural convergence" describes new ways audiences are relating to media content, their increased skills at reading across different media and their desires for a more participatory and complex media culture.[34]

Will Brooker and Deborah Jermyn describe convergence this way: "The contemporary phenomenon of overflow, then, transforms the audience relationship with the text from a limited, largely one-way engagement based around a proscribed time slot and single medium into a far more fluid, flexible affair which crosses media platforms—Internet, mobile phone, stereo system, shopping mall—in a process of convergence."[35] Jenkins determines that even "blogging is a form of grassroots convergence. By pooling their information and tapping grassroots expertise, by debating evidence and scrutinizing all available information, and, perhaps most powerfully, by challenging one another's assumptions, the blogging community is 'spoiling' [Jenkins defines this as the tracking down of, and presenting, information soon to be on television] the American government."[36] That is, bloggers manage to get information so quickly and present it apace, often ruining the orchestrated presentation campaigns of both the government and the commercial news media.

This is a far cry from the production-centered view of mass culture (where the passive consumer—the phrase itself is something of an oxymoron—is relatively ignored) of the past. Theodor Adorno wrote: "The culture industry fuses the old and familiar into a new quality. In all its branches, products which are tailored for consumption by masses, and which to a great extent determine the nature of that consumption, are manufactured more or less according to plan.... The culture industry intentionally integrates its consumers from above.... The customer is not king, as the culture industry would have us believe, not its subject but its object. The very word mass-media, specially honed for the culture industry, already shifts the accent onto harmless terrain. Neither is it a question of primary concern for the masses, nor the techniques of communication as such, but of the spirit which sufflates them, their master's voice."[37] A focus on convergence will likely convince one that this has never been completely true and that, today, with a new media spectrum that is both interactive and participatory, it is even less so. Jenkins defines these two terms: "Interactivity refers to the way that new technologies have been designed to be more responsive to consumer feedback.... Participation, on the other hand, is shaped by the cultural and social protocols. So, for example, the amount of conversation possible in a movie theater is determined more by the tolerance of audiences ... than by any innate property of cinema itself."[38] The blogs are both, being interactive in that the software programs were designed as platforms for feedback and that their usage is controlled by convention.

The avenues envisioned for the purposes of customer feedback of the sort Herbert Gans described have become something more, bringing the customer more intimately into the creation process than ever before, as happened during the creation of the film *Snakes on a Plane* (David Ellis, 2006) starring Samuel L. Jackson. According to *The Hollywood Reporter*, the very title may have been retained because of fan input:

Movie fans ... seized upon the title and started spontaneously creating fan sites, blogs, T-shirts, poems, fiction and songs. The title itself, sometimes abbreviated as "SoaP," has emerged as Internet-speak for fatalistic sentiments that range from c'est la vie to "shit happens."

"The title is so clear and so straightforward," said Brian Finkelstein, a Washington, D.C., native who created the blog Snakesonablog.com and who hopes to score tickets to the movie's premiere. "You know exactly what you're going to get."

Like Harry Potter, whose first suggestion that he's got magic on his hands comes when he discovers he can talk to snakes in their language, New Line got the message. Deciding that so many anonymous fans couldn't be wrong, the studio decided to revert to the movie's original title.

Jackson publicly endorsed the move. "That's the only reason I took the job: I read the title," Jackson told entertainment site Collider.com. He added, "You either want to see that, or you don't."[39]

To reiterate: like Harry Potter, who heard what snakes were saying when others could not, the movie's makers heard the fans when others had not. They did not need magical powers, though: the blogs provided that. Unfortunately for the filmmakers, that magic, responding to fan input (whose influence may have extended beyond the title), did not prove enough to create a successful film.

The growing force of fan art threatens to explode interactivity into a diffusion of control, forcing it away from the creators. Even those, like George Lucas, who have opened the door to it just slightly in an attempt to control it rather than just fight it, are eventually going to lose as pressure from the other side grows. Because of copyright, much fan art (like Japanese *doujinshi*, semi-private comic books often based on commercial products) has to fly below the corporate radar, but it is still having an impact on the original creators. Because fan art is a potential source of huge revenues even for those original creators, it will eventually force its way into a place within the "legitimate" structures of mass-culture creation—another example of "mass" becoming "massed."

So, what we are seeing today is a situation where mass culture, the creation and distribution of material for the people, is finding itself pushed back by massed culture, the manipulation of the items of mass culture by its consumers, through new avenues of interactivity and participation. People are manipulating the works of mass culture and are creating their own contributions to massed culture in ways that can catch attention never before so easily available. In the past, this was difficult, not because the creations of mass culture were so much better, but because they were so much more highly polished and self-contained and more easily distributed in a one-dimensional manner.

The result has been (and will be, even more so) something of a shock to the creators of mass culture because, as John Fiske notes, "by ignoring the complexity and creativity by which the subordinate cope with the commodity system and its ideology in their everyday lives, the dominant underestimate and thus devalue the conflict and struggle entailed in constructing popular culture within a capitalist society."[40] Not seeing something is not the same as it not existing. The desires, and even creative acts, occurring outside of commercial mass culture creation have always existed. Now, they have new avenues for expression, including the blogs, and are beginning to challenge the hegemony of the purveyors of mass culture—as the pushback against increasingly restrictive copyright provisions, among other things, indicates.

In fan art relating specifically to *Star Wars* (George Lucas, 1977 and following), those items closest to the actual creations of George Lucas are considered to be the most authentic. This provides a new standard for authenticity—lack of remove in conception from the first creator. This is significant, because one of the more interesting aspects of the Web is the destruction of even the possibility of "authenticity" as Walter Benjamin described it, and even of the possibility of the "original"—along with all that might mean in questions of ownership. Recognizing what this might mean, Benjamin argued that "the technique of reproduction detaches the reproduced object from the domain of tradition. By making many reproductions it substitutes a plurality of copies for a unique existence. And in permitting the reproduction to meet the beholder or listener in his own particular situation, it reactivates the object reproduced. These two processes lead to a tremendous shattering of tradition which is the obverse of the contemporary crisis and renewal of mankind. Both processes are intimately connected with the contemporary mass movements."[41] Ownership is the basis of tradition; shatter tradition, and ownership goes, too. But that does not mean that pedigree disappears as well, as the *Star Wars* fans have shown.

As the writers on American culture from the 1950s discovered, looking back in their later years, writing about any revolution from within it is fraught with danger. In 2007, I watched a man in his sixties moderating a panel on media change. He could barely contain his fury at what he saw happening around him. His fury, I am sure, was based in part on fear, fear of a situation today which, from his viewpoint, seems nearly out of control. "None of us," writes Jenkins, "really knows how to live in this era of media convergence, collective intelligence, and participatory culture. These changes are producing anxieties and uncertainties, even panic, as people imagine a world without gatekeepers and live with the reality of expanding corporate media power."[42] People who once thought they understood the world and technology are seeing their once solid base turn to quicksand.

People imagining "a world without gatekeepers" while experiencing "the reality of expanding corporate media power" are certainly aware that the ideal they long for may instead be replaced by one of greater control than ever before. This has been the upshot of many revolutions of the past, and may be what will happen this time. On the other hand, the possibilities represented by the Internet may now be too great for any entity to manage them effectively, new gatekeepers constantly finding that the fences they have erected around their gates are quickly undermined. Gatekeeping, however (or its possibility), remains quite healthy on the Web, for all the seeming cacophony. Alan Toner describes the gatekeeping situation of today this way:

Having solved the problem of broadcast-scope, producers find that the problem is now how to find an audience. This question in fact entails two elements: how people decide what they want (preference formation) and the cost of finding what they're looking for when they already know that they want it (search-costs). Industrial media manufacturers solved these questions by investing hugely in marketing and then by either buying up distributors/ retailers (vertical integration) or through partnerships. The online world divides   the   model   of   preference-formation   between   the   traditional mechanisms of marketing combined with user-based recommendation systems, driven by proprietary algorithms. The latter tend to be used by more experienced users, other people find things through scattershot use of search engines. Sourcing the data is the preserver [*sic*] of search engines, either on the web as a whole, or on a site where you could reasonably expect to find the product (ebay, amazon, etc.).

Users' reliance on search places Google in a position of enormous power, and the search engine has permeated people's experience of the web to the point where they forget that it's even there: surveys have shown that people often run searches for Google or Yahoo from the Google search itself! Much has been made of the fact that the search results are decided democratically, on the basis of the pattern of links clustered around search phrases, but in fact we can only take google's word on it. Should google decide that a site is inappropriate it simply disappears.[43]

Though it may sometimes seem, today, that there are no longer any gatekeepers, they do exist—simply on a different level.

Even if "the people" triumph, it remains true, as Jenkins warns, that there "are no guarantees that we will use our new power any more responsibly than nation-states or corporations have exercised theirs. We are trying to hammer out the ethical codes and social contracts that will determine how we will relate to one another just as we are trying to determine how this power will insert itself into the entertainment system or into the political process. Part of what we must do is figure out how—and why—groups with different backgrounds, agendas, perspectives, and knowledge can listen to one another and work together toward the common good. We have a lot to learn."[44] That we do. And it is the links provided by the Web (in part), that are making it possible for us to do so.

Perhaps it is true to some degree of all cultures, but Americans have been obsessed with links since colonial days. Not only were the trade links with England necessary for survival for the early settlers, but mail links within the colonies kept isolated villages from feeling that they were facing the "wilderness" alone. As an expansive culture, new links to far places were constantly sought, rivers and mountain passes bringing connection to new places, canals and steamboats, roads and railroads augmenting them, making them faster, stronger, and more permanent. Barriers encountered were only to be overcome, through bridges and tunnels and, later, simply by overflight.

Scholar of early American literature and culture Wayne Franklin sees a process of discovery, exploration, and settlement in the history of this country, each step containing its own particular way of looking at the landscape. Just so with the landscape of the newly opened virtual world where we have seen, these last few years, a rush to settlement as chaotic as the run for land in Oklahoma in 1889. To me, "discovery" is a better metaphor for the establishment of the Web than the more accurate "invention," for the Web has come to be seen as a "place" rather than a thing. Certainly, there has been an ongoing process of discovery in relation to our online "world," and it continues within the individual as she or he steps into the unknown landscape of the Web, and it has been one of using the vocabulary developed in an "old" world to create, in many respects, or expand into the "new" one.

Like William Bradford, writing of his experiences as the *Mayflower* landed, the early discoverers of the worlds of the Web "had no friends to welcome them nor inns to entertain or refresh their weatherbeaten bodies; no houses or much less towns to repair to, to seek for succor."[45] It was all new, and it had to be made up as they went along—including the language for it. It should be no surprise, then, that they repeated the process of those early discoverers, then explorers, and later settlers.

Generally, it is the discoverers who start the naming process, mapping the new territory in terms of the old—but sketchily, at best. Still, the parameters are set for what will come. When Tim Berners-Lee and Robert Cailliau first proposed the World Wide Web, they wrote:

It will aim:

- to provide a common (simple) protocol for requesting human readable information stored at a remote system, using networks;
- to provide a protocol within which information can automatically be exchanged in a format common to the supplier and the consumer;
- to provide some method of reading at least text;
- to provide and maintain at least one collection of documents, into which users may (but are not bound to) put their documents. This collection will include much existing data;
- to provide a keyword search option, in addition to navigation by following references, using any new or existing indexes;
- to provide the software for the above free of charge to anyone.[46]

Like discoverers of the past (as opposed to inventors, which they really were, as well), Berners-Lee and Cailliau were not looking to exploit what they had found, but to name it and, thereby, to open it up for exploration by others. Here is how Berners-Lee described the Web early on: "The WWW world consists of documents, and links. Indexes are special documents which, rather than being read, may be searched. The result of such a search is another ("virtual") document containing links to the documents found."[47] As we have all found since, the WWW world consists of much, much more.

"Documents and links." In a way, these are just like early maps. They documented coast lines and currents, and created links through the possible (and then actual) trade routes shown. Once Berners-Lee had shown the way, explorers flooded in, uncovering possibilities and establishing claims. And these, like all good explorers, moved on as the settlers came, setting up camp, adding final detail to the maps as they built their towns, their Web sites, and established a network of links beyond anything the explorers—let alone discoverer Berners-Lee—could have imagined.

Running through this process from the discoverer through the explorer and to the settler is emphasis on the link. Be it through language back to the place of origin or between newly established sites, the link is key to growth. And Americans, probably more than any other people on earth, understand both the importance of links and the meaning of their breaking.

The real revolution connected to technology at the end of the twentieth century was not simply one of computers. In fact, invention and technological progress did no more than *allow* the revolution; they were themselves neither the revolution itself nor its causes. The *real* revolution has to do with information and communication.

In 2000, the University of California at Berkeley's School of Information Management and Systems released a study estimating that the "world produces between 1 and 2 exabytes of unique information per year, which is roughly 250 megabytes for every man, woman, and child on earth."[48] The report goes on to say: "It is clear that we are all drowning in a sea of information. The challenge is to learn to swim in that sea, rather than drown in it. Better understanding and better tools are desperately needed if we are to take full advantage of the ever-increasing supply of information described in this report."[49] A new study just three years later concluded that "Print, film, magnetic, and optical storage media produced about 5 exabytes of new information in 2002."[50] That is much more than a doubling of information production between 1999 and 2002. If we were drowning in information then, what is our situation now?

It is actually much better. Though we have not yet learned how to deal adequately with the onslaught of information, we are making headway—and that, really, is the revolution we are in the midst of, not one of quantity of information, but in managing it.

Even the blogs themselves, especially the ones acting as aggregators, are part of the attempt to manage the information explosion. As is the growing culture of linking on the Web, pressure towards *always* providing a pathway to the source of any bit of information, expanding and regularizing the network at the same time. The search engines, as they expand and refine, are another part of this. What we have yet to achieve is any means of quickly evaluating the information we receive. We have not yet learned to be adequately *neterate*.

However, the sheer mass of information and users on the Web is beginning to act as something of an antidote to the proliferation of "bad" information. Take for example, the question of Wikipedia: Many of my fellow college professors tell their students not to use Wikipedia as a source. Because it lacks a rigid editorial system (though it has developed more of one than it had at first), many professors do not trust it. Now, to be fair, I do not want my students to cite Wikipedia either, though for another reason, the same reason I do not want them citing the *Encyclopedia Britannica* or any other encyclopedia: neither is sufficiently authoritative. Both are starting points for exploration, not final destinations of the sort I want students to establish. Though I do not particularly care about the number of errors in either *Britannica* or Wikipedia (which does not really matter, if they are simply being used as introductory material in a search for deeper discussion), I was interested to see that there is not really that much difference between them, in the rate of errors, anyway—at least, not according to a study published in *Nature* magazine, which "revealed numerous errors in both encyclopaedias, but among 42 entries tested, the difference in accuracy was not particularly great: the average science entry in Wikipedia contained around four inaccuracies; Britannica, about three."[51] No encyclopedia should be seen as an end point for information assemblage; instead, each should be seen simply as a useful place for stopping and taking a look around.

Interestingly, Wikipedia is developing its own corrective process and replacement for a vertical editorial process through the extreme breadth of its horizontal process (though, as I have said, it has found it necessary to add a certain minimum of gatekeeping). Here, too, the horizontal and the vertical are integrating.

Chapter 6

Online Community, Online Utilization: The Christian Blog

Blogs and Other Online Entities Discussed in Chapter 6

Bending the Twigs, http://bendingthetwigs.blogspot.com
Bene Diction Blogs On, http://www.benedictionblogson.com
Between Two Worlds, http://theologica.blogspot.com
Bible Belt Blogger, http://spirituality.typepad.com/biblebelt
Careful Thought II, http://carefulthought.wordpress.com
Christianblog, http://www.christianblog.com
Christianity in the Raw's Blog, http://theologos.vox.com
Christian Studies, http://christianstudies.wordpress.com
Christian Thoughts, http://urbanchristianz.blogspot.com
Clippedwings, http://clippedwings.vox.com
Deep Furrows, http://deepfurrows.blogspot.com
A Guy in the Pews, http://aguyinthepew.blogspot.com
Moral Science Club, http://moralscienceclub.blogspot.com
MyChurch, http://www.mychurch.org
Pure Church, http://purechurch.blogspot.com
Simple Values, http://www.simplevalues.org
Take a Risk, http://www.xanga.com/Sarahbi

Is there no more to a blog than one might find in a church newsletter, as Nicholas Lemann seems to think is the case? To answer this question, I have explored a little bit of the religious blogosphere, hoping to discover just how the blogs are being used by just those people who once may have run the mimeograph machine in the church basement, producing those newsletters and providing a little bit of the glue to the church community. To my frustration and surprise, I was not able to see very much of what is going on, for the extent proved just too great, forcing me to limit my survey to just a small sampling of Christian blogs. There are, of course, blogs devoted to every religion imaginable. But the depth and diversity that I found in just this small sampling of Christian blogs made it clear to me, at least, that what we are seeing here is far beyond anything ever imagined for so simple and static a vehicle as a newsletter. As a matter of fact, what one finds in the Christian blogosphere is nothing less than inspiring and eye-opening in both extent and depth.

The purpose of this chapter is not to present a comprehensive survey of the religious blogosphere, and not even of the Christian subset. Instead, it is intended to provide a simple introduction to the incredible variety within the blogs, using the Christian blogs glimpsed here as examples of the careful thought and discussion that occurs regularly on the blogs. Because there is so much out there, what follows cannot be considered even representative. It is merely a taste of the possibilities and thoughts one can find online in one subset of the blogosphere.

It should be no surprise to anyone familiar with the Christian Bible that the blogs were quickly embraced by both individuals and groups within church communities. Blogging, after all, follows almost without fault the instructions of Jesus from the Sermon on the Mount (Matthew 5:14–16): "You are the light of the world. A city seated on a mountain cannot be hid. Neither do men light a candle and put it under a bushel, but upon a candlestick, that it may shine to all that are in the house. So let your light shine before men, that they may see your good works, and glorify your Father who is in heaven." What is surprising is the myriad of ways that Christians have found for shining their light—as many ways as any group of bloggers anywhere. In fact, the religious blogs, which the Christian ones dominate, may be the most diverse and vibrant of all the possible classifications within the blogosphere. The reason for this may be that the religious people attracted to the blogosphere are not looking for community in quite the way that other bloggers are.

Certainly, these bloggers do seek community, but it is based less on external agreement than on recognition of personal revelation. This may seem strange, for most religious bloggers come out of hierarchical religious traditions. There are few Quaker bloggers, for example, or Hinayana Buddhist ones. In most other situations, the blogger is reaching out to find those with similar interests, looking to externals. The Christian blogger more often is looking within for the things that may resonate with others, surely, but that arises from the individual and goes to the group, and not quite so much vice versa, as it is in most other blogging situations. In a sense, the religious blogger may best be seen as a cross between the political blogger—to whom relations to the external political world are the defining entities—and the social networkers—to whom the individual and his or her relations to their friends is paramount. This crossing of types provides a textured body of diaries of an intricacy and detail not found elsewhere.

There are, of course, many Christian blogs that are really political blogs coming from a background in the political right (or left, though there are many fewer of these). In their links, such blogs tend towards news sources and commentary rather than towards sites with specific spiritual foci. For the purposes of my exploration, I have given less emphasis to such blogs. In general, they are more predictable and less interesting than the other Christian blogs, falling into line with particular political movements and showing less of the intricacies of the individual personalities found in the more personal and reflective religious blogs.

For, in looking over Christian blogs, one is soon impressed by the breadth of thought and concern, and of the fluid nature of American Christianity, even within areas straitjacketed by preconceptions, such as evangelicalism. Take, for example, this passage from a guest post by D. W. Congdon on Faith and Theology:

> I grew up in your textbook American evangelical home: strong nuclear family, large extended family (presently over 50 first cousins), rooted in Scripture (devotions every night; Bible memory verses at every dinner), committed to biblical inerrancy and a male-female complementarianism (i.e., hierarchicalism), avid believers in six-day creationism, distrustful of anything related to the secular academy, loyal Republicans, Baptist heritage, descendants of Jonathan Blanchard (founder of Wheaton College), home-schooled, raised with strong moral principles, and active in our local non-denominational church at every level of ministry. And this description only scratches the surface.
>
> In writing this post, therefore, I do not come with any experience in moving from one established Christian tradition to another. I grew up and remain an American evangelical of sorts. But within the course of my life-time, evangelicalism became a much more fluid, malleable, and diverse entity. Within a single decade, I saw the rise of evangelical feminism, evangelical leftist politics, evangelical engagement with evolution (beyond creationism and ID), and most importantly, an evangelical engagement with ancient and contemporary theology in ways that had not been the case before. Of course, we might also mention the rise of the emerging church movement within American evangelicalism. Regardless of whether one sees this as a positive or negative development, it is at the very least indicative of how evangelicalism has expanded over recent years.[1]

Throughout the Christian blogosphere is a recognition of the inevitability of change and even of growth. The humility that is seen so rarely in the public "Christians" on the 24-hour news shows is generally front and foremost on the blogs. Rare is the railing against progress, technology, or the modern world that many nonbelievers and agnostics have come to expect—though that really should not be surprising. After all, these writers are all comfortable with blog technology. Most would certainly be called *neterate*. They are clearly people who look beyond what they already know.

Like all successful bloggers, Christian bloggers show their excitement at blog-ging in an almost evangelical way. That is, they want others to get involved and want to help them make their blogs work. Following in the footsteps of bloggers in almost every arena, Abraham Piper concocted a list of advices for Christian bloggers, addressed, in the best Christian tradition, to himself:

> Blog readers, I discovered, simply don't have time for me to write any old way I feel like. They're understandably impatient—but that doesn't mean they're uninterested. They want content—but they want it quick and easy.
>
> So I created a checklist of blog-writing essentials that I try to follow with each post—the main question being: *How can I write so that people will actually read this?*
>
> It's motivated by the golden rule, really: I enjoy and am served by blogs that follow these writing guidelines, so I want to follow them, too.
>
> Here's what I preach to myself when I sit down to blog:
>
> **Be yourself**
>
> You have ideas, and people are reading because they're interested. So <u>be you</u>.
>
> **Write less**
>
> Don't write any more than is necessary to make your point.
>
> This has nothing to do with whether or not long posts are good. People are just unlikely to read them, good or not.
>
> **Write to be scanned**
>
> Compose your posts so that your point is accessible to those who are not reading word-for-word, because *most people aren't.*
>
> Here's a list of what will usually make text scannable:
>
> - Putting your point at the beginning.
> - Composing short, one-point paragraphs.
> - Organizing with headers and sub-headers.
> - Setting lists apart with bullets or numbers.
> - Highlighting important words and phrases with bold or italics (but not all caps).
>
> **Use common keywords**
>
> *Vocabulary affects visibility*, so usually it's good to write with words that people are likely to search when they are interested in your topic.
>
> For instance, if someone is curious about the Bible, they will probably search "Bible," not "Scripture" or "God's Word," even though these are perfectly good synonyms.
>
> **Link a lot**
>
> With discretion, link to anything that will support your content.
>
> Also, linking does not mean condoning; so don't be afraid to send people to sites you disagree with. If you discuss the <u>KKK</u>, it may be useful to link to their site. (If only to show how lame it is—my goodness!)
>
> **Don't tease with titles**
>
> The best headlines are both eye-catching and content-rich. They are interesting and they state the main point of the post.

Bad: "Big News at Crossway!"

Good: "Justin Taylor Is Voting for Clinton"

Allow exceptions

Guidelines are not commandments. Break these as necessary—but do it on purpose.[2]

This last, of course, echoes George Orwell's advice at the end of "Politics and the English Language."

Another Christian blogger, Thabiti Anyabwile, took advantage of the first anniversary of his blog to write:

And in the last year, here are a few things I've learned and gained from regularly blogging and from those who blog.

1. *A bit more sanctification.* Boy, there's nothing like hitting "publish post" after writing some screed or critique or essay on some position and anticipating the response of others and the potential effect on someone to sanctify me a bit. The blogosphere is some time exhibit A for the truth of James 3:6—"And the tongue is a fire, a world of unrighteousness. The tongue is set among our members, staining the whole body, setting on fire the entire course of life, and set on fire by hell." And I'm ashamed of comments that I've made that prove this. Blogging has been sanctifying in speech.

2. *A lot more friends.* I'm one of those who envisioned this blog thing as essentially another chat room for lonely types ... Christians, yes, but lonely and in need of a real hobby. So, now, I'm either one of the lonely chat room types or, more likely the case, I've been again judgmental and flat wrong. I can't praise and thank God enough for the many people He's blessed me to meet in the last year. You may not know this ... but it's lonely being African American and Reformed and living in the Caribbean!

3. *It would be impossible to list all I've learned from fellow bloggers.*

4. *Christ is all!* That's the conclusion for me. After reading over hundreds of pages and thousands of lines, after writing my share, upon reflection, at its best, blogging reminds me that Christ is All! He is the One who unites me with so many other of His people across continents and time zones and cultures and educational levels and economic standings and every other natural boundary. I'm reminded by the blogosphere that Christ unites us to Himself as one new man and unites us to each other. When I've stumbled or misspoken, when others have been the same, I've lost count of the number of responses and emails and corrections and rebukes and encouragements that keep me and others coming to the cross of Christ, clinging to Him, rejoicing in Him, confessing and receiving yet more grace, growing in godliness, deepening our

affections for the Savior … and in the end, becoming more like Him. I'm thankful to the Lord for all the small and wonderful ways He's surprised me with Himself through this interesting thing called a "blog."[3]

Growth and community: these seem to be the points for satisfaction to Anyabwile—as they clearly are to most Christian bloggers. They are not looking to convert, but to talk about their religion in an atmosphere of acceptance and understanding. This fits well with the horizontal model of the blogs in general.

Not all Christian blogging does center on the individual, however. Just as in the rest of the blogosphere, the vertical has an important place, as well—in the guise of the church. There are sites devoted to specific churches and communities, and ever broader ones. Following the lead of MySpace, for example, a Web site called MyChurch has opened to provide a Christian parallel, but with significant differences. Where MySpace provides an open space for social networking, MyChurch is much more closed and controlled. In addition, MyChurch works through churches, and not simply individuals. In fact, it makes churches, and not the individual, the center of the site, stating that it is a "community space for your church" that can "extend church between Sundays" and will "expand your church walls."[4] Individuals are given their own pages, but these are tied to church affiliations.

With MyChurch, as with the rest of the blogs, there is no sense of creation of a "parallel" or virtual world of any sort. Just look at how it describes itself in the previous example, using "extend" and "expand" rather than claiming to offering something "new" or "different." So far, though I don't think that this is the most fruitful branch of the Christian blogosphere, the approach seems to be working:

> Owner and operator JC Media reports that MyChurch.org receives 2.5 million page views a month. It allows pastors to record and upload sermons and congregants to discuss them. Users can embed Bible passages into blogs, and organize and register for local events. The site allows access to electronic bulletins, classifieds, recent sermons, a U.S. church map, prayer requests, podcasts, comments, photos, and personal profiles, of course.
>
> "Conversations we've never had time for are coming together online," Pastor Dan Beasley, of the Calvary Community Church in Maryland, said in a prepared statement. "The profiles and pictures are revealing things about us that might take years to come out. We're seeing folks show their true gifts. People we didn't know as teachers are emerging in the blogs, and encouragement and mercy are shown in the comments."[5]

If any place in the blogosphere resembles a church newsletter at all, it is MyChurch. Its dynamic possibilities, however, make it about as much like a newsletter as a one-speed bicycle is like a Harley-Davidson motorcycle. Both may have two wheels, a seat, and handlebars, but not much else is similar.

Though MyChurch seems to be a success, and may prove to be an enduring part of both church life and the blogosphere, it will never surprise anyone, either in content or presentation. Beholden to the established church structures that provide its base, it will always be among the last to come onboard to anything new—as anyone who has ever tried to introduce change into any religious organization knows. Because churches do not have to respond with the same immediacy of many other institutions to cultural changes, it is extremely difficult to get them to move at all, and takes quite some time.

Individual belief, on the other hand, can change without synods or rulings by bishops.

For Americans, whose ancestors sometimes built churches in their pioneer communities before they had a preacher, let alone had decided on a denomination, the individual as responsible for his or her beliefs has always been something of a given in the United States. David Riesman describes the result of this tradition as "the invisible church: the union of people who, without organization, that is, formal organization, but through piety and through print (the Bible) feel close to one another and feel they 'belong' through some invisible set of bonds which are irontight. They are as sure of the existence of this church as a spy is sure of the writing he has just done with invisible ink; in both cases, the future will reveal the presence of the now-invisible."[6] The church is their creation. That is, it comes through them and after them, but need not precede them. Much like the blogs.

Frank Lockwood, the religion editor for the *Arkansas Democrat-Gazette* and a committed blogger and proprietor of Bible Belt Blogger, may have more of a political slant to his own blog (which is to be expected, for a reporter), but he is in an enviable position to look over the Christian blogosphere and comment upon it. He writes:

A religion blog can be an amen corner or a town-hall forum. It can be a bully pulpit or it can serve as an open microphone. It can appeal to a group of like-minded individuals or try to attract a broad cross-section.

With Bible Belt Blogger, I try to welcome everybody. I'm not there to preach or proselytize. I'm there to keep the discussion going. I'm kind of a facilitator. At times, I'm a referee.

Initially, my blog was a lonely place. Nobody knew about it when it debuted in July 2006. Nobody visited. But then, a debate broke out in the "comments" section and ten months later, it's still going. I've probably had 3,000 comments posted so far. (When I switched from the *Lexington Herald-Leader* in Kentucky to the *Arkansas Democrat-Gazette* in Little Rock, I had to erase some of the content which belonged to my old employer. The comments linked to those stories were also erased. Even so, I currently have 2327 comments on the site.)

I knew next to nothing about blogs when I started, but I've discovered that they're addictive. Oddly enough, you form virtual friendships with these people. You get to know their world views. Their pet peeves. You get to the point where you can almost complete each other's sentences.

It's a lot of work. I have to read every comment before it goes up to make sure it's not obscene, libelous or an ad hominem attack. If there's a factual error, I try to gently point it out. Blogs can rally large groups of like-minded people, and they've been incredibly influential in the religious community. The best source for information (and misinformation) about the Episcopal Church comes from blogs. There are conservative and liberal blogs that post news stories from around the globe concerning the split in the Anglican Communion. If there's a dispute in the Diocese of Lake Malawi in Central Africa, you'll read about it on a blog long before you see it in the *New York Times*. If a parish breaks away in central Kentucky, you'll find out about it on-line, long before you hear about it on NPR.

Bloggers were widely credited with helping to elect an outsider as president of the Southern Baptist Convention last summer. They help rally people from around the country who otherwise would never connect. Blogs can cater to religious "niche markets" in a way that older media outlets can't.

People need to read (and watch television news) with a skeptical eye. Some of the information—be it printed, on-line or over the airwaves—is wrong. Some of it is biased. Some of it lacks nuance. But over time, you learn who is trustworthy and who is error-prone.

Plus a good blogger will let you know where he or she is getting his or her information. I read the Drudge Report every day. A few people sniff at that. "How can you be sure he's right?", etc. Well, Drudge usually lets you know where he's getting his information. If he's linking to a story in the *New York Times*, I can be fairly confident that the story is legitimate …

Thus far, I haven't seen many blogs used (effectively at least) to convert the unconverted. I think blogs are better at rallying like-minded people or at sparking an intellectual debate than as evangelism tools.[7]

Lockwood is surely right: if my analysis of the blogosphere in general is at all correct, it will never become a place for conversion, be it religious, political, or elsewhere. The seeker may come to a blog, but the blogger can never come to the speaker—unless approached first. Successful proselytizing, evangelists from the first-century Christians to the Salvation Army have learned, has to occur where the target people are. And Lockwood's experience, in general, reflects the standard of the blogosphere: rarely is a blogger immediately successful (unless they come to the blog with an established reputation). It takes time and patience to succeed in the blogosphere, no matter the target community.

Watching with some surprise as Christian blogs exploded in number even in the early days of the blogosphere, in 2002, blogger Martin Roth divided Christian blogs into four groups:[8]

1. Catholic Blogs, which focus almost exclusively on church issues. When I first started looking into Christian blogs, I was surprised just how many were by Catholics. Roth (remember he was writing in 2002) found them focusing on church structures, especially in light of the various sexual abuse scandals. That seems to have changed. I did not find any where that was a major topic. In fact, the Catholic blogs seemed rather positive about the church.

2. Emerging-Church (Youth) Blogs, which try to deal with contemporary social and cultural problems. Emerging-church conversations seem particularly well suited to the blogs. However, identifying them as a particular strain distinct from others is a little difficult. In a sense, almost every Christian blog could be said to have elements of the emerging-church movement within it.

3. Expansive Blogs, where religion is but one of a variety of topics. These don't focus solely on religion, but on almost any topic that comes to the writer's mind. I would include many homeschooling blogs in this category, along with quite a few that have a political focus but religious overtones.

4. Experience Blogs, where the focus is on particular and personal relationships to the Lord in daily life. There is a depth to these blogs that can often be surprising, an openness, a willingness to make self-examination the center of conversation, but rarely in any sort of egotistical manner.

Perhaps a fifth could be added: Outreach Blogs, which describe the works of Christian life. These record the works that people are engaged in—not evangelical, but supportive. Missionary work where the focus is nutrition or health; soup kitchens; outreach to unwed mothers. I even saw one describing a project to change the oil in the cars of single working moms.

One blog of this last sort is part of the Simple Values Web site and ministry of Sharon Poarch. She has be instrumental in organizing rebuilding efforts along the Gulf Coast in the aftermath of hurricane Katrina, going down there a number of times herself. The trip in the early part of 2007 ended up as an eye-opener for the group and is recorded on the Simple Values blog. The last entry contains this:

> Please pray for this family and others like them in this neighborhood, that God will continue to shed His light on them.
> We saw a lot that week that we never expected ... guns stuck down the back of jeans, people living in squalor ... and people in need of a Savior, not a fix from the next drug available.

We hear it was so much worse six months ago … a people forgotten and
left to do themselves in … one way or another.

What they and so many others caught up in such situations—people
further burdened by the hurricane, people of low income, the elderly, single
parents—what they need is a hope … not a dead end street.

…and there are many more like them all up and down the Gulf Coast.[9]

The story is a wonderful one, and deserves telling on its own (and in more
detail than the blog gives). On the blog, it was particularly dramatic, for the
story was told while it was happening, one of the real advantages of the blogs
in any situation such as this. Briefly, the group was asked to redo a house in a
Black community that had not been touched, really, since the hurricane. The
owner, an elderly woman, was staying nearby with a daughter. A son and a
friend were "camped out" in the house, with no running water. They were not
much interested in the rebuilding work or in morning prayer: "The mission
field is not always with people who openly welcome you or who seem grateful
for help. Seasoned missionaries soon realize this. Appreciation just isn't considered a necessary part of the equation for why we do what we do."[10] Soon,
however, the group began to realize that the two men were dealing drugs out
of the house, and were not stopping because of the White Christians working
around them! Poarch let the team leader handle the problem: "Joel said he
was going to have a talk with the grandmother and just let her know what was
going on. In that loving and matter of fact way that Joel is so gifted with, he
explained to the grandmother what work we hoped to accomplish this week
and offered ideas of some things she and her family could do to help. Joel
then explained the little enterprise her boys had going in the front yard all day
and that he thought she ought to know about it. Joel told her that we wanted
to get a lot of work done this week but the boys' activity needed to move on
away from here. The grandmother and daughter told us they agreed and that
this should not be happening. They said they'd take care of the problem right
away." What happened the next day can be found on the Simple Values blog,
but it shows what patience, faith, and love can accomplish—as well as how
the blogs can bring the works of faith back home and to a broader community
in general.

What is important about this story is that it now becomes more than simply
a story to bring back home when it is used on a blog—it becomes part of the
small group's faith and its record in a way that the photographs (also on the
blog) could never do by themselves. In this way, Christian bloggers are cement-
ing both their works and their faith through the Web and their blogs. The fact
that such a story could be blogged almost as it happened brings both an immediacy and an importance to it that could not otherwise have been attained.

One thing seen over and over again on Christian blogs is the search for a
new congregation, generally resulting from the blogger's family moving to a

new community. One thing that struck me was that these searches are rarely exclusionary or judgmental, instead accepting the differences while seeking just the right fit. Mark Byron writes of his own search:

> Another interesting possibility is Victory Baptist, which is just down the road from our apartment. They seem Holy Spirit friendly, with a theme verse from Acts 1:8—"But you will receive power when the Holy Spirit has come upon you, and you will be my witnesses in Jerusalem and in all Judea and Samaria, and to the end of the earth."
>
> We've been partial to Vineyard churches, but the one in Lexington is a good hike away, a bit east of the UK campus on the NE side of town, and seems a bit on the left-side of Vineyards; they were running a "Doing Justice" series in March that focused on African development. It seems to be a bit more on the emergent side of things than our more Bapticostal Vineyard in Lakeland, which was founded by a Southern Baptist pastor who got blasted by the Holy Spirit and then given the left foot of disfellowship from the Baptists.
>
> If the Lexington Vineyard may be to the left, Porter Memorial Baptist a couple of miles to the west of our new locale definitely *isn't*. They showed up on Bene's [Bene Diction Blogs On] radar back in 2005 when a men's meeting got more than a bit on the jingoistic and militaristic side and a video of the event made the rounds of some left-leaning sites.... It seemed only a notch more patriotic than some of the Baptist churches I've hung my hat at in the past.[11]

Perhaps it should be no surprise to anyone familiar with Christianity in America that there are Christian blogs from so many and different perspectives. After all, the same is true of our churches.

One of the things that Christian bloggers, like political bloggers, have learned over the past few years, is that the blog can be a tool towards refining relations with political figures, even if that means contacting them by "snail mail." Glenn Penner, for example, writing on Persecuted Church Weblog, gives this "advice" for writing politicians:

> Over the years, I have seen a number of such examples of well-intentioned but ultimately useless correspondence. To that end, here are a few tips on how to write a letter that no one will read:
>
> 1. Quote the Bible. As much as I respect the Scriptures, using biblical passages in a letter to a politician will almost guarantee that it will not be taken seriously. You will appear to be a religious fanatic and not someone who has seriously thought about an issue.
> 2. Express your anger. Want your letter to be dismissed as hate mail? Use exclamation marks liberally, write in a preaching tone and include veiled threats of divine judgment.

3. Write to the wrong person. Not all letters of protest about federal policy should be written to the Prime Minister. Sometimes it is better to write to your local Member of Parliament or to a Minister. Find out who is the best person to receive a letter before you send it out.

4. Use a form letter or a petition. Personal, handwritten letters are better received than form letters and especially a petition. VOMC typically avoids making these available because of their relative ineffectiveness. The only person that they really benefit is the person writing is because of how easy they are to use. But is this really the point?

5. Write long letters. Enough said. Letters to politicians should be no more than a page long. Anything longer and you may be wasting your time and ink.

6. Cover many topics. Hey, while you have his or her attention, why not address a number of things that are bothering you? Instead, stick to one subject, write on it well and succinctly and then finish. Avoid the temptation to sneak other concerns in the back door.

7. Don't identify yourself. Keep your identity a secret. Surely this will add an air of mystery to your letter. Right ... all the way to the paper shredder.

8. Refuse to use proper titles. Show disrespect for them by referring to them by their first name. Address your letter to "Dear Scumbag." This will really get their attention! In truth, remember that politicians, ambassadors and all other government leaders are entitled to the respect that you can give them even if they make you angry sometimes. If you want to be taken seriously, address them by their proper title and salutation.[12]

One of the most cherished—and reviled—features of the blogs is the rant, the expression of outrage and frustration that wells up to the point where it has to be expressed ... either to a backyard wall or on a blog. Christians are not immune to the rant. In fact, some of them can rant with the best:

The core of a family is a mom and a dad. Every kid needs a mom and a dad. Those who treat us like we would like our actual family to treat us are not really biologically family, no matter how many times ya wanna click your hills and wish it wasn't so. Call families and marriages for what they are: dysfunctional and a poor representation of what they should be, but they ain't your family. On the other hand, I think civil unions aren't a bad thing for same-sex couples. Last time I checked, this was a free country, and consenting adults may act as they choose unless they are hurting or impinging on the rights of others.

Abortion is not a form of birth control. It is for a medical emergency. What i find very interesting is that for poor women who have abortions,

there is no choice for them. They are usually compelled because of their circumstances to have the procedure done. If they had the money, many of
these women would carry the kid to term. It is, I notice, the middle and
upper middle class that really has a choice, and when they abort a kid, they
do it because they have the money, it is a convenience they can afford. The
abortion industry is a billion dollar industry, and it has few, if any, regulations in place. There is a lot of money that changes hands ...

The great enemy of democracy is multinational corporations. Those who
run these things were not elected by anyone, and yet they determine so
much. I used to have a quote about fascism being corporatism by Mussolini,
but I lost the quote. The industrial/military complex is long gone, but it has
been replaced by the joining of the politico/media/lawyer cabal, and is even
more of a threat than what was during Cold War.

Global warming is a crock—it's just another system of control (Read M.
Creighton's *State of Fear*). Should we be conservationists? You bet! Is there a
problem with pollution? Of course. But should we fall under the modern
delusion that we are the masters of our circumstances and our fate and
decide to form nature into our own idea of what we think she should be?
Get this: Greenland was once so warm that the Viking set up farming communities ... and there was no industrial revolution happening at the time.
Should we still strive for clean air and water? Hell yes. The cloud of smog
that over hangs our major cities should and can be cut back. Fear is the big
seller, it gives politicians an issue, lawyers a chance to litigate, and the media
a story. ("It Could Happen Tomorrow!") But most of the debate going on
now is about power, control. Scientist, politicians, the Media ... they all are
vying to control the issue.

I seem to stand alone on my common sense platform—common sense is
the arch enemy of ideology. I'd be hit from both the Left and the Right for
this blog if I was doing it for a living or had anything close to a wide readership. I'll vote in '08, but please, God, send me someone I can actually vote
for that is qualified to lead.... [13]

Feel better now, blogger Martin Burry? Certainly, release is an important function of the blogs.

Many of those who are not familiar with the blogs are put off by the rants
on first encountering them. The ranters, though, rant on secure in their awareness that no one *has* to read them. And that few who really will pursue them
are likely to disagree—unless, like me, they simply appreciate a good rant, no
matter the topic. Unless stifled by desires for propriety, the blog rant stands a
good chance of becoming something of a genre on its own, examined and discussed in academic essays and on conference panels.

Sometimes, the rants get out of hand, but they are just as often a little
more gentle than Burry's and reflect the real frustrations of people with

artistic bent, say, who are as yet unable to succeed within the world of commercial art:

> My problem isn't that I haven't written a *good* book, it's that the book has two major problems: Too dark of themes for the Christian market and too much God for much of anyone else. "Secular" audiences, as the Christian markets call them, don't want to hear about a young girl shaking off her Catholic roots and finding a God that she can identify with on a personal level. The rape and all of that is fine, in fact, I could find several books that dealt with similar themes. Of course, none of them were first time novels, something that was also pointed out to me many many times. Apparently I need to write something fluffier and that can be marketed directly to a specific audience, and then they'll consider publishing the good stuff.[14]

In the case of the rant, it is not the community or the point that is important, merely the saying—though this writer certainly would like it if a publisher happened across the blog, was intrigued, and contacted her to find out more about the book. Unfortunately, many have used the rant to characterize the blogosphere as a whole when, quite clearly (as this chapter shows) much else is going on.

Much of what I found within the Christian blogosphere reminds me of nothing so much as the words of a group of Quaker elders assembled at Balby in England in 1656 with a quote from 2 Corinthians: "Dearly beloved Friends, these things we do not lay before you as a rule or form to walk by, but that all with the measure of Light which is pure and holy may be guided, and so in the light walking and abiding these may be fulfilled in the Spirit—not from the letter, for the letter killeth, but the Spirit giveth life." The role of the Christian blog has, for the most part, been one not of preaching but of demonstration and advice, often even addressed to oneself and arising from personal experience:

> So, after tearing down cynicism and delusion, what is it I'm saying I want to see? Reality married with hope.
>
> 1. See the needs of the world around us. Be fierce in your hatred of it. But don't get bogged down in the bigness of it and give up. Rather than focusing on AIDS in Africa, focus on AIDS in a small village in Mozambique. Change the lives of orphans in a chosen orphanage in Russia, rather than give up hope at the thought of all the orphans in the world. Remember that changed lives pay it forward! If you change the lives of a few, they will be inspired to change lives and so on. It does start with you and you can make a difference.
> 2. Be realistic in your expectations of people and accept that your friends, spouse, children, and family members will hurt you. Don't be shocked when it happens. Instead, be prepared and armed with a wealth of

forgiveness and a bank account of grace. Make note of every time you say or do something thoughtlessly or purposefully hurtful and put the grace you want to receive in that checking account. Write a grace check to the next person who hurts you.

3. Love lavishly and deeply. Love well. Don't hold back your heart just because people will hurt you. People will also love you and give you forgiveness and grace. The only way to heal wounds of pain is to allow them to be bandaged with love. Sounds cheesy, I know, but it's true. Therapy can help and I don't diss it, but it won't fix it completely. Buying stuff, being busy, accomplishing much, doing good deeds, having a good time, vacations: they soothe for a moment. But they won't remove the root because they're not the right tools.

Conclusion: Don't expect more than you should. Keep the faith. Let your hope endure. Love well. Jesus is the greatest example of this. The One who knew the hearts and thoughts of men walked among us who sinned against HIM, who betrayed Him, who rejected Him, and still went to the cross because He believed in the goodness of God's plan for salvation, His hope for us to be saved was enduring, and He loved us deeply and lavishly and withheld nothing from us, but gave His all.[15]

As should be clear by now, much of what is found in the Christian blogosphere has its analog in the blogosphere as a whole, including the group blog where individuals "congregate" to share opinions and to argue within certain assumptions of political belief or, in this case, religious faith. One such group, ChristianBlog, describes itself as follows:

ChristianBlog.Com is an online community of family oriented Christian Bloggers, and is devoted to providing an easy to use gathering place for Christians from around the world! ...

We have dedicated volunteers who review each and every blog entry to make sure that all content that is posted is family safe and Christian based. This means *(for some)* that ChristianBlog.Com might not be the best place for you ...

We are unlike nearly every other "blog" websites that exists! Our purpose and goal is not just to provide blogs for folks ... but rather to create an atmosphere where Christians actively participate in *other Christians* blogs! Through the use of a simple and free registration Christians can easily and quickly share their thoughts, faith, daily insights, and just life-in-general! By joining together we create a unique online community of Christian bloggers![16]

Group Christian blogs, the claim of ChristianBlog notwithstanding, are not really that different from other group blogs. All of them, except for the social-networking blogs, coalesce around a particular set of beliefs and attitudes. Their simple premise is that there is strength in numbers—something the group blogs are proving in a variety of venues.

To many Christians, the idea of a public expression of faith is a significant part of their belief, making the blogs almost a "godsend," allowing them to do easily and broadly what they had already been doing privately or among friends. No longer is it possible to make excuses about not having the time to get involved in discussions of faith and religion, for that can now be done in the odd spare moments snatched from just about any other activity—yet still in public. Blogger Jim Jordan makes an analogy to Alcoholics Anonymous when he writes:

> A mature Christian is a Christoholic. I know it sounds like alcoholic but that's the point. It's harder to be holier than thou when you're called a Christoholic. We can't get enough of Christ and we can't help ourselves. How embarrassing! Christian is too good a name for us. You know, Christian literally means "little Christ." No wonder being called a Christian goes to people's heads.
>
> Christoholic is much better. It sounds out of balance, sloppy, humiliating and uncoordinated—which means it's spot on when characterizing a Christian who contemplates Christ every day. It fits the bill of someone who stumbles all the time and RECOGNIZES that they stumble. And it summarizes a person who cannot get enough of Jesus Christ.
>
> So there. Good evening, my name is Jim Jordan and I'm a Christoholic. (Crowd waves "Hi, Jim!") How about you?[17]

As with AA, another important aspect of religion is encouragement, of finding a group of like-minded people or ones who, at least, are going through problems one faces oneself. This is important to Christians just as it is to alcoholics, for it is quite easy to drift away from careful living in what Quakers call "the light."

> Ever wonder why you find it so hard to grow in God? Do you ever feel frustrated by your level (or lack) of spirituality? I can't give you all the reasons you might not be growing in God, but I can definitely point out one: You.
>
> If you've been a Christian for any length of time, you know how hard it is to "go through." How hard it can be to face trial after trial, tribulation after tribulation. How long sleepless nights lead to long empty days until you finally feel you've HAD ENOUGH! That if this "season" wasn't over, it was definitely time for it to be over. So you take matters into your own hands.
>
> You begin to pray a little less. And hang out with your friends a little more. Or watch a little more tv. Or pay a little more attention to that cutie who sits across from you at work.

Anything to avoid doing what you need to do: spend more time with God. Get through these circumstances. Spiritually grow.

I find that many of us cut off our spiritual growth in one of two ways. We either begin to neglect our spiritual activities (prayer, Bible study, meditation and fasting) or throw ourselves into physical activities to avoid thinking about those things. Our bodies (or our flesh) can operate in direct opposition to God in many ways, and we often pursue physical activity in order to avoid the things of God. You know what I mean—you start to eat a little more or tv becomes oh so appealing suddenly. You engage in more sex, do a little more drinking or hang out more than usual.

Here's a sad truth to all that activity: you can delay, but you cannot deny. You can avoid what God is trying to tell you, detour from your trial or tribulation, but it is never going to go away.

Until you deal with what is required of you, you will have to re-visit that territory again and again—until you get it right.

So next time you find yourself in a tough spot, learn to bear it. Go through what you have to go through, cry when you need to cry and.... get past it. God truly designs trials to bring out the best in us, so be assured that the "you" that waits on the other side of the circumstances will be well worth the pain you had to go through to get there![18]

While blogs cannot bring outsiders in very easily, they certainly do provide something to grasp for those who might find themselves beginning to slip away from their systems of belief. The active nature of the blogs even ensures that someone will respond to just about any cry for help. No one with access to the blogosphere is ever totally alone.

Still, one of the limitations of blogs of all sorts is that they usually are not much good for outreach, for rarely are people willing to spend much time with blogs that present views at odds with their own. Though the majority of Christian bloggers are comfortable with this, and use their blogs to help bolster each other rather than trying to change people's minds on any particular issue, some do try, joining in the discussions within other online manifestations of community for the purposes of conversion. The results are rarely satisfying for anyone, the evangelist driven off with bad feelings on all sides.

Though there are quite a number of issues raised on Christian blogs, few of them draw the responses that homeschooling does. The homeschooling movement has grown most rapidly within religious communities and the blogs allow for efficient communication among homeschoolers, allowing swapping of ideas and programs, and providing a certain level of emotional support. Even though there are now huge numbers of homeschoolers, their numbers are almost insignificant when held up against the total number of children in America. The blogs help keep the adherents of homeschooling from feeling alone, reinforcing the motivations that led to its adoption in the first place:

> Our primary goal in homeschooling is to teach our children to love God
> and to serve Him in everything they do. We teach science as the study of
> His creation; mathematics as His order for the universe; literature, art, and
> music as the fruits of His inspiration; history as His plan for humanity;
> health and physical education as taking care of His precious gift of our
> bodies; and religion as His instructions for how we should live our lives here
> on Earth. We strive to provide our children with the tools (spiritual, aca-
> demic, and practical) that they will need in their future vocations.[19]

Though faith may be strong, there is emotional satisfaction in finding others
who agree, and who are striving in a similar manner.

Related to homeschooling (though one should not assume that Christian
homeschoolers are creationists or adherents of Intelligent Design), evolution,
of course, rises as a topic on Christian blogs quite often, but frequently in
ways that do not fit the stereotype of the Christian as a creationist:

> And most public opinion polls show nearly half of all Americans reject
> evolution.
>
> Why?
>
> Now part of the explanation is that these commenters and most Americans
> are unfamiliar with the quite strong evidence for evolution—from the fossil
> record, biogeography, and most recently from genetics. All strongly support the
> theory that species evolve through natural selection. The recent genetic evidence
> is particularly compelling. As Dr. Francis Collins has repeatedly said, there is
> no reputable biologist or geneticist who doubts that evolution accurately
> described the development of species. Indeed, it is foundational to biology.
>
> But I think that the hostility to evolution may arise from a more funda-
> mental issue than lack of knowledge—acceptance of evolution suggests a
> very different view of how God acts in the world than that explained in
> Genesis and other biblical accounts of God's actions in the world. Under
> this view of God, when God wants something done, God acts directly—he
> creates every species directly and individually, he parts the Red Sea, and he
> smites Israel's enemies.
>
> Acceptance of evolution, however, suggests that God acts in more indi-
> rect ways, and this is disturbing to anyone brought up to believe a more
> direct view of God's action in the world.[20]

Contentions about evolution are common within the Christian blogosphere,
where there are advocates for every position. Discussion, however, is a lot less
acrimonious than one might be led to believe through depictions of the debate
within the commercial news media. Though there certainly are people who
insist that dinosaurs and humans once lived side-by-side, the debate, in general, is much more sophisticated and informed.

If the blogs are any indication, the American Christian community is much more inquisitive than its stereotypical image suggests. There is an emphasis on growth and change within a Christian context. The idea of questioning and constantly learning certainly shows itself as important to the Christian blogs, as this brief post, along with its short updates, shows:

> I've just finished reading *Murder in the Cathedral* by T. S. Eliot. It's a drama in verse, a historical fiction of the martyrdom of St. Thomas Becket. To summarize, God acts and everyone else reacts to this action. The question for the reader is: where do you stand? I may add a quote to this a bit later.
>
> {a bit later ...}
>
> OK. I've read this before and it's all right, but what is the big deal about it? To me, it's kind of a *fait accompli*. The versification is fine but a bit heavy on the rhymes. Some good lines here and there. I can't say that I ever have had much sympathy, much resonance, with Eliot. And listening to his recording of *The Wasteland* in college didn't help either.
>
> {several days later ...}
>
> It occurs to me that I didn't read this work with an open mind. That is, I read it in a way similar to how I (too often, but less now than once) sometimes read or listen to Scripture: yes, yes, I've heard all this before. Even now, some stray impressions have sneaked past the barbed-wire of my world-weariness, suggesting that this little drama has something to do with my life.[21]

These are not the words of someone so limited by belief that he cannot change or grow, but of a person with sufficient intellect and curiosity to be able to recognize the barriers he has created in his own life and to manage to overcome them.

Home Bible study has been at the core of protestant Christianity since the Reformation, and has become important to Catholics as well. Daily readings and discussion are an important part of the faith of many. So, it is no surprise that the Bible and the history of belief have become an important part of Christian blogs:

> The purpose of this site is to present studies of the Bible, and examine Christianity from a historical and theological perspective. Contemporary Christianity is well known for its division into many different sects, and a common aim of many Christians is to determine what is right doctrine (orthodoxy), and right practice (orthopraxy), as originally taught by the apostles.
>
> The return to apostolic Christianity is considered a Holy Grail by many Christians, and an impossible endeavour by others. Some Christians believe that apostolic Christianity is irrelevant to subsequent Christians, some

believe it is impossible to define apostolic Christianity, and some believe that apostolic Christianity can be (and has been), legitimately replaced by developments and innovations in doctrine and practice by later generations.[22]

The point is not to *tell* what is true, but to outline the differences in belief and to explore their backgrounds in the Bible and the long history of Christian faith.

Christian bloggers can even manage to bring their faith into such mundane problems as the unmet need to lose weight, making even that into an entry into discussion of how, even in faith, there can be disagreement:

> I'm getting to the point in life where exercise is not just a nice-to-do thing. In the few years since I retired from the service I've managed to pack on about 15 pounds, and unfortunately, it doesn't come off as easily as it went on. Along with the exercise has to come a change in diet, and I've grudgingly had to admit that a healthy lifestyle is necessary for a healthy body. It's a lot more fun (and productive) when all the parts work together.
>
> The church is no different, and Paul makes frequent reference to the health and unity of the (church) body. Romans 14 and 15 go into detail about our relations as believers with other believers. These other believers are the members of the body that he refers to 1 Corinthians 12. The unity of the body is not a lockstep, robotic approach to faith, but rather, a united front that we should be showing to a faithless world. In Romans 15:5–7, he says:
>> "May the God who gives endurance and encouragement give you a spirit of unity among yourselves as you follow Christ Jesus, so that with one heart and mouth you may glorify the God and Father of our Lord Jesus Christ. Accept one another, then, just as Christ accepted you, in order to bring praise to God." (Romans 15:5–7, NIV)
>> We are going to disagree with other believers, and that's okay. As a kidney, I can get fed up with the spleen and that whiny endocrine gland, but we all need to function together.[23]

As with so much else, the Christian blogs demonstrate not only that the blogs themselves are a great deal more complex and interesting than dismissive stereotypes might lead one to believe. Like other bloggers, Christian bloggers are not generally close-minded advocates of simplistic positions. If they were, they probably would not blog (or would not blog for long), for the very nature of the blogs demands an openness to disagreement. One can "shout" and "pound one's feet," but one also must—to succeed in the blogosphere—respect the views of others, just as we find ourselves doing in most face-to-face situations.

It is true: one rarely really encounters those whose views are quite counter to one's own on the blogs (unless one goes out and seeks them) but, even among friends, complete agreement is unusual. Just as when we discuss over coffee, we find that, in the blogosphere, we tailor our presentation of our beliefs to the immediate community. We find, in fact, that we must. Response is part of the new writing found on the blogs in ways that had been distanced from much written behavior since the advent of print. Religious bloggers, like the rest of the blogosphere, are now able to participate in a discussion greater than anything possible just a decade ago.

Church newsletters? Sure, the Christian blogs may be that—but they are also, as I hope I have shown, a great deal more.

Conclusion

I t will be decades before we have a clear view of what the blogs are, exactly, and how they have affected American—and world—society. That, however, does not mean we should not be talking about them, arguing over them and on them. Our views, while not conclusive, will be part of our final cultural evaluation of the blogs, no matter what that turns out to be.

As people become increasingly *neterate*, I am sure that the hysteria over the dangers of the online extensions of our world will begin to die down. We are scared of what we do not know and of what we cannot control. Right now, even the most net savvy of us knows little of what the Web may really become—the changes are too fast and generally too unexpected for any of us to be able to grasp the whole. And efforts to control the Web—or any aspect of the current communications revolution—seem to backfire almost as soon as they are introduced. Eventually, we will come to terms with the Web, but the process will be neither the expected nor the planned.

In writing this book, I spent a great deal of time reading the critics of technological culture of half a century ago. Though I find little of what they said relevant to our current situation, they all helped me understand a little more clearly (or so I believe right now) what is happening today. My hope is that a scholar fifty years in the future, in looking back on this book, will have the same experience.

BLOGROLL

One thing about a blogroll is that it is never complete or comprehensive. This one certainly is not. Like any blogroll, these are simply some of the blogs I have visited over the past months—not all of them, by any means, but ones that, for one reason or another, caught my attention for a moment.

Together, they provide nothing more than a starting point into the blogs, and from my particular biases (not that I agree with the positions of every one of them). If you use these online, you will find that most have their own blogrolls. If you like what you see on a particular blog, click on some of the blogroll recommendations. By that pattern, you will begin to create your own personal blogroll.

One of the biggest problems on the Web is deciding what information you can trust, which is why the blogroll, and a personal list of favorites, is so important. Over time, a reader of blogs begins to be able to discern between those that have no substance (or nothing of interest to the particular reader) and those that do. The reader starts to learn to trust certain writers and sites, and to use them to spread out to others, beginning to negotiate the cacophony of the Web in something of an orderly manner.

There is more on the Web than any of us (or any book, any list) can encompass. We need to develop personal ways of focusing on only what we really need or want— that is part of becoming *neterate*. Blogrolls, and personal lists of favorites, are a good start towards that.

If you use the list here either as a starting point for exploring the blogs or as an experienced blog reader seeking broader exposure, rest assured, you will find little about breakfast cereals and less by "social isolates" in pajamas. These bloggers are all dynamic writers intent on engaging their readers, either in dialogue or just in thought. They are all trying to further communities of one sort or another. Rarely are they simply showing off or bragging—their agendas are much more expansive than that. These are not necessarily the best of the blogs, or the most representative. They are merely blogs I have encountered that sparked interest.

Because I have provided lists of the relevant blogs referred to in the chapters of this book, I have not broken the blogs listed here into sections (and be warned: this is not simply a compilation of those lists). Many of these provide a hint to their topics through their names, though some do not. It is important, in approaching the blogs, to experiment and to rely on serendipity. All I will say about these blogs is that each has something to offer. No visit to any will be completely wasted.

Althouse, http://althouse.blogspot.com
AMERICAblog, http://www.americablog.com
Andrew Keen: On Media, Culture, and Technology, http://andrewkeen.typepad.com
The Angry Black Woman, http://theangryblackwoman.wordpress.com
Bending the Twigs, http://bendingthetwigs.blogspot.com
Bene Diction Blogs On, http://www.benedictionblogson.com
Between Two Worlds, http://theologica.blogspot.com
Bible Belt Blogger, http://spirituality.typepad.com/biblebelt
Bitch Ph.D., http://bitchphd.blogspot.com
Blogging Brande, http://bloggingbrande.blogspot.com
BlogHer, http://blogher.org
Blog Time Passing, http://lancestrate.blogspot.com
BoingBoing, http://boingboing.net
Burningbird, http://burningbird.net
Cahiers de Corey, http://joshcorey.blogspot.com
Careful Thought II, http://carefulthought.wordpress.com
Caveat Lector, http://cavlec.yarinareth.net
Christian Blog, http://www.christianblog.com
Christianity in the Raw's Blog, http://theologos.vox.com
Christian Studies, http://christianstudies.wordpress.com
Christian Thoughts, http://urbanchristianz.blogspot.com
Clippedwings, http://clippedwings.vox.com
Cognitive Diss, http://cognitive-diss.blogspot.com
Confessions of an Aca-Fan, http://www.henryjenkins.org
The Constant Observer, http://spap-oop.blogspot.com
Creating Passionate Users, http://headrush.typepad.com
Creek Running North, http://www.faultline.org
Crooked Timber, http://www.crookedtimber.org
Crooks and Liars, http://www.crooksandliars.com
Crowdsourcing, http://crowdsourcing.typepad.com
Culture Industry, http://kulturindustrie.blogspot.com
Daily Kos, http://www.dailykos.com
Deep Furrows, http://deepfurrows.blogspot.com
Diaryland, http://diaryland.com
Digby's Hullabaloo, http://digbysblog.blogspot.com
Double Articulation, http://doublearticulation.blogspot.com
Drew's Marketing Minute, http://www.drewsmarketingminute.com
ePluribus Media, http://scoop.epluribusmedia.org
Every Other Day, http://www.kickingwind.com
Ezra Klein, http://ezraklein.typepad.com
Eschaton, http://atrios.blogspot.com
FireDogLake, http://www.firedoglake.com
Freedom to Tinker, http://www.freedom-to-tinker.com
Free Exchange on Campus, http://www.freeexchangeoncampus.org
Ghostfooting, http://ghostfeet.wordpress.com
Grasping Reality With Both Hands, http://delong.typepad.com

Greenpoint Dog Log Blog, http://www.newyorkshitty.com
Greg Palast: Journalism and Film, http://www.gregpalast.com
A Guy in the Pews, http://aguyinthepew.blogspot.com
Heatstrings, http://heatstrings.blogspot.com
Heavens to Betsy, http://annamartinebell.blogspot.com
Huffington Post, http://www.huffingtonpost.com
If I Ran the Zoo, http://tehipitetom.blogspot.com
Information Wants to Be Free, http://meredith.wolfwater.com/wordpress/index.php
Informed Comment, http://www.juancole.com
Instapundit, http://www.instapundit.com
Isola di Rifiuti, http://isola-di-rifiuti.blogspot.com
James Harris, http://jamboharris.blogspot.com
kNOw Future Inc. http://knowfuture.wordpress.com
LanguageHat, http://www.languagehat.com
Language Log, http://itre.cis.upenn.edu/~myl/languagelog
Lawyers, Guns and Money, http://lefarkins.blogspot.com
Lessig Blog, http://www.lessig.org/blog
The Little Professor, http://littleprofessor.typepad.com
LiveJournal, http://www.livejournal.com
Lorcan Dempsey's Weblog, http://orweblog.oclc.org
Mark Byron, http://markbyron.typepad.com/main
Martin Roth Christian Commentary, http://martinrothonline.com
Michael Peverett, http://michaelpeverett.blogspot.com
Moral Science Club, http://moralscienceclub.blogspot.com
MyDD, http://www.mydd.com
My Left Wing, http://www.myleftwing.com
Nomades Advanced Technologies Interactive Workshop, http://www.natiw.ch/blog
One Flew East, http://www.audsandens.blogspot.com
On the Left Tip, http://onthelefttip.blogspot.com
O'Reilly Radar, http://radar.oreilly.com
Pandagon, http://pandagon.net
Persecuted Church Weblog, http://persecutedchurch.blogspot.com
Powerline, http://www.powerlineblog.com
Prelinger Library Blog, http://prelingerlibrary.blogspot.com
Pure Church, http://purechurch.blogspot.com
Roger Ailes, http://rogerailes.blogspot.com
Rosenblumtv, http://rosenblumtv.wordpress.com
Samizdat Blog, http://samizdatblog.blogspot.com
Shadmia's World, http://shadmia.wordpress.com
Sharp Sand, http://www.sharpsand.net
Simple Values, http://www.simplevalues.org
Startling Bleats of Tomorrow, http://lileks.com/bleats/index.html
Swoonrocket, http://swoonrocket.blogspot.com
Take a Risk, http://www.xanga.com/Sarahbi
Talking Points Memo, http://www.talkingpointsmemo.com
Tenser, Said the Tensor, http://tenser.typepad.com/tenser_said_the_tensor

Tenured Radical, http://tenured-radical.blogspot.com
The Try-Works, http://www.tryworks.org
The Unconventional Truth, http://theunconventionalcouchsurfingtruth.blogspot.com
University Diaries, http://margaretsoltan.phenominet.com
The Valve, http://www.thevalve.org
Waggish, http://www.waggish.org
With Hands Held High, http://whhh.blogspot.com

Notes

Preface

1. Keen, Andrew, "Blogs Are Boring," *Andrew Keen: On Media, Culture, and Technology*: http://andrewkeen.typepad.com/ (viewed 6/6/07).

2. Reid, David, "The Evolution of the Web," *Nomades Advanced Technologies Interactive Workshop*: http://www.natiw.ch/blog/index.php/?p=40#more-40 (viewed 6/6/07).

3. Mentor, "Couchsurfing 2.0 Not Really 2.0," *The Unconventional Truth*: http://theunconventionalcouchsurfingtruth.blogspot.com/2007/05/couchsurfing-20-not-really-20.html (viewed 6/6/07).

4. Shadmia, "Is Google Big Brother?" *Shadmia's World*: http://shadmia.wordpress.com/2007/06/04/is-google-big-brother/ (viewed 6/6/07).

5. Rosenblum, Michael, "The Empire Strikes Back," *Rosenblumtv*: http://rosenblumtv.wordpress.com/2007/06/06/the-empire-strikes-back/ (viewed 6/6/07).

6. Howe, Jeff, "Andrew Keen's Cult of the Amateur," *Crowdsourcing*: http://crowdsourcing.typepad.com/cs/2007/06/andrew_keens_cu.html (viewed 6/6/07).

Chapter 1: An Introduction to the Blogs

1. Habermas, Jürgen, *The Structural Transformation of the Public Sphere: An Inquiry into a Category of Bourgeois Society*, trans. Thomas Burger (Cambridge, MA: MIT Press, 1991), 27 (1962).

2. Habermas, 30.

3. Habermas, 141.

4. Habermas, 160.

5. Habermas, 161.

6. Barlow, Aaron, *The Rise of the Blogosphere* (Westport, CT: Praeger Publishers, 2007).

7. Habermas, 36.

8. Habermas, 36.

9. Rosen, Jay, "Why We're Doing This," *Assignment Zero*: http://zero.newassignment.net/about (viewed 4/27/07).

10. Habermas, 37.

11. Rosedale, Philip, "Alter Egos," *Forbes*, May 7, 2007, Vol. 179, Issue 10, 76–80.

12. *Second Life*: http://secondlife.com/whatis/ (viewed 4/14/07).

13. Dick, Philip, "How to Build a Universe That Doesn't Fall Apart Two Days Later," *I Hope I Shall Arrive Soon* (Garden City, NJ: Doubleday, 1985), 6.

14. Dick, 5.

15. *Second Life*, http://secondlife.com/ (viewed 4/14/07).

16. *Second Life*: Create an Avatar, http://secondlife.com/whatis/avatar.php (viewed 4/14/07).

17. Poster, Mark, "Postmodern Virtualities" (Oxford: Blackwell, 1995): http://www.humanities.uci.edu/mposter/writings/internet.html (viewed 4/15/07).

18. Burke, Kenneth, *Permanence and Change* (New York: New Republic, 1936), 220.

19. Sapir, Edward, "The Status of Linguistics As a Science," in *Edward Sapir: Selected Writings in Language, Culture, and Personality*, David Mandelbaum, ed. (Berkeley: University of California Press, 1986), 162 (160–166).

20. Skinner, B. F., *Verbal Behavior* (Englewood Cliffs, NJ: Prentice-Hall, 1957), 408. Quotes reprinted with permission of B. F. Skinner Foundation.

21. Gans, Herbert, "The Creator-Audience Relationship in the Mass Media: An Analysis of Movie Making," in Bernard Rosenbery and David Manning White, eds., *Mass Culture: The Popular Arts in America* (Glencoe, IL: Free Press, 1957), 317 (315–324).

22. Aspan, Maria, "New Republic Suspends an Editor for Attacks on Blog," *The New York Times*, 9/4/06: http://www.nytimes.com/2006/09/04/technology/04republic.html?ex=1315022400&en=cc629c6ec5d5805d&ei=5088&partner=rssnyt&emc=rss.

23. "Sock Puppets," FAQs, *dKosopedia*: http://www.dkosopedia.com/wiki/DailyKos_FAQ#Sock_Puppets (viewed 4/23/07).

24. Ong, Walter, *Orality and Literacy*, 2nd edition (New York: Routledge: 2002), 17.

25. Skinner, 394.

26. Skinner, 382.

27. State Examinations Commission (Ireland), Junior Certificate Examination 2006, English, Chief Examiner's Report: http://www.examinations.ie/archive/examiners_reports/cer_2006/JC_English_2006.pdf.

28. Skinner, 385.

29. Skinner, 384.

30. Skinner, 277–278.

31. Skinner, 373.

32. Skinner, 376.

33. Skinner, 280.

34. Dumenco, Simon, "Web 2.0? Not so Fast—Say Hello to Web 1.9 (if that)," *Advertising Age*, April 16, 2007, Vol. 78, Issue 16, 32.

35. Skinner, 376–377.

36. Skinner, 374.

37. Whorf, Benjamin, "The Relation of Habitual Thought and Behavior to Language," in *Language, Culture, and Personality, Essays in Memory of Edward Sapir*, Leslie Spier, ed. (Menasha, WI: Sapir Memorial Publications Fund, 1941), reprinted in *Language Thought and Reality: Selected Writings of Benjamin Lee Whorf*, John Carroll, ed. (Cambridge, MA: MIT Press, 1956), 156 (134–159).

38. Ong, 115.

39. Ong, 116.

40. Ong, 116.

41. See Ulmer, Gregory, *Internet Invention: From Literacy to Electacy* (New York: Longman, 2002).

42. Ong, 119–120.

43. Ong, 120.

44. Ong, 122.

45. Ong, 123.

46. Ong, 127.

47. Peirce, Charles, "How to Make Our Ideas Clear." In *Philosophical Writing* (New York: Dover Books, 1955), 30.

48. Ong, 128–129.

49. Gray, 22–24.

50. Gray, 24.

51. Gray, 25.

52. Ong, 133–134.

53. Lichtenstein, Bill, "The Transmission of Experience," *The Infinite Mind*, 10/18/06: http://www.lcmedia.com/mind475.htm.

54. Rosedale, 77.

55. The Weblog Awards 2006: http://2006.weblogawards.org/ (viewed 4/24/07).

56. Academic Blog Portal: http://www.academicblogs.org/wiki/index.php/Main_Page (viewed 4/24/07).

57. DeLong, Brad, "The Invisible College," *The Chronicle of Higher Education*, 7/28/06: http://chronicle.com/free/v52/i47/47b00801.htm (viewed 4/24/07).

58. Burstein, Miriam, email correspondence with the author, 4/26/07.

59. Tribble, Ivan, "Bloggers Need Not Apply," *The Chronicle of Higher Education*, 7/8/2005: http://chronicle.com/jobs/2005/07/2005070801c.htm.

60. Baker, Stephen and Heather Green, "Blogs Will Change Your Business," *Business-Week*, 5/2/2005: http://www.businessweek.com/magazine/content/05_18/b3931001_mz001.htm.

61. McClellan, Drew, email to Aaron Barlow, 5/30/07.

62. Conlin, Michelle, "Web Attack," *Business Week*, April 16, 2007, Issue 4030, 54–56.

63. Keen, Andrew, *The Cult of the Amateur* (New York: Doubleday, 2007), 18.

64. "About Club for Growth," *The Club for Growth*: http://www.clubforgrowth.org/about.php (viewed 4/25/07).

65. "About TPM Café," *TPM Café*: http://www.tpmcafe.com/node/4 (viewed 4/24/07).

66. Herring, Susan, et al., "Bridging the Gap: A Genre Analysis of Weblogs," *BROG Papers*: http://www.blogninja.com/DDGDD04.doc (viewed 4/20/07).

67. Lileks, James, *Lileks.com*: http://lileks.com/index.html (viewed 4/25/07).

CHAPTER 2: THE BLOGS IN SOCIETY

1. Keen, Andrew, *The Cult of the Amateur* (New York: Doubleday, 2007), 3.

2. Keen, 64–65.

3. Farkas, Meredith, "Balancing the Online Life," *American Libraries*, January 2007, Vol. 38, Issue 1, 42–45, 42.

4. http://radar.oreilly.com/archives/2007/03/call_for_a_blog_1.html.

5. http://headrush.typepad.com/creating_passionate_users/2007/03/as_i_type_this_.html.

6. Nakashima, Ellen, "Sexual Threats Stifle Some Female Bloggers," *The Washington Post*, 4/31/07: http://www.washingtonpost.com/wp-dyn/content/article/2007/04/29/AR2007042901555_pf.html.

7. Moulitsas, Markos (writing as "Kos"), "Death Threats and Blogging," *Daily Kos*: http://www.dailykos.com/storyonly/2007/4/12/22533/9224 (viewed 4/20/07).

8. Clarke, Chris, "This Just In: Markos Moulitsas Is an Idiot," *Creek Running North*: http://faultline.org/index.php/site/comments/this_just_in_markos_moulitsas_is_an_idiot/ (viewed 4/20/07).

9. Leary, Patrick, "Free Speech, Quality Control, and Flame Wars: Sticking to the Topic on SHARP-L and VICTORIA," *Academe*, January/February 2007, Vol. 93, Issue 1, 50–52, 50.

10. "What Is BlogHer's Long-Term Vision?" *BlogHer*: http://blogher.org/node/927 (viewed 4/29/07).

11. Riesman, David, "The Ethics of We Happy Few," *Individualism Reconsidered* (New York: Free Press, 1954), 46–47.

12. Harris, Chris, "Five Reasons Not to Blog," *School Library Journal*, April 2007, Vol. 53, Issue 4, 24.

13. Harris, 24.

14. Harris, 24.

15. Harris, 24.

16. Harris, 24.

17. Harris, 24.

18. Anahita, Sine, "Blogging the Borders: Virtual Skinheads, Hypermasculinity, and Heteronormativity," *Journal of Political and Military Sociology*, Summer 2006, Vol. 34, Issue 1, 144.

19. Anahita, 151.

20. Holloway, Sarah, and Gill Valentine, *Cyberkids: Children in the Information Age* (London: RoutledgeFalmer, 2003), 10.

21. Holloway and Valentine, 10.

22. Claburn, Thomas, "Digg Rebellion Shows That Crowd Is Law," *Information Week*, 5/2/07: http://www.informationweek.com/software/showArticle.jhtml;jsessionid=3ETMP1SE2SYF4QSNDLPSKH0CJUNN2JVN?articleID=199203386.

23. Howe, Irving, "Notes on Mass Culture," *Mass Culture: The Popular Arts in America* (Glencoe, IL: Free Press, 1957), Bernard Rosenberg and David Manning White, eds., 496 (496–503), reprinted from *Politics*, Vol. 5, Spring, 1948, 120–123.

24. Howe, 497.

25. Howe, 399.

26. Peirce, Charles, "How to Make Our Ideas Clear." In *Philosophical Writings* (New York: Dover Books, 1955), 25–26.

27. MacDonald, Dwight, "A Theory of Mass Culture," *Diogenes* 3 (Summer, 1953), reprinted in Bernard Rosenberg and David Manning White, eds., *Mass Culture: The Popular Arts in America* (New York: Free Press, 1957), 60 (59–73).

28. McLuhan, Marshall, *Understanding Media* (Cambridge, MA: MIT Press, 1964), 22–23.

29. Friedberg, Anne, "The Virtual Window," in David Thorburn and Henry Jenkins, eds., *Rethinking Media Change: The Aesthetics of Transition* (Cambridge, MA: MIT Press, 2003), 345–346 (337–353).

30. Postman, Neil, *Amusing Ourselves to Death* (New York: Viking, 1985).

31. Holloway and Valentine, 12.

32. Barlow, Aaron, *The Rise of the Blogosphere* (Westport, CT: Praeger Publishers, 2007).

33. Lemann, Nicholas, "Amateur Hour," *The New Yorker*, August 7, 2006, Vol. 82, Issue 24, 44–49, 47.

34. Burke, Kenneth, *Permanence and Change* (New York: New Republic, 1936), 17.

35. Lemann, 48.

36. Lemann, 48.

37. Cohn, David, "What Are Citizen Journalists Good For?" *newassignment.net*: http://www.newassignment.net/blog/david_cohn/jan2007/04/what_citizen_jou (viewed 3/11/07).

38. "Why Bloggers Should Use Creative Commons Licenses," *iCommons*: http://icommons.org/2007/03/28/why-bloggers-should-use-creative-commons-licences/ (viewed 4/20/07).

39. Skinner, B. F., *Verbal Behavior* (Englewood Cliffs, NJ: Prentice-Hall, 1957), 387.

40. Campbell, Erik, "The Accidental Plagiarist: Thoughts on the Anxiety of Influence, the Influence of Anxiety, and the Trouble with Originality," *Virginia Quarterly Review*, Spring 2007, Vol. 83, No. 2, 238–256, 243.

41. Campbell, 252.

42. Lethem, Jonathan, "The Ecstasy of Influence," *Harper's Magazine*, February, 2007, 64.

Chapter 3: The Blogs from Within

1. Barlow, John Perry, "Is There a There in Cyberspace?" *Utne Reader*, March 1995: http://www.eff.org/Misc/Publications/John_Perry_Barlow/HTML/utne_community.html (viewed 6/1/07).

2. Carroll, Lewis, *Through the Looking Glass*, chapter 1: http://www.literature.org/authors/carroll-lewis/through-the-looking-glass/chapter-01.html (viewed 8/16/07).

3. Strate, Lance, "Through the Blogging Glass," *Lance Strate's Blog Time Passing*: http://lancestrate.blogspot.com/search/label/on%20blogging (viewed 5/15/07).

4. Burke, Kenneth, *Permanence and Change* (New York: New Republic, 1936), 54.

5. Burke, 55.

6. Felten, Ed, "Digg Users Revolt Over AACS Key," *Freedom to Tinker*: http://www.freedom-to-tinker.com/?p=1153 (viewed 5/3/07).

7. Rose, Kevin, "Digg This: 09-f9-11-02-9d-74-e3-5b-d8-41-56-c5-63-56-88-c0," *Digg*: http://blog.digg.com/?p=74 (viewed 5/3/07).

8. Felten, Ed, "Why the 09ers Are So Upset," *Freedom to Tinker*: http://www.freedom-to-tinker.com/?p=1154 (viewed 5/3/07).

9. Jenkins, Henry, "The Poachers and the Stormtroopers: Cultural Convergence in the Digital Age," a talk presented at the University of Michigan, Spring, 1998. http://legalminds.lp.findlaw.com/list/rre/msg00012.html (viewed 5/4/07).

10. Riesman, David, "Some Observations Concerning Marginality," *Individualism Reconsidered* (New York: Free Press, 1954), 155.

11. Quine, Willard Van Orman, *Word and Object* (Cambridge, MA: MIT Press, 1960), ix.

12. Zimmer, Benjamin, "The First 'Fitzmas,'" *Language Log*: http://itre.cis.upenn.edu/~myl/languagelog/archives/002604.html (viewed 5/2/07).

13. Dewey, John, *The Public and Its Problems* (New York: Henry Holt, 1927), 148.

14. Dewey, 150.

15. Dewey, 151–152.

16. Riesman, David, "Values in Context," *Individualism Reconsidered* (New York: Free Press, 1954), 18.

17. Popper, Karl, *The Open Society and Its Enemies*, Vol. II: "The High Tide of Prophecy: Hegel, Marx, and the Aftermath" (New York: Harper, 1962), 213.

18. Miss Heather, "A Few Thoughts About the 2007 Brooklyn Blogfest," *Newyork shitty.com*: http://www.newyorkshitty.com/?p=1098 (viewed 5/13/07).

19. Dr. Virago, "K'zoo Report #2: Breakfast of Champions," *Quod She*: http://quod-she.blogspot.com/2007/05/kzoo-report-2-breakfast-of-champions.html (viewed 5/16/07).

20. Rosenbaum, Ron, "How to Trick an Online Scammer into Carving a Computer Out of Wood," *The Atlantic*, June 2007, Vol. 299, No. 5, 83.

21. Froomkin, A. Michael, "Habermas@Discourse.Net: Toward a Critical Theory of Cyberspace," *Harvard Law Review*, January 2003, Vol. 116, No. 3, 749–873, 820–821.

22. Powers, Shelley, "Poor Impulse Control," *Burningbird*: http://burningbird.net/category/weblogging/page/2/ (viewed 4/16/07).

23. Boulding, Kenneth, *The Image: Knowledge in Life and Society* (Ann Arbor: University of Michigan Press, 1956), 71–72.

24. Herring, Susan, et al., "Conversations in the Blogosphere: An Analysis 'From the Bottom Up,'" *Proceedings of the Thirty-Eighth Hawai'i International Conference on System Sciences* (Los Alamitos: IEEE Press, 2005), 10: http://www.blogninja.com/hicss05.blogconv.pdf (viewed 4/20/07).

25. RenaRF, "Bloggers Just Sit on Their Butts," *On the Left Tip*: onthelefttip.blogspot.com/2006/10/bloggers-just-sit-on-their-butts.html (viewed 5/10/07).

26. RenaRF, email correspondence with the author, 5/17/07.

27. Auerbach, David Benjamin (writing as "Waggish"), "Thoughts on Genre: Blogs and Genre," *Waggish*: http://www.waggish.org/2005/07/thoughts_on_genre_blogs_and_genre.html (viewed 4/20/07).

28. Arata, Luis, "Reflections on Interactivity," in David Thorburn and Henry Jenkins, eds., *Rethinking Media Change: The Aesthetics of Transition* (Cambridge, MA: MIT Press, 2003), 219 (217–225).

29. Barthes, Roland, "From Work to Text," in *Image, Music, Text*, trans. Stephen Heath (New York: Hill and Wang, 1977), 155 (155–164).

30. Barthes, 157.

31. Barthes, 157.

32. Barthes, 157.

33. Barthes, 158.

34. Barthes, 159.

35. Barthes, 161.

36. Barthes, 162.

37. Barthes, 164.

38. Gray, Jonathan, *Watching the Simpsons: Television, Parody, and Intertextuality* (New York: Routledge, 2007), 3.

39. Bérubé, Michael, *Rhetorical Occasions: Essays on Humans and the Humanities* (Chapel Hill: University of North Carolina Press, 2006), 289.

40. Bérubé, 289.

41. Kennedy, Shirley Duglin, "Us Versus Them," *Information Today*, April 2007, Vol. 24, Issue 4, 15–17, 15–16.

42. Digby, "I Love My Navel So Much . . .," *Digby's Hullabaloo*: http://digbys blog.blogspot.com/2007/05/i-love-my-navel-so-much-by-digby.html (viewed 5/15/07).

43. Greenwald, Glenn, "Blog News," *Unclaimed Territory*: http://glenngreenwald .blogspot.com/2007/02/blog-news.html (viewed 2/1/07).

44. Moulitsas, Markos, "In the Blog World, No Individual Is Indispensable," *Daily Kos*: http://www.dailykos.com/storyonly/2007/5/3/01255/96752 (viewed 5/3/07).

CHAPTER 4: THE BLOGS, POLITICAL ISSUES, AND THE PRESS

1. Cambridge, Darren, "Two Faces of Integrative Learning Online," *Electronic Portfolios: Emergent Findings and Shared Questions*, eds. Darren Cambridge, Barbara Cambridge, and Kathleen Yancey (Sterling, VA: Stylus, in press).

2. Berners-Lee, Tim, "Overview of the Web," *W3.org*: http://www.w3.org/History/ 19921103-hypertext/hypertext/DataSources/Top.html (viewed 5/30/07).

3. Pursell, Carroll, *The Machine in America: A Social History of Technology*, 2nd edition (Baltimore: Johns Hopkins University Press, 2007), 326–327.

4. Boulding, Kenneth, *The Image: Knowledge in Life and Society* (Ann Arbor: University of Michigan Press, 1956), 99.

5. Boulding, 99–100.

6. Keen, Andrew, *The Cult of the Amateur* (New York: Doubleday, 2007), 63.

7. Burke, Kenneth, *Permanence and Change* (New York: New Republic, 1936), 14.

8. Burke, 18.

9. Keen, Andrew, *The Cult of the Amateur* (New York: Doubleday, 2007), 16.

10. http://www.catb.org/jargon/html/S/Sturgeons-Law.html (viewed 4/27/07).

11. Jenkins, Henry, *Convergence Culture: Where the Old and New Media Collide* (New York: New York University Press, 2006), 211.

12. drational, "On Why Greg Palast Is Dangerous," *Daily Kos*: http://www.daily-kos.com/story/2007/5/26/83915/0129 (viewed 5/29/07).

13. Palast, Greg, "Greg Palast Is Dangerous," *Greg Palast: Journalism and Film*: http://www.gregpalast.com/greg-palast-is-dangerous/#more-1740 (viewed 5/29/07).

14. DHinMI, "Does Greg Palast View You with Contempt?" *Daily Kos*: http:// www.dailykos.com/story/2007/5/19/191917/548 (viewed 5/29/07).

15. xaxnar, "Been There, Done That—Greg Palast vs. Daily Kos or the Great Foot-Shooting Free for All," *Daily Kos*: http://www.dailykos.com/story/2007/5/29/ 64433/2367 (viewed 5/29/07).

16. "A New Measure of Quality. A Collaborative Approach," *ManyOne*: http:// www.manyone.net/ (viewed 6/4/07).

17. Bradley, Bill, *The New American Story* (New York: Random House, 2007), 336.

18. "Communicate+Collaborate+Educate: Inspire," *Digital Universe*: http://www.dufoundation.org/project.php (viewed 6/4/07).

19. Kha'nh, Truong Phuoc, "Search for sailor called off," *SilliconValley.com*: http://www.siliconvalley.com/search/ci_5248721?nclick_check=1 (viewed 5/4/07).

20. Howe, Jeff, "The Rise of Crowdsourcing," *Wired* 14.06, June 2006, http://www.wired.com/wired/archive/14.06/crowds.html (viewed 2/11/07).

21. Burge, Randy, Sidebar to "Assignment Zero First Take: Wiki Innovators Rethink Openness," *Wired*: http://www.wired.com/techbiz/media/news/2007/05/assignment_zero_citizendium (viewed 5/6/07).

22. "Journalism Gets Crowdsourced," *Assignment Zero*: http://zero.newassignment.net/assignmentzero/crowdsourced_journalism# (viewed 4/30/07).

23. http://www.tpmmuckraker.com/archives/002329.php (viewed 4/30/07).

24. http://www.signonsandiego.com/news/metro/20070112-9999-1n12lam.html (viewed 4/30/07).

25. "White House Pushes Out Another Prosecutor": http://www.tpmmuckraker.com/archives/002340.php (viewed 4/5/07).

26. "What's the White House Doing to Prosecutors?": http://www.tpmmuckraker.com/archives/002347.php (viewed 4/5/07).

27. "Gonzales Appoints Political Loyalists into Vacant U.S. Attorneys Slots": http://www.realcities.com/mld/krwashington/news/nation/16555903.htm (viewed 4/5/07).

28. Boehlert, Eric, "*Wash. Post* Still Blind to Liberal Blogger Success," *Media Matters for America*: http://mediamatters.org/columns/200705150002 (viewed 5/16/07).

29. Kurtz, Howard, "Jeff Gannon Admits Past 'Mistakes,' Berates Critics," *The Washington Post*, 2/19/05: http://www.washingtonpost.com/wp-dyn/articles/A36733-2005Feb18.html (viewed 4/20/07).

30. Lippmann, Walter, *Public Opinion* (New York: Free Press, 1997), 214–215.

31. Cho, AvaHome, and Roxy, "The Gonzales Seven," *ePluribus Media Journal*: http://www.epluribusmedia.org/features/2007/20070127_gonzales_seven_p1.html (viewed 3/15/07).

32. "Resurrecting Jim Crow: The Erratic Resume of the Voting Section Chief," *ePluribus Media Journal*: http://www.epluribusmedia.org/features/2007/20070505_resurrecting_jim_crow.html (viewed 5/8/07).

33. Holbrooke, Richard, "A Loss for All of Us," *The Washington Post*, 5/2/07: http://www.washingtonpost.com/wp-dyn/content/article/2007/05/01/AR2007050101418.html (viewed 5/6/07).

34. Packer, George, "Postscript: David Halberstam," *The New Yorker*, 5/7/07: http://www.newyorker.com/talk/2007/05/07/070507ta_talk_packer (viewed 5/6/07).

35. Kurtz, Howard, "Alberto Gone-zales?" *The Washington Post*, 3/16/07: http://www.washingtonpost.com/wp-dyn/content/blog/2007/03/16/BL2007031600594_pf.html (viewed 5/5/07).

36. Kmiec, Douglas, "Gonzales Case Merely a Footnote," *Chicago Tribune*, 4/24/07: http://www.chicagotribune.com/news/nationworld/chi-0704230345apr24,1,5984423.story?coll=chi-newsnationworld-hed (viewed 5/6/07).

37. "A Scandal That Keeps Growing," *The New York Times*, 5/6/07: http://www.nytimes.com/2007/05/06/opinion/06sun1.html (viewed 5/6/07).

38. Kuttner, Robert, "The Race," *Columbia Journalism Review*, March/April 2007, Vol. 45, Issue 6, 22–32.

39. Kuttner, 22.

40. Kuttner, 24.

41. Kuttner, 24.

42. Dewey, John, *The Public and Its Problems* (New York: Henry Holt, 1927), 146.

43. Gillmor, Dan, "From Dan: A Letter to the Bayosphere Community," *Bayosphere . . . of by and for the bay community*: http://bayosphere.com/blog/dan_gillmor/20060124/from_dan_a_letter_to_the_bayosphere_community (viewed 5/1/07).

44. Fine, Jon, "Down and Out in the 'Burbs'," *Business Week*, 3/26/07, Vol. 4027, 28.

45. Fine, 28.

46. Cho, "The iBrattleboro Wizards—Pioneers in Net Based Citizen Journalism," *ePluribus Media Community Site*: http://scoop.epluribusmedia.org/story/2006/9/8/174221/9258 (viewed 1/22/07).

47. iBrattleboro.com, "Frequently Asked Questions," http://www.ibrattleboro.com/statpages/index.pho/20030315191156231 (viewed 3/10/07).

48. Jenkins, Henry, "The Poachers and the Stormtroopers: Cultural Convergence in the Digital Age," a talk presented at the University of Michigan, Spring, 1998. http://legalminds.lp.findlaw.com/list/rre/msg00012.html (viewed 5/4/07).

49. Smith, Craig, email with the author, 5/18/07.

CHAPTER 5: THE BLOG IN POPULAR CULTURE

1. Rosenberg, Bernard, "Mass Culture in America," in Bernard Rosenberg and David Manning White, eds., *Mass Culture: The Popular Arts in America* (Glencoe, IL: Free Press, 1957), 5.

2. Jenkins, Henry, *Convergence Culture: Where the Old and New Media Collide* (New York: New York University Press), 136.

3. Evans, Woody, "Google Myth," *Ghostfooting*: http://ghostfeet.wordpress.com/2007/04/02/google-myth/ (viewed 5/12/07).

4. Dick, Philip K., *The Man Who Japed* (New York: Ace Books, 1956), 153.

5. MacDonald, Dwight, "A Theory of Mass Culture," *Diogenes*, Summer 1953, No. 3, 1 (1–17).

6. MacDonald, 2.

7. Boulding, Kenneth, *The Image: Knowledge in Life and Society* (Ann Arbor: University of Michigan Press, 1956), 55–56.

8. Gans, Herbert, "The Creator-Audience Relationship in the Mass Media: An Analysis of Movie Making," in Bernard Rosenbery and David Manning White, eds., *Mass Culture: The Popular Arts in America* (Glencoe, IL: Free Press, 1957), 315 (315–324).

9. Orwell, George, *1984* (London: Signet, 1977), 2–3.

10. Nicole, "1984–2007," *With Hands Held High*: http://whhh.blogspot.com/2007/05/1984-2007.html (viewed 5/26/07).

11. Dick, Philip K., *The Man Who Japed* (New York: Ace Books, 1956), 44–45.

12. Wilson, Richard Guy, et al., *The Machine Age in America: 1918–1941* (New York: Abrams, 1986).

13. Dick, Philip K., *The Man in the High Castle* (New York: Berkeley, 1974), 150.

14. Adams, Henry, *The Education of Henry Adams* (Boston: Houghton Mifflin, 1961), 388.

15. Wainaina, Binyavanga, "Glory," *Bidoun*, No. 10, Spring 2007: http://www.bidoun.com/issues/issue_10/04_all.html#article (viewed 5/23/07).

16. Wainaina, Binyavanga, "Glory," *Bidoun*, No. 10, Spring 2007: http://www.bidoun.com/issues/issue_10/04_all.html#article (viewed 5/23/07).

17. Bowers, Christine, "How Banking on a Mobile Phone Can Help the Poor," *Passport*: http://blog.foreignpolicy.com/node/3131 (viewed 5/26/07).

18. Thoreau, Henry, *Walden* (Charlottesville: University of Virginia American Studies Program, 2003): http://xroads.virginia.edu/~HYPER/WALDEN/hdt04.html (viewed 3/3/07).

19. Marx, Leo, *The Machine in the Garden* (New York: Oxford University Press, 1964), 191.

20. Pursell, Carroll, *The Machine in America: A Social History of Technology*, 2nd edition (Baltimore: Johns Hopkins University Press, 2007), xii.

21. Bradley, Bill, *The New American Story* (New York: Random House, 2007), 337.

22. Lewis-Kraus, Gideon, "A World in Three Aisles: Browsing the Post-Digital Library," *Harper's Magazine*, May 2007, Vol. 314, No. 1884, 47 (47–57).

23. Anders, Gunther, "The Phantom World of TV," trans. Norbert Guterman, *Dissent*, 1956, Vol. 3, 16 (14–24).

24. Anders, 17.

25. Anders, 19.

26. Thoreau, Henry, *Walden* (Charlottesville: University of Virginia American Studies Program, 2003): http://xroads.virginia.edu/~HYPER/WALDEN/hdt04.html (viewed 3/3/07).

27. Anders, 17.

28. Anders, 17.

29. Anders, 17.

30. Anders, 17.

31. Anders, 17.

32. Rabassiere, Henry, "In Defense of Television," *Dissent*, 1956, Vol. 3, 329 (327–332).

33. Jenkins, 3.

34. Jenkins, Henry, "The Poachers and the Stormtroopers: Cultural Convergence in the Digital Age," a talk presented at the University of Michigan, Spring, 1998: http://legalminds.lp.findlaw.com/list/rre/msg00012.html (viewed 5/4/07).

35. Brooker, Will and Deborah Jermyn, "Conclusion: Overflow and Audience," *The Audience Studies Reader*, Will Brooker and Deborah Jermyn, eds. (London: Routledge, 2003), 325.

36. Jenkins, 215.

37. Adorno, Theodor, "Culture Industry Reconsidered, *The Adorno Reader*, Brian O'Connor, ed. (Oxford: Blackwell, 2000), 232.

38. Jenkins, 133.

39. Kit, Borys, "Fan Frenzy for 'Snakes' Is On a Different Plane," *Hollywood Reporter*, 3/23/06: http://www.hollywoodreporter.com/hr/search/article_display.jsp?vnu_content_id=1002234847 (viewed 5/12/07).

40. Fiske, John, *Understanding Popular Culture* (London: Routledge, 1989), 18–19.

41. Benjamin, Walter, "The Work of Art in the Age of Mechanical Reproduction": http://www.marxists.org/reference/subject/philosophy/works/ge/benjamin.htm (viewed 5/10/07).

42. Jenkins, 170.

43. Toner, Alan, "Google, Viacom: Gatekeepers Old and New?" *kNOw Future Inc.: law, technology and cinema, washed down with wine*: http://knowfuture.wordpress.com/2007/05/17/google-viacom-gatekeepers-old-and-new (viewed 5/20/07).

44. Jenkins, 245–246.

45. Bradford, William, *History of Plymouth Plantation*, 1651: http://www.fordham.edu/halsall/mod/1650bradford.html#How%20they%20sought%20a%20place%20of%20habitation (viewed 5/20/07).

46. Berners-Lee, Tim and Robert Cailliau, "WorldWideWeb: Proposal for a HyperText Project," *W3.org*: http://www.w3.org/History/19921103-hypertext/hypertext/WWW/Proposal.html (viewed 5/20/07).

47. Berners-Lee, Tim, "Executive Summary," *W3.org*: http://www.w3.org/History/19921103-hypertext/hypertext/WWW/Summary.html.

48. "How Much Information? 2000": http://www2.sims.berkeley.edu/research/projects/how-much-info/summary.html#about (viewed 5/20/07).

49. "How Much Information? 2000": http://www2.sims.berkeley.edu/research/projects/how-much-info/summary.html#about (viewed 5/20/07).

50. "How Much Information? 2003": http://www2.sims.berkeley.edu/research/projects/how-much-info-2003/execsum.htm (viewed 5/20/07).

51. Giles, Jim, "Internet Encyclopedias Go Head to Head," *Nature Online*, December 14, 2005: http://www.nature.com/news/2005/051212/full/438900a.html (viewed 5/20/07).

CHAPTER 6: ONLINE COMMUNITY, ONLINE UTILIZATION: THE CHRISTIAN BLOG

1. Congdon, D. W., "Encounters with Tradition (2): From Evangelical to Post-evangelical," *Faith and Theology*: http://faith-theology.blogspot.com/2007/06/encounters-with-tradition-2-from.html (viewed 6/7/07).

2. Piper, Abraham, "Tips for Better Blogging," *Between Two Worlds*: http://theologica.blogspot.com/2007/06/tips-for-better-blog-writing.html (viewed 6/7/07).

3. Anyabwile, Thabiti, "A Year in the Blogosphere," *Pure Church*: http://purechurch.blogspot.com/2007/06/year-in-blogosphere.html (viewed 6/7/07).

4. "Learn More," *MyChurch*: http://www.mychurch.org/info/learnmorepg1.php (viewed 5/4/07).

5. Jones, K. C., "Churches Create Religious Alternative to MySpace," *Information Week*, May 1, 2007: http://www.informationweek.com/internet/showArticle.jhtml?articleID=199202900&cid=RSSfeed_IWK_News (viewed 5/4/07).

6. Riesman, David, "Some Observations Concerning Marginality," *Individualism Reconsidered* (New York: Free Press, 1954), 155.

7. Lockwood, Frank, email to the author, 4/27/07.

8. Roth, Martin, "Blogging for the Lord," *Martin Roth Christian Commentary*: http://martinrothonline.com/MRCC1.htm (viewed 2/17/07).

9. Poarch, Sharon, "Final Days in Gulfport, MS," *Simple Values*: http://www.simplevalues.org/cgi-bin/csNews/csNews.cgi?database=ARCHIVE_FOR_BLOG%2edb&command=viewone&id=283&op=t (viewed 4/29/07).

10. Poarch, Sharon, "Back in Gulfport," *Simple Values*: http://www.simplevalues.org/cgi-bin/csNews/csNews.cgi?database=ARCHIVE_FOR_BLOG%2edb&command=viewone&id=273&op=t (viewed 4/29/07).

11. Byron, Mark, "Worship the Prince of Peace at Man O' War," *Mark Byron*: http://markbyron.typepad.com/main/2007/06/worship_the_pri.html (viewed 6/6/07).

12. Penner, Glenn, "How to Write a Letter That No One Will Read," *Persecuted Church Weblog*: http://persecutedchurch.blogspot.com/2007/05/how-to-write-letter-that-no-one-will.html (viewed 6/6/07).

13. Burry, Martin, "Groan—Politics," *Christianity in the Raw's Blog*: http://theologos.vox.com/library/post/groan-politics.html (viewed 39/07).

14. Clippedwings, "To Publish or Not to Publish, *Clippedwings*: http://clippedwings.vox.com/library/post/to-publish-or-not-to-publish.html (viewed 6/6/07).

15. Sarahbi, "Expectations: The Continuum between Reality and Cynicism," *Take a Risk*: http://www.xanga.com/Sarahbi/591181182/expectations-the-continuum-between-reality-and-cynicism.html (viewed 6/6/07).

16. "About Christianblog.com," *Christianblog*: http://www.christianblog.com/about/ (viewed 4/25/07).

17. Jordan, Jim, "Welcome to Christoholics Anonymous," *Moral Science Club*: http://moralscienceclub.blogspot.com/2006/04/welcome-to-christoholics-anonymous.html (viewed 3/24/07).

18. Triggs, Sonya, "Stunting Your Spiritual Growth," *Christian Thoughts*: http://urbanchristianz.blogspot.com/2006/09/stunting-your-spiritual-growth.html (viewed 3/23/07).

19. Crimson Wife, "Our Educational Philosophy," *Bending the Twigs* http://bendingthetwigs.blogspot.com/2007/03/our-educational-philosophy.html (viewed 4/15/07).

20. Blanchard, Chuck, "Some Thoughts on Evolution," *A Guy in the Pews*: http://aguyinthepew.blogspot.com/2007/06/some-thoughts-on-evolution.html (viewed 6/7/07).

21. Deep Furrows, "Murder in the Cathedral," *Deep Furrows*: http://deepfurrows.blogspot.com/2007/01/murder-in-cathedral.html (viewed 3/14/07).

22. Fortigurn, "Introduction," *Christian Studies*: http://christianstudies.wordpress.com/2007/05/04/introduction (viewed 6/7/07).

23. Steve, "Exercise and the Unity of Believers," *Careful Thought II*: http://carefulthought.wordpress.com/2007/05/10/exercise-and-the-unity-of-believers/ (viewed 5/21/07).

BIBLIOGRAPHY

Adams, Henry. *The Education of Henry Adams*. Boston: Houghton Mifflin, 1961.

Adorno, Theodor. "Culture Industry Reconsidered." In Brian O'Connor, ed., *The Adorno Reader*. Oxford: Blackwell, 2000.

Anahita, Sine. "Blogging the Borders: Virtual Skinheads, Hypermasculinity, and Heteronormativity." *Journal of Political and Military Sociology*, Summer 2006, Vol. 34, No. 1 143–164.

Anders, Gunther. "The Phantom World of TV," trans. Norbert Guterman, *Dissent*, 1956, Vol. 3, 14–24.

Arata, Luis. "Reflections on Interactivity." In David Thorburn and Henry Jenkins, eds., *Rethinking Media Change: The Aesthetics of Transition*. Cambridge, MA: MIT Press, 2003, 217–225.

Baker, Stephen, and Heather Green. "Blogs Will Change Your Business." *BusinessWeek*. 5/2/2005. http://www.businessweek.com/magazine/content/05_18/b3931001_mz001.htm.

Barlow, Aaron. *The Rise of the Blogosphere*. Westport, CT: Praeger Publishers, 2007.

Barthes, Roland. *Image, Music, Text*. Trans. Stephen Heath. New York: Hill and Wang, 1977.

Benjamin, Walter. "The Work of Art in the Age of Mechanical Reproduction," http://www.marxists.org/reference/subject/philosophy/works/ge/benjamin.htm.

Bérubé, Michael. *Rhetorical Occasions: Essays on Humans and the Humanities*. Chapel Hill: University of North Carolina Press, 2006.

Boulding, Kenneth. *The Image: Knowledge in Life and Society*. Ann Arbor: University of Michigan Press, 1956.

Bradley, Bill. *The New American Story*. New York: Random House, 2007.

Brooker, Will, and Deborah Jermyn, eds. *The Audience Studies Reader*. London: Routledge, 2003.

Burke, Kenneth. *Permanence and Change*. New York: New Republic, 1936.

Cambridge, Darren. "Two Faces of Integrative Learning Online." In Darren Cambridge, Barbara Cambridge, and Kathleen Yancey, eds., *Electronic Portfolios: Emergent Findings and Shared Questions*. Sterling, VA: Stylus, in press.

Campbell, Erik. "The Accidental Plagiarist: Thoughts on the Anxiety of Influence, the Influence of Anxiety, and the Trouble with Originality." *Virginia Quarterly Review*. Spring 2007, Vol. 83, No. 2, 238–256.

Claburn, Thomas. "Digg Rebellion Shows That Crowd Is Law." *Information Week*. 5/2/07. http://www.informationweek.com/software/showArticle.jhtml;jsessionid=3ETMP1S E2SYF4QSNDLPSKH0CJUNN2JVN?articleID=199203386.

Conlin, Michelle. "Web Attack." *Business Week*, April 16, 2007, Issue 4030, 54–56.

DeLong, Brad. "The Invisible College." *The Chronicle of Higher Education*, 7/28/06. B8. http://chronicle.com/free/v52/i47/47b00801.htm.

Dewey, John. *The Public and Its Problems*. New York: Henry Holt, 1927.

Dick, Philip. "How to Build a Universe That Doesn't Fall Apart Two Days Later." *I Hope I Shall Arrive Soon*. Garden City, NJ: Doubleday, 1985. http://deoxy.org/pkd_how2build.htm (6/3/07).

Dick, Philip. *The Man in the High Castle*. New York: Putnam, 1963.

Dick, Philip. *The Man Who Japed*. New York: Ace Books, 1956.

Dumenco, Simon. "Web 2.0? Not so fast—say hello to Web 1.9 (if that)." *Advertising Age*, April 16, 2007, Vol. 78, Issue 16, 32–32.

Durham, Meenaksi, and Douglas Kellner, eds. *Media and Cultural Studies Keyworks*. Oxford: Blackwell, 2001.

Farkas, Meredith. "Balancing the Online Life." *American Libraries*. January 2007, Vol. 38, Issue 1, 42–45.

Fiske, John. *Understanding Popular Culture*. London: Routledge, 1989.

Franklin, Wayne. *Discoverers, Explorers, Settlers: The Diligent Writers of Early America*. Chicago: University of Chicago Press, 1979.

Friedberg, Anne. "The Virtual Window." In David Thorburn and Henry Jenkins, eds., *Rethinking Media Change: The Aesthetics of Transition*. Cambridge, MA: MIT Press, 2003, 337–353.

Froomkin, A. Michael. "Habermas@Discourse.Net: Toward a Critical Theory of Cyberspace." *Harvard Law Review*. January 2003, Vol. 116, No. 3, 749–873.

Gans, Herbert. "The Creator-Audience Relationship in the Mass Media: An Analysis of Movie Making." In Bernard Rosenberg and David Manning White, eds., *Mass Culture: The Popular Arts in America*. Glencoe, IL: Free Press, 1957, 315–324.

Gray, Jonathan. *Watching the Simpsons: Television, Parody, and Intertextuality*. New York: Routledge, 2007.

Habermas, Jürgen. *The Structural Transformation of the Public Sphere: An Inquiry into a Category of Bourgeois Society*. Trans. Thomas Burger. Cambridge, MA: MIT Press, 1991.

Harris, Chris. "Five Reasons Not to Blog." *School Library Journal*. http://www.schoollibraryjournal.com/articles/cag430167.html. April 1, 2007.

Herring, Susan, et al. "Bridging the Gap: A Genre Analysis of Weblogs." *BROG Papers*. http://www.blogninja.com/DDGDD04.doc (5/30/07).

Holloway, Sarah, and Gill Valentine. *Cyberkids: Children in the Information Age*. London: RoutledgeFalmer, 2003.

Howe, Irving. "Notes on Mass Culture." In Bernard Rosenberg and David Manning White, eds., *Mass Culture: The Popular Arts in America*. Glencoe, IL: Free Press, 1957, 496–503. Reprinted from *Politics*, Spring 1948, Vol. 5, 120–123.

Howe, Jeff. "The Rise of Crowdsourcing." *Wired*. June 2006. Vol. 14, Issue 6. http://www.wired.com/wired/archive/14.06/crowds.html.

Jenkins, Henry. *Convergence Culture: Where the Old and New Media Collide*. New York: New York University Press, 2006.

Jenkins, Henry. "The Poachers and the Stormtroopers: Cultural Convergence in the Digital Age," a talk presented at the University of Michigan, Spring 1998. http://legalminds.lp.findlaw.com/list/rre/msg00012.html.

Keen, Andrew. *The Cult of the Amateur: How Today's Internet Is Killing Our Culture*. New York: Doubleday, 2007.

Kennedy, Shirley Duglin. "Us Versus Them." *Information Today*. April 2007, Vol. 24, Issue 4, 15–17.

Kuttner, Robert. "The Race." *Columbia Journalism Review*. March/April 2007, Vol. 45, Issue 6, 22–32.

Leary, Patrick. "Free Speech, Quality Control, and Flame Wars: Sticking to the Topic on SHARP-L and VICTORIA." *Academe*. January/February 2007, Vol. 93, Issue 1, 50–52.

Lemann, Nicholas. "Amateur Hour." *The New Yorker*, August 7, 2006, Vol. 82, Issue 24, 44–49.

Lethem, Jonathan. "The Ecstasy of Influence." *Harper's Magazine*, February 2007, Vol. 311, 59–71.

Lewis-Kraus, Gideon. "A World in Three Aisles: Browsing the Post-Digital Library." *Harper's Magazine*, May 2007, Vol. 314, No. 1884, 47–57.

Lippmann, Walter. *Public Opinion*. New York: Free Press, 1997.

MacDonald, Dwight. "A Theory of Mass Culture." *Diogenes*. Summer 1953, No. 3, 1–17.

McLuhan, Marshall. *Understanding Media*. Cambridge, MA: MIT Press, 1964.

Marx, Leo. *The Machine in the Garden*. New York: Oxford University Press, 1964.

Nakashima, Ellen. "Sexual Threats Stifle Some Female Bloggers." *The Washington Post*. 4/31/07. http://www.washingtonpost.com/wp-dyn/content/article/2007/04/29/AR2007042901555_pf.html.

Ong, Walter. *Orality and Literacy*, 2nd edition. New York: Routledge, 2002.

Orwell, George. *1984*. New York: Harcourt, Brace, 1949.

Peirce, Charles. *Philosophical Writing*. New York: Dover Books, 1955.

Peter, Laurence, and Raymond Hull. *The Peter Principle*. New York: Morrow, 1969.

Popper, Karl. *The Open Society and Its Enemies*, Vol. II: "The High Tide of Prophecy: Hegel, Marx, and the Aftermath." New York: Harper, 1962.

Poster, Mark. "Postmodern Virtualities." *The Second Media Age*. Oxford: Blackwell, 1995.

Postman, Neil. *Amusing Ourselves to Death*. New York: Viking, 1985.

Pursell, Carroll. *The Machine in America: A Social History of Technology*, 2nd edition. Baltimore: Johns Hopkins University Press, 2007.

Rabassiere, Henry. "In Defense of Television," *Dissent*, Vol. 3, 1956, 327–332.

Riesman, David. "The Ethics of We Happy Few." *Individualism Reconsidered*. New York: Free Press, 1954.

Rosedale, Philip. "Alter Egos." *Forbes*, May 7, 2007, Vol. 179, Issue 10, 76–80.

Rosenberg, Bernard. "Mass Culture in America." In Bernard Rosenberg and David Manning White, eds., *Mass Culture: The Popular Arts in America*. Glencoe, IL: Free Press, 1957, 3–12.

Rosenberg, Bernard, and David Manning White, eds. *Mass Culture: The Popular Arts in America*. Glencoe, IL: Free Press, 1957.

Sapir, Edward. *Edward Sapir: Selected Writings in Language, Culture, and Personality*. David Mandelbaum, ed. Berkeley: University of California Press, 1986.

Skinner, B. F. *Verbal Behavior*. Englewood Cliffs, NJ: Prentice-Hall, 1957.

Thoreau, Henry David. *Walden*. Charlottesville: University of Virginia American Studies Program, 2003. http://xroads.virginia.edu/~HYPER/WALDEN/hdt04.html.

Thorburn, David, and Henry Jenkins, eds. *Rethinking Media Change: The Aesthetics of Transition*. Cambridge, MA: MIT Press, 2003.

Tribble, Ivan. "Bloggers Need Not Apply." *The Chronicle of Higher Education*. 7/8/2005. http://chronicle.com/jobs/2005/07/2005070801c.htm.

Ulmer, Gregory. *Internet Invention: From Literacy to Electacy*. New York: Longman, 2002.

Wainaina, Binyavanga. "Glory." *Bidoun*. No. 10, Spring 2007, http://www.bidoun.com/issues/issue_10/04_all.html#article.

Whorf, Benjamin. "The Relation of Habitual Thought and Behavior to Language." In Leslie Spier, ed., *Language, Culture, and Personality, Essays in Memory of Edward Sapir*. Menasha, WI: Sapir Memorial Publications Fund, 1941. Reprinted in John Carroll, ed., *Language Thought and Reality: Selected Writings of Benjamin Lee Whorf*. Cambridge, MA: MIT Press, 1956, 134–159.

INDEX

Adams, Henry, 120
Adorno, Theodor, 129
Amusing Ourselves to Death (Neil Postman), 49
Anahita, Sine, 43
Anders, Gunther, 125–127
Anthony, Piers, 8
Anxiety of Influence, The (Harold Bloom), 54–55
Anyabwile, Thabiti, 141–142
Arata, Luis, 76
Auerbach, David Benjamin, 75–77, 80
"AvaHome," 100

Baran, Paul, 86
Barlow, John Perry, 59–61
Barnes & Noble, 88, 91
Barthes, Roland, 76–78, 80
Benjamin, Walter, 130–131
Berners-Lee, Tim, 86, 93–94, 133–134
Bérubé, Michael, 42, 79, 80–83
Bloom, Harold, 54–55
Boehlert, Eric, 98
Boulding, Kenneth, 72, 116
Bowers, Christine, 122
Bradley, Bill, 95
Brooker, Will, 128
Burke, Kenneth, 9, 51, 62, 63, 89–90
Burry, Martin, 148–149
Burstein, Miriam, 27
Byron, Mark, 147

Cailliau, Robert, 133
Cambridge, Darren, 85

Campbell, Erik, 55–56
Clarke, Chris, 38–39, 41
Cohn, David, 52
Cole, Juan, 31–32, 42
Congdon, D. W., 139

DeLong, Brad, 27, 70
Dewey, John, 66–67, 69, 104, 111
"DHinMI," 92
Dick, Philip K., 7, 114, 118–119
"Dr. Virago," 70
"drational," 91–92
Dumenco, Simon, 17

Evans, Woody, 114

Farkas, Meredith, 36
Felten, Ed, 63–64
Firmage, Joe, 94–95
Franklin, Wayne, 132–133
Froomkin, Michael, 71

Gans, Herbert, 11, 116, 129
Gibson, William, 44
Gillmor, Dan, 104–106
Gordon, Greg, 97–98
Gray, Jonathan, 24–25, 78–79
Greenwald, Glenn, 81–83
Grotke, Chris, 106
Grotstein, Josh, 106

Habermas, Jürgen, 2–5, 9, 20
Halberstam, David, 101–102
Harris, Chris, 41–43
Holbrooke, Richard, 101–102

Holloway, Sarah, 44
Howe, Irving, 46
Howe, Jeff, 4, 96

Infinite Mind, The, 26
Irish State Examinations Commission, 14

Jenkins, Henry, 65, 90, 108, 113–114,
    127–128, 132
Jermyn, Deborah, 128
Jordan, Jim, 152–153

Keen, Andrew, 31, 35–36, 89–90
Kennedy, Shirley Duglin, 80
Kiel, Paul, 97
Kmeic, Douglas, 103
Kurtz, Howard, 102
Kuttner, Robert, 103

Leary, Patrick, 39
Lemann, Nicholas, 51–52, 67, 138
LePage, Lise, 106
Lethem, Jonathan, 56
Liberman, Mark, 66
Lichtenstein, Bill, 26
Lileks, James, 33
Lippmann, Walter, 98–99
Lockwood, Frank, 143–144
Lonely Crowd, The (David Riesman), 40
Lucas, George, 130

MacDonald, Dwight, 115–116
Macroscope (Piers Anthony), 8
Man in the High Castle, The (Philip K.
    Dick), 119–120
Man Who Japed, The (Philip K. Dick),
    114–115, 118
Marshall, Josh Micah, 32, 97–98
Marx, Leo, 123
McClellan, Drew, 29–30
McLuhan, Marshall, 48, 115
"Miss Heather," 69
Moulitsas, Markos, 32, 38–39, 46, 67, 83

Negroponte, Nicholas, 120–122
Neuromancer (William Gibson), 44
"Nicole," 117

1984 (George Orwell), 117

Ong, Walter, 2, 9–10, 19–24
Orality and Literacy (Walter Ong), 19–24
O'Reilly, Tim, 37–38
Orwell, George, 117

Packer, George, 101–102
Palast, Greg, 91–92
Peirce, Charles Sanders, 24, 47
Penner, Glenn, 147–148
Permanence and Change (Kenneth
    Burke), 9
Perry, Greg, 123
Peter, Laurence, 86
Peter Principle, The (Laurence Peter and
    Raymond Hull), 86
Piper, Abraham, 140–141
Pixel Press, 21
Poarch, Sharon, 145–146
Popper, Karl, 68–69
Poster, Mark, 7
Postman, Neil, 49
Powers, Shelly, 71–72
Prelinger, Megan Shaw, 124–125
Prelinger, Rick, 124–125

Quine, Willard Van Orman, 65

Rabassiere, Henry, 127
"RenaRF," 72–74
Riesman, David, 40, 65, 68, 143
Ritchen, Fred, 21
Roeg, Jim, 61
Rood, Justin, 97
Rose, Kevin, 63–64
Rosedale, Philip, 5, 26
Rosen, Jay, 4, 37, 52, 91, 96,
    101, 106
Rosenbaum, Ron, 70–71
Rosenberg, Bernard, 113–114
Roth, Andrew, 31
Roth, Martin, 145

Sapir, Edward, 10, 19
Sapir-Whorf Hypothesis, 19
Second Life, 5–10, 21, 26, 43

Siegel, Lee, 11
Sierra, Kathy, 38, 41
Skinner, B. F., 2, 9–18, 55, 77
Smith, Craig, 109–111
Soltan, Margaret, 29
Strate, Lance, 61
Structural Transformation of the Public Sphere, The (Jürgen Habermas), 2–5
Sturgeon, Theodore, 90

Taylor, Marisa, 97–98
Thoreau, Henry David, 123, 126
Toner, Alan, 131
"Tribble, Ivan," 28–29, 70

Ulmer, Gregory, 20

Valentine, Gil, 44
Veblen, Thorstein, 51–52, 89
Verbal Behavior (B. F. Skinner), 11–18, 55

Wainaina, Binyavanga, 120–122
Wales, Jimmy, 37
Whorf, Benjamin, 19
Wikipedia, 22, 37, 95, 97, 134–135

"xaxnar," 92–93

Zimmer, Benjamin, 66

About the Author

AARON BARLOW teaches technical writing and composition at New York City College of Technology of the City University of New York. He is the author of *The DVD Revolution: Movies, Culture, and Technology* (Praeger, 2005) and *The Rise of the Blogosphere: American Backgrounds* (Praeger, 2007).